# AYAHUASCA IN MY BLOOD

25 Years of Medicine Dreaming

by
Peter Gorman

Cover Image by M.C. Escher (Snakes, 1969)

Photo back cover: Julio's house (Photo by Peter Gorman)
Photo front flap: The Author (Photo by Italo Gorman)
Photo back flap: Peter Gorman, left, with Julio Jerena
and Lynn Chilson in 2002" (Photo by Pasha)

Book Design by Johan Fremin

Illustrations by Morgan Maher

Copyright by Peter Gorman, 2010

First Edition, Published by the Gorman Bench Press, 2010
ISBN #: 978-0-557-48442-3

To my sons, Italo and Marco,
and my daughter, Madeleina

# TABLE OF CONTENTS

## PART I
## AYAHUASCA: VINE OF THE LITTLE DEATH

## PART II
## When Ayahuasca Speaks: An Unexpected Venture into Healing

## PART III
## Red Magic, An Introduction to Ayahuasca Healing

# ACKNOWLEDGEMENTS

THIS BOOK would not have been possible without the expert and kind help of a lot of people. At the top of the list is my teacher Julio Llerena (Jerena) Pinedo, a man who understood ayahuasca on deep levels. He is closely followed by Moises Torres Vienna, my jungle survival teacher and friend for many years, who shared how to live in the deep green with me; by Pablo, an indigenous Matses headman and curandero—healer—who knew more about plants than anyone I've ever encountered, and who, despite language barriers, imparted a great deal of Matses lore to me. And then there is Bertha Grove, a medicine woman from the Southern Ute tribe outside of Durango, Colorado, who allowed me to participate in several healing ceremonies there. And Lady, Julio's daughter, who knew the medicine needed to keep me from losing my leg after a poisonous spider bite out in the jungle. And Julio's son-in-law Juan, and my long-time friend Jhonny Java and my whole Peruvian team: Ruber, George, Sidalia, Gasdalia, Mauricio, MaBel, Kay, German, Corina and my former wife Chepa and her mother Lydia and father Demetrio. And my friends Lynn Chilson and Bill Weinberg and Larry Lavalle and Chuck Dudell and my kids and a host of other people who pushed me to learn despite the odds. Of course, there is Morgan Maher to thank also, for his wonderful illustrations.

And then especially Johan Fremin, who thought these stories would make a good book and backed that up by making it so.

# GLOSSARY

**AGUA DE FLORIDA**—Florida Water. An inexpensive orange-scented cologne used by healers throughout Peru as a holy water.

**AYAHUASCA**—A *Quechua* word meaning "vine of the soul" or "vine of the dead," *ayahuasca* is often colloquially referred to as "vine of the little death" because the user feels as though his ego has dissolved, or died. *Ayahuasca* is also known as *caapi, natema, pinde,* or *yagé* in various languages by the indigenous groups that employ the beverage.

The standard preparation of *ayahuasca* involves the simmering of cracked sections of *Banisteriopsis caapi* vine with *Psychotria viridis*—*chacruna*—leaves over a period of several hours, during which black tobacco (*Nicotiana rustica*) smoke is continually blown into the mixture. In Ecuador, leaves of the *Diplopteris cabrerena* are frequently used instead of *Psychotria viridis.*

Various additional plant products are frequently added to the brewing of *ayahuasca*, most frequently the bark of the *capirona* (*Calycophyllum spruceanum*), the *catahua* (*Hura crepitans*) and the *lupuna negra* (*Trichilia tocachana*) trees. Bark scraped from the roots of the bush known as *chiric sanango* (*Brunfelsia grandiflora*) is also commonly added.

Most *ayahuasqueros* select the additives they will use based on their medicinal properties and the needs of their clients.

*Ayahuasca* is used as a sacrament by a number of small religious groups, including the *Uñiao de Vegetal* and the *Santo Daime* churches that originated in Brazil.

**AYAHUASQUERO**—A healer who works primarily with *ayahuasca.*

**BRUJERIA**—The actions, generally negative, taken by a *brujo.*

**BRUJO AND BRUJA**—A healer who has fallen off the path of healing and uses his or her abilities to cast spells for spite, envy or money. A negative sorcerer for hire.

CAMALONGA—Seeds from the yellow oleander, *Thevetia peruviana* . They are thought to be able to protect one from brujeria. They are generally put whole into a bottle of *aguardiente* along with male and female camphor pieces, and male and female chopped onion and garlic from the mountains and coast of Peru. Utilizing elements from all three regions of Peru—the coast, mountains and jungle—is thought to be particularly effective against *brujeria*.

*Curanderos* who cure specifically with *camalonga* are called *camalongeros*.

CHACRUNA—*Psychotria viridis*. The standard leaves utilized with the *B. caapi* vine to make *ayahuasca*. Male leaves only are used; they are distinguishable because they have tiny protrusions near their tip on the underside of the leaf. *Ayahuasca* is sometimes made with *Chaliponga—Diplopterys cabrerena* leaves instead of *chacruna*.

CURANDERO—A traditional healer who may work in any number of modalities. He may heal with plants, by utilizing *ayahuasca* or *San Pedro* or *Toé*, he or she (the curandera) may work with smoke or stones or several other things. All traditional healers are considered *curanderos* or *curanderas*.

EGG-HEALER—One of the oddest, and no doubt oldest healing methods in Peru, egg-healing involves a *curandero* who passes a raw egg over his or her patient's body while chanting and blowing black tobacco smoke. A good egg-healer is said to be in communication with the unborn spirit of the chicken within the egg, and requests that that spirit absorbs the illness of the patient into its unformed body. While ridiculous to Westerners on the face of it, egg-healings are considered a vital, medical practice by Peruvians.

FLOWER BATH—Among lowland healers it is thought that negativity, whether it be physical or spiritual in nature, has a presence that affixes itself to people, like a black gob of ether. In the tradition of *ayahuasca* use in the region of Pucallpa, several hundred miles south of Iquitos, *curanderos* are trained to make baths with a variety of flowers which can eliminate that negativity from their patients.

ICARO—The name for the songs sung or whistled by curanderos during their ceremonies. Many *curanderos* in northwest Amazonia say that they learned their songs directly from the ayahuasca or other plants during ceremonies, and view them as gifts from the spirits of the plants. Other traditions pass the songs down from one generation of healers to the next.

LA PURGA—The deep vomiting produced by *ayahuasca*.

MAPACHO—The name for both the various black *Nicotiana* species of tobacco grown in the Amazon—most often *Nicotiana rustica*—as well as the cigarettes made from it. The tobacco (a genus of the *Solanaceae* family) is used both as a medicinal and spiritual aid.

**MAREADO**—To be dizzy or lightheaded or nauseous. In colloquial use in Peru's Amazon it signifies drunkenness, particularly to be *ayahuasca*-drunk.

**MATSES INDIAN**—Also known as Mayoruna, the Matses, along with their close relations, the Matis, Matsis and Marubo, live in the border region of Peru and Brazil, primarily on the Galvez, Alto Yavari, Lobo, and Blanco Rivers. Their language is in the Panoan language family. Until recently, they were known for the striking hash-mark tattoo that circled their mouths and ran up their cheeks nearly to their ears. That, along with wearing long bamboo splints in their nose (women) or upper lip (men) gave them the look of a jaguar. In their belief system, looking like a jaguar gave them the ability to hunt like a jaguar. The tattooing has ceased over the last 20 years for all but the most remote communities.

**MESTIZO**—A Spanish term indicating a person of mixed blood, specifically someone with both European and Amerindian bloodlines.

**PALO SANTO**—A willowy tree, *Bursera graveolens*, palo santo means "holy wood" or "saint wood" in English. Small pieces of the tree are burned as fragrant incense that is used throughout Central and South America to clear negative energy from people and spaces.

**SACHA**—An indigenous word that signifies "of the jungle" or "jungle-like", or "similar to". A tapir is called a *sachavaca*, or "jungle cow," for instance, and the medicine plant known as *sacha jergon* is so named because its flower and bulb look like a *jergon*—a pit viper—ready to strike.

**SACHA JERGON**—A tuber whose Latin name is *Dracontium loretense* it has long been used throughout the Peruvian lowlands in conjunction with *uña de gato* (cat's claw) as a general tonic. During the past several years it has also been used as an adjunct therapy, along with cat's claw, in the treatment of both AIDS and cancers, not only in Peru but in U.S. hospitals as well.

**SHACAPA**—A leaf-bundle rattle used throughout Amazonia during healing ceremonies, particularly during *ayahuasca* ceremonies.

**SHAMAN**—A *curandero* whose work includes contact with the spirit world.

**SHAMANISM**—A range of traditional beliefs and practices concerned with communication with the spirit world. A practitioner of shamanism is known as a shaman. The word originates among the Tungus people of Siberia, but now includes any system in which spirit-world communication is vital.

**SOPLA**—The act of blowing a fine line of smoke or a mist from a *curandero's* perfumes or medicines. The *sopla'ing* is done with the intention of cleaning or clearing negative energy from a person or space.

**TOÉ**—Also known as *datura*, it is a drink made from any of a number of plants from the *Solanaceae* (Nightshade) family, specifically those from both the *Brugmansia* and *Brunfelsia genera*. Very powerful, very toxic, the leaves are frequently added to the *ayahuasca* preparation to increase both the potency and duration of the psychotropic effect. A participant will know if *datura* leaves have been added to the *ayahuasca* if his or her lips, fingers and toes go numb.

An herbalist friend from Lima, Dr. Solomon Melchor Arroyo, has classified several uses of various *datura* preparations, including divination, future seeing and the stealing of a person's willpower, which has led many Peruvians to speak of *datura* as "the plant of the demon." In Colombia, and Bogotá in particular, certain *datura* preparations are used on unsuspecting tourists which leaves the tourist awake but susceptible to suggestion. There are many stories of tourists who have gone to the bank and withdrawn all of their money under the influence of *datura* and who have no recollection of it the following day.

Medicinally, various *datura* preparations are used for treating fever, swollen joints, muscle cramps, rheumatism, snake bite, yellow fever, infections and a number of other diseases and symptoms. Additionally, *toé* is frequently used by *curanderos* as a diagnostic tool, much the same way ayahuasca is used.

**UÑA DE GATO**—*Uncaria tomentosa* is a woody shrub that grows along the banks of the Amazon and its tributaries throughout lowland Peru. It gets its colloquial name, *uña de gato*, cat's claw, because of the sharp, claw-like appendages that grow on its branches. Extracts from the plant, both liquid and powder, have long been used in Peru as a general tonic and for relief from rheumatism, arthritis and bursitis. It has been used as an adjunct therapy for AIDS treatment throughout Peru for several years, as one of its beneficial qualities is to sharply increase T-cell levels. Most recently it has been used as an adjunct medicine in the treatment of cancers by such high-profile clinics as New York Hospital and the Mayo Clinic.

**VIROTÉ**—Invisible darts shot at one *curandero* from another with the intent of doing harm. The act falls into the category of *brujeria*. The *virotés* can be sent from long distances.

⊛

# INTRODUCTION

AMONG THE indigenous peoples of the world, there are several plants considered to be, in essence, master teachers of the human race. Several plants, in particular are said to possess the ability to allow a human, on their ingestion, to expand his or her perception and to temporarily access other levels of reality normally prohibited to all but visionaries, the dying, the very young and those in moments of extreme stress. Among these is *Brugmansia grandiflora*, also known as *datura* or *toé*, the trumpeted flowers of which possess the ability to transport man to worlds beyond imagination—though few are strong enough to use it. *Lophophora williamsii*, *peyote*, is the ancient cactus of northern Mexico and the Southwest US. Its cousin is *San Pedro, Trichocereus pachanoi*, the cactus of the Inca and before them the people they conquered, both shape-shifters. *Amanita muscaria* is a mushroom so potent that Siberian shamans ingested it, then offered their urine—filled with the power of the mushroom bolstered and balanced by the spirit of the shaman—to the mushroom's devotees to drink. Also among them are *Iboga tamarinth*, the West African plant teacher, and *ayahuasca*—also known as *yagé, natem, hoasca*, depending on the region—the visionary and curative vine of the Amazon.

This is the story of my experience with *ayahuasca* over a period of 25 years as its student. The first time I experienced a cup of the foul-tasting tea I had no idea of what it was, how important it was to the people of Amazonia, or how my life would change because of it. That first time it was just something to try. But something extraordinary happened, something that drew me back for a second cup the following year. Then a third. With each, the vine exposed a little more of her spirit, and with it I was led deeper and deeper into my consciousness. I had no idea that what lay ahead of me would take me beyond the limit of bearable fear, teach me to heal, help me through the bitter and painful breakup of my family, and finally put me back together again, just as I was, but somehow completely different. I can say that during those 25 years I have visited countless worlds and spent time, often awestruck, with unimaginable entities. I have been tickled by invisible hands from other worlds until I was rendered immobile from joy. I have been attacked by forces I did not know existed, and once was given the gift of a moment of absolute unconditional love.

It's been an incredible journey of the heart and one I'm thrilled and honored to have been allowed to take.

The best part, of course, is that my schooling has just begun.

⊛

# PROLOGUE

I'M GOING to begin with a supposition: that all matter has a life force. By that I mean that all matter is sentient.

And all matter dates from the first moment of time. You and I can trace our lineage back to that moment, when we were just cosmic dust balls billions of years from becoming slime creatures and millions of years away from coming out of the primordial soup and clambering up onto land.

The same would hold true for a mountain, a rock, a flower. Everything we know and millions of things we don't know trace back to that first moment when matter came into existence. If we were to look at a mountain, for instance, and apply my supposition—imagine what that mountain has gone through since the dawn of time, imagine what it has experienced, and now imagine what it would be like to be able to communicate with that mountain about those experiences. It's my belief that that's doable; it's my failure that I don't know how to communicate with that being, its will, its personality. But that doesn't mean it's not doable, just that I fail at it.

Imagine the same for an ocean, for a fish that's just been bitten by a predator, for a plant.

Plants, like everything else, are our co-dwellers in the universe. But humanity has a special relationship with plants. Since the beginning of humanity plants have provided the bulk of our food, our clothing, our shelter. Some provide us with the loveliest scents; some with extraordinary color. They're the source of our medicines. They go so far as to take the poisonous carbon dioxide that humans exhale and turn it back into life-giving oxygen. That's some relationship. Of course it may be that plants only invented us to distribute their seeds, so I'm not suggesting they live to cater to us. But they do provide us with much of what we need to exist on this planet.

Among the flora of the world as we know it, several plants are not just allies, they are considered master plant teachers. You might extend that to read master plant teachers of humanity. These plants might be considered gate-keepers of a sort. These plants are the plants that allow us, we humans, to slow down enough to communicate with the mountains; to speed up enough to communicate with a hummingbird; to visit the other realms past and present and simultaneous that are here but that we don't ordinarily see or hear within the bandwidths of our senses.

When I say other realms that are already here, what I mean are other realities that co-exist with ours. Imagine a dog whistle. You blow it, you hear nothing. Your cat hears nothing. Birds hear nothing. But a dog will yelp in pain at the sound.

So while you couldn't hear it, it was still there. Your hearing just didn't have a broad enough band. Now, what I'm suggesting the master plant teachers do is broaden the bands of our senses so that we see, hear, feel, touch, taste and sense things we can't under ordinary circumstances. There are several that are commonly known, though there are undoubtedly others whose existence humanity has either not yet discovered or whose existence is being closely guarded by the peoples who use them.

These teachers all have, I believe, will and intent, and have made the choice to be teachers to humanity. They all, also, have built-in mechanisms that ensure that humanity has to want to ingest them, has to want the knowledge they can impart once they have opened the gates they guard for us. Most of them prevent frivolous or accidental use simply by being physically difficult to ingest. One might pick a peyote button and eat it with little difficulty, but to eat the 30 or 50 or 100 one would need to talk with its spirit is a very difficult thing. Similarly, the vile taste of *datura* or *ayahuasca*—coupled with the intense purging and often terrifying visionary states they induce—makes frivolous or accidental use almost impossible.

So while the rose suggests we come to her to bathe in her glorious scent, the master plant teachers warn us away from them. You pretty much have to want what they have to offer, and be willing to prove it with physical discomfort, before they will share.

But once they do, well, when those gates are once opened, they will never quite close all the way again. Your broadened band of senses will never quite be able to forget seeing or interacting with the spirits you encountered, the spirits that are sharing your/our space. In other words, the spirits never leave once you've made their acquaintance.

Of course, if you don't want to learn that ghosts or spirits are everywhere, if you don't want to learn what a flower is "thinking" or how a tree feels when you prune its branches, you may not want to deal with those medicines.

In my own case, some of the teachings have taken years and dozens of sessions to learn; others have been very simple but no less profound. Once, years ago, I was in an ayahuasca dream and asked the spirits what I could do to make a better living as a writer. Without hesitation a spirit said: "Drink less. Write more."

That was it. The whole answer. So I drank less, wrote more and pretty soon was able to support my family on what I earned as a journalist.

※

Realizing that inviting the spirit of a master plant teacher like *ayahuasca* into your life has lasting repercussions is just one of the frequently overlooked but important aspects of these plants. There are several others as well.

Healing is a vital element of all of the master plant teachers. With *ayahuasca*, with which we are concerning ourselves, that healing occurs on physical, emotional and spiritual levels—sometimes all in the same session. In northwestern Amazonia, where I have spent my time with *ayahuasca*, illness is almost always seen as a symptom of a disorder or disturbance on another plane. Accessing that plane and identifying that disorder will frequently eliminate the symptom. *Ayahuasca* is one of the methods *curanderos*—healers—use to access those other planes.

In that same region, things like *mal ojo*, the evil eye; *celoso*, jealousy, and other forms of negative energy, whether produced by a person or by a *brujo*—sorcerer—paid by someone, are considered to produce very real results. That's because of a belief, or awareness, that intentions, like everything else, have a life force. And that force, good or bad, affects what it touches.

At its most basic level, a person living on a river might go to a *curandero* and say that he's got a problem. His problem is that his chickens keep dying and he doesn't understand why. He asks the *curandero* to drink *ayahuasca* to see what's causing it.

The *curandero* drinks, contacts his spirit allies and asks them the cause of the problem. They in turn might show him that a neighbor who is angry with the chicken farmer is adding a touch of poison to the chicken's feed at night.

But the work doesn't end there. A good *curandero* would look further, to see what might have caused such anger, and see that the chicken farmer, at some earlier time, had caused a problem for the neighbor.

When the *curandero* comes out of his dream he has good news and bad news for the chicken farmer. The good news is he's identified the problem. The bad news is that until the chicken farmer acknowledges the initial wrong he did to his neighbor, the poisonings will continue and the chickens will keep dying.

One time, a man who kept hurting himself shortly after he sold his plantains went to visit my teacher Julio and said he suspected someone was giving him the evil eye. He asked Julio to drink *ayahuasca* to see who it was. Julio did, and when he came out of his dream he told the man that no one was giving him the evil eye. "Then why do I keep getting hurt?" asked the man.

"Because every time you have money you get drunk in that little cantina in Herrera, and then when you leave you trip on the broken step," Julio chuckled. "So you can either stop drinking when you sell your plantains or you can fix that step."

On one occasion, just outside of Iquitos, I was present when a man came to a *curandero* named Juan. The man was beside himself. He was certain that his wife was cheating on him and about to leave him for another man and he couldn't bear the thought. He wanted to know whether it was true and who the man was.

On this occasion, Juan, the man and I all drank. And all of us saw the same thing: We saw the woman—I only presumed it was the wife in question, as I didn't know her—speaking with a man on a busy square.

When the dream was over the man was even more distraught. "I knew it! She's no good and she's leaving me," he sobbed.

Juan asked the man to try to revisit the scene in the *ayahuasca* dream. He asked the man if he could identify the place. The man did: It was the Plaza 28, one of the city's main plazas and not far from the center of town.

Juan then asked the man to try to calm down enough to see the man in the vision clearly. This time when the man grew even more distraught: "She's cheating with a priest!"

Juan laughed. "No. She's not cheating. Did you hear what they were talking about?"

The man said he hadn't.

"She was telling him that you are so jealous that you always think she's cheating. And then you hit her. And now, even though she still loves you, she cannot take your jealousy and the beatings anymore. So she was talking with the priest about getting a divorce."

The man started to deny it, then began to sob and admitted that what Juan said was true. He kept beating her because he thought she was so beautiful that everyone wanted her and he didn't want her to leave him.

Those healings are quite typical of the work a *curandero* does with the people he treats. But *ayahuasca* healing is not limited to those sorts of things. In sessions with Don Julio, I've had guests clear up physical ailments, emotional problems, solve mid-life crises.

One unusual type of healing that is common with *ayahuasca* deals with soul-loss, a condition most Westerners have never even heard of, and if they have, it's not something they would believe is real. Soul-loss is a condition in which a person's soul, or life-force, flees the body, generally during a traumatic experience, leaving the body nearly lifeless. If the life force is not reunited with the body quickly, the person will frequently die, and if he or she doesn't die, will be little more than vegetable.

Several years ago, an old indigenous Matses woman who lived not far from Julio was washing clothes in her canoe on the river. She looked into the water and saw her recently deceased husband. He was calling to her to join him. Then she saw her own grave next to his. This we learned later. What those who were there saw was the woman suddenly lurch forward and fall from the canoe, screaming. She climbed onto the riverbank and began racing headlong through tall grass toward the village she lived in. In her panic she stumbled on a fallen tree trunk hidden in the grass and fell, hitting her head.

Her nephews brought her to Julio while I happened to be there. They had to carry her from the canoe. Her breathing was very shallow, her eyes were rolled back in her head. She did not respond to touch.

Julio had her laid down on a hut floor and began to treat her. He chanted, cleansed her with smoke and *Agua Florida*—the ubiquitous holy water of northwest Amazonia—then went into a trance that lasted perhaps an hour. During the trance he was as lifeless as she, except for moments of agitation when his fists would clench, his shoulders shudder, and he would speak unintelligibly. He began to sweat profusely. When he came out of the trance his clothes were soaked through and he told the Matses men to bring her back the next day at the same time.

She left as lifelessly as she'd arrived, and she arrived the next day as lifelessly as she'd left.

The second day's treatment was much like the first, except that Julio forced a little bit of a plant decoction he'd had his son Jairo make into the woman's mouth. And this time, when Julio was in his trance and would tense up, the woman began to tense up as well. She was still unconscious, but moaned perceptibly, and gritted her jaw.

When he was finished, he told her nephews to bring her back to finish her treatments the next day at the same time.

When she was gone, Julio related that he'd seen the woman see her husband in the river calling to her. Then she'd seen her grave. It was such a shock that her soul fled, leaving her to fall from the canoe, then race mindlessly until she'd fallen. He thought she would be better the next day.

During the third treatment, while Julio began to chant, the woman began to move. She moaned, clenched her jaw and folded her hands into fists. She began to move her torso. Within an hour she opened her eyes and there was recognition in them. Julio chanted and cleansed and the woman was given a little more of the plant medicine—this time she tried to object to it—and her movements began to take on a solidity. An hour later and she was angrily asking Julio what he was doing and why was she there.

Another hour and she could be helped to her feet and, with assistance, walked back to the canoe. She'd gotten her soul back.

The next day she returned, still weak, and Julio asked what had happened to cause her soul to flee. She told the same story Julio had told two days earlier.

*Ayahuasca* is frequently called *la purga*, the purge, because users tend to physically purge themselves. Generally, within 20 to 40 minutes of drinking *ayahuasca*, the user will be overcome with an impossible-to-resist urge to vomit that's sometimes accompanied by a similarly uncontrollable urge to excrete.

A lot of people who drink the medicine hate that part of it, but the purge is one of the most effective healing elements of *ayahuasca*—touching on the physical, emotional and spiritual levels at the same time.

In northwest Amazonia, among the most typical illnesses are gastro-intestinal problems. The reasons for that out on the river include a lack of refrigeration; sun-drying fish that later gets wet and then is dried again, a perfect set-up for parasites; game often carries parasites that, if not cooked well enough, can be transmitted to humans. In the city, meat and fish in the markets in Iquitos will often be salted but are otherwise uncooked, and can go un-refrigerated in the tropical heat and humidity for weeks, until it's sold.

*Ayahuasca* cleans out those parasites better than any other medicine available in the region.

But for those suffering emotional and spiritual issues, *la purga* is equally effective. Normally, it's recommended that a person drinking *ayahuasca* fast for at least several hours and often for a full day before drinking. That ensures an empty stomach. But it won't diminish the purging effects.

The difference in the purge on an empty stomach, however, is that instead of vomiting lunch, the participant will have a chance to vomit some of the bile of their lives, things they carry around which clutter up their mental and spiritual arenas uselessly. Most of us don't even realize what we are carrying. None of us can remember the first time we were scolded by what was, until then, the loving voice of our mother or father, but it certainly left a scar. Few of us remember all of the hearts we broke, or the lies we told breaking them. Many of us do remember those who broke our hearts and every little lie that was told in doing it. That's emotional junk that we're better off tossing. Guilt for something we cannot fix? Get rid of it.

*Ayahuasca's* spirit reaches down into the depths of your soul and roots around for those things, then brings them to the surface—in the frightening moments of ego-dissolution—in a wretched reliving of them, and then allows you to eliminate them. It's not like vomiting at all: It's as if great chunks of physical matter are explosively hurled from the bottom of your bowels—the vomiting often sounds like a waterfall in reverse, the water rushing up the rocks and violently cascading from your mouth. My guests swear they vomited heaps; in truth they rarely vomit more than the few ounces of *ayahuasca* they drank as they have nothing physical in their stomachs to eliminate.

Another element of healing that's frequently overlooked must be touched on. *Curanderos* in both the Amazon and elsewhere often have to suck illnesses—physical, emotional, spiritual—from their patients. But illnesses, like all other matter, are sentient and have the same will to live as other things.

The person who explained that to me originally was Bertha Grove, a medicine woman from the Southern Ute tribe outside of Durango, Colorado. She was elderly but powerful. I had attended several all-night peyote ceremonies with the Utes, during which Bertha was always present. It had taken probably a year to get permission to attend the first; after several, I asked permission to bring my sister, an acupuncturist. Bertha said okay and Pat joined me.

The ceremony that evening was being held for a youngster who was quite ill. At one point during the ceremony Bertha stood, took the boy and began to suck the top of his head. In a few minutes she stopped and briefly stepped outside the teepee.

In the morning, outside the teepee, Bertha called to my sister and I. "You both saw what I did in there, didn't you?" she asked. We said we had.

"I sucked that boy's sickness out. But I don't know if you understand that that sickness wants to live. It's just as willful as you or me. And now if I suck that sickness out and spit it out it's going to be lying on the ground just waiting for someone to step on it and then that person is going to get sick. They might not get the same sickness the boy had because sickness can change its shape and affect different people different ways, but it will always be sickness or something bad.

"So when we Indians suck out a sickness we don't swallow it. We spit it out and always wrap it up in something—not that you can see, something like invisible gauze—and send it off somewhere to a place where it will never be allowed to land on someone else and make them sick. I send mine to a far off planet that's very cold and barren. Other healers send theirs to their own places.

"Now the reason I'm telling you this," she said to my sister, "is that last night I saw you. I saw that you are an excellent healer. But you have a problem. You're taking sickness out of people and you don't know to get rid of it so it's just staying on you. You're covered in a lot of sicknesses and you've got to stop because even though you're strong you are going to get real sick, real soon if you don't get rid of all that."

Six months later my sister did get sick. She got a host of illnesses that were apparently unrelated but which would leave her crippled and in pain for the next 20 years.

✵✵✵

Another point I think needs making—as it frequently comes up in conversations related to the use of *ayahuasca*, *San Pedro*, *peyote*, and probably with all of the master plant teachers—is the question of the value of a *curandero*. The question that arises is whether or not a curandero (in the case of *ayahuasca* or *San Pedro*) or a "Roadman" (in the case of *peyote*) is necessary. The answer, I think, is that they're not necessary—the plants will teach you something whether there is a *curandero* or not. But I think that the work of a good *curandero* can add whole dimensions to the experience.

On a physical level, the *curandero* is the master preparer of the ayahuasca. He must be compared to a chef, rather than a cook. More than that, however, his interactions with the spirits of the plants he's working with are what's of great value. The plants must give up their chemicals to whoever puts them in a pot and boils them.

But the *curandero*, through his relationship with the sentient side of the plant, can encourage those plants to give up more than their chemical components, to give up their spirit. This is not to be dismissed.

*Curanderos* have generally spent years becoming intimate with the spirits of the plants. Moreover, the *curandero* might have several plant allies, and depending on the needs of those drinking on a given day might have a variety of admixture plants he can add to the basic recipe. And each of those plants bring their individual spirits and personalities to the ceremony the *curandero* is running.

And running the ceremony is really what a *curandero* does. It might look to an outsider as if he or she is just sitting on a stool, chanting and shaking a leaf-rattle, but he is doing much more than that. He is seeing what each person is dreaming, his *icaros*, songs, sending some further out into their dreams and pulling others back down to earth at the same time. The *curandero* is healing everyone simultaneously as well, even those who don't know they need it. He is asking his plant spirit allies to work with everyone, and his allies respond.

Until you've experienced it, that is a difficult thing to believe. One former guest explained it this way, just hours after his first *ayahuasca* experience. The guest was named Lynn, and he was one of two males among my six guests. He said he was sitting on the hut floor and not having much of a reaction to the medicine. "And at one point in the ceremony, I mentally called out to Julio to show me something," he said. "Anything that would indicate that I hadn't taken a very expensive trip for nothing.

"I had my eyes open while I was thinking that," he said. "And as soon as I did, Julio suddenly stood and grew to about 14 feet tall and his chakras began spinning with the most fantastic lights, shooting colors all over the space and me. And then he very clearly said. 'Now can I get back to the work I was doing on the women?'

"In that moment," Lynn said, "I understood something fantastic happens out in that realm—a realm that I wasn't certain even existed until that point in time."

# PART I

# AYAHUASCA: VINE OF THE LITTLE DEATH

*Prepare your priest, oh, medicine, good medicine;*
*Still the heart, oh saints and spirits;*
*Prepare me for the little death, the good death,*
*Oh spirits who live beneath the sea.*
*At every moment take care of us;*
*Bless these bodies, protect us as we sleep*
*And the spirits fly about us in the trees.*

*from an ayahuasquero's chant.*

## Chapter One

# NIGHT OF VISIONS

J ULIO JERENA sat on his porch, leaning against the front wall of his home, a stilted hut on the Rio Aucayacu in Peru's Amazonia. Around us night had fallen. The heat of the day had subsided but the air was still thick with the incessant buzz of insects and the dank smells of the jungle. The moon, half-full and hung askew, began to rise above the trees across the little river.

I'd known Julio for several years. He was a *curandero*, a jungle doctor who worked with plant medicines. The missionary family who lived not far from him on the Aucayacu called him a *brujo*, a sorcerer, to dissuade the other families who lived on the river from going to him. They rarely succeeded: He simply understood illness and cures too well.

The eerie yellow light from a small kerosene lamp illuminated Julio's frame and face: He was old, small, wiry and tired from chopping wood and maintaining a fire all day. He had a shock of white hair. Sunken cheeks highlighted his prominent nose. The veins in his neck stood out through his thin skin. His ears were too big by far. But his eyes, clear and dark and almost luminous, captured my attention. They had a quality about them that was ageless and strong, warm and understanding.

Among the medicines he used was *ayahuasca*, a liquid extracted from cooking sections of the *Banisteriopsis caapi* vine, *chacruna* leaves and a number of tree barks. It's used throughout Amazonia for both its curative and spiritual properties.

"When I use ayahuasca I can see inside a person and tell what is wrong," he explained once during one of our rare verbal conversations. "The spirits let me look very closely and tell me what to do."

Julio interrupted my thoughts by asking for a match. He took it and lit a *mapacho*, a hand-rolled black-tobacco cigarette common to the region.

"*Muy bueno*," he said, exhaling the thick smoke into the open neck of an old brown bottle filled with ayahuasca. The smoke, he said, prevented evil spirits from contaminating it.

He chanted while he smoked: His voice was gruff and the words ran together incomprehensibly. Next to him his 12-year-old son, Antenor, played a guitar he'd fashioned by stretching a boar skin over the hard shell of a giant armadillo and affixing a neck to it. His fingers flew about the fretless neck effortlessly, picking out the chant's haunting melody on the taut strings.

Julio, Antenor and the rest of us—my guide, Moises; a friend of mine, Larry Lavalle; and I—were sitting in a circle. In the center of it was an old piece of blue plastic sheeting, upon which Julio had placed a number of things: the ayahuasca bottle, a handful of mapacho cigarettes, a bottle of sweet orange *Agua Florida*, a bottle of *camalonga*—sacred oleander seeds mixed with camphor, garlic cloves and onion in *aguardiente*, strong cane liquor—and a *shacapa*, a fan rattle made of leaves. He also had an old book of Catholic saint stories, a bottle of Tabu cologne, and a small stone axe head he'd found in the foothills of the Andes years earlier.

*Medicine Bottles, Mapachos and Julio's Book*

Julio chanted until he'd finished two of the mapachos, then corked the bottle and took the ayahuasca into his bedroom, the only walled section of the hut. He would leave it there in the dark for an hour to give it a chance to settle after it has been "smoked," so that good spirits could gather around it.

"*Bueno*," he said after he returned and resumed sitting. "*Una hora mas.*"

We sat silently, listening to the beautiful music coming from Antenor's odd guitar. He'd never played a real one so had no idea that what he had made was all wrong—for frets he'd dug out little canals in the neck, and he only had five strings—but its music was nonetheless clear and filled the night air with warmth and melancholy.

When he finally grew tired and put the instrument down, his father smiled. "*Ah, bueno,*" he said in the harsh, guttural Spanish of the region. "*Todo bien.*" Good. Everything was good.

He looked to each of us. "*Ahora,*" he began. "Have you any questions you would like to ask?"

"Yes," said Larry, a strapping 40-year-old from Brooklyn with Mediterranean coloring and chiseled features who'd been living in Los Angeles. "What kind of visions do you have when you drink ayahuasca, don Julio?"

Julio smiled again. "Many things. I see boats, planes, people, spirits. I talk with them and they tell me things. Some of them are dead family members or old friends. Some of them are the ancients, some are plant spirits. There are a lot of different spirits who speak with me. Some of them are good and some of them are not. But they are only spirits."

He turned to Antenor, who was going to drink ayahuasca for the first time that night. "If you get afraid, you must remember that. They are only spirits."

He might have said it to all of us. It was always a little frightening to drink ayahuasca, and occasionally terrifying. The visions it produced were not always the visions one wanted to see, and even when they were, they were difficult to reconcile with ordinary reality. I had learned that several years earlier, with my first ayahuasca experience.

⚬⚬⚬

It was 1984 and I had been traveling in Peru with Larry and another friend, Chuck Dudell. We had spent time in the Cordillera Blanca and later at Machu Picchu, and had finally flown to Iquitos, the part of the trip I had most looked forward to. Iquitos is the city where the Amazon River, traveling south to north until that point, hits a slightly raised land mass and turns east, toward the Atlantic. Iquitos is that land mass. It was there—after we'd taken a trip upriver to a town called Requena—that we'd met Moises, a 55-year-old *mestizo* guide with tattooed arms, a cocky air and a good smile. He had approached us on the street, explained that he was a former military man whose specialty was jungle survival training and offered to take us into the jungle for a few days.

When he learned that we had already looked into a number of established guide services but had turned them down because we were looking for something different, he beamed.

"*Perfectamente!* I am the only guide in Iquitos who will take you into the real jungle," he said in pidgin English. "No tourist camps. *Pura selva.* pure jungle. I can even arrange for you to drink ayahuasca."

It was obvious that he expected us to know what he meant but we didn't, and when we asked him what it was, he laughed. "*Alucino.* Jungle medicine."

*Moises Torres Vienna*

Though all of us had done a fair share of hallucinogens, none of us were familiar with ayahuasca. Moises, who claimed no knowledge of drugs outside the jungle, doubted it would be like anything we'd done before. "*Muy diferente,*" he said. "*Muy especial.* It is the fastest way to know the jungle. It will make the jungle your friend and give you night vision. And if it likes you, you'll be able to visit any part of the world you want to see."

Two days later, we set off about dawn in a flat-bottomed boat heading up the Amazon River.

By mid-morning we had left the big river and were traveling up a smaller one in two dugout canoes Moises had rented from a local fisherman. By noon we had reached the home of a woman Moises described as a Shipibo Indian *curandera*. She was beautiful, strong and old, and Moises assured us that her ayahuasca would produce incredible visions.

Unfortunately, she refused to make it for us. We were dilettantes, she said, who had no business using ayahuasca, and no amount of cajoling on Moises' part would entice her to change her mind.

We set off by foot on a path to the home of another person who might make us ayahuasca. We traveled along the river through a dense stretch of jungle to the home of a man named Alphonse. It was a hard walk. There were several nearly impossible bridges to cross—just a log or two across deep stream beds, some of them several yards wide. The logs were slippery and unanchored: At each we crossed with a painstaking caution that Moises found hilarious.

When we finally arrived at the unwalled platform hut where Alphonse lived, he was not home. Moises explained to one of his wives what we wanted and she explained that it was too late in the day to begin making ayahuasca. She said we ought to come back in the morning. Moises persisted and the woman eventually agreed to pass the message along in return for some small presents.

We left the camp, hiked for an hour, and returned. This time Alphonse was there. He was a bull of a man wearing raggedy clothing and an old painter's cap. My first impression was that he was a dangerous man, but that vanished almost immediately. His smile was broad and radiant.

He was sitting by a great aluminum pot, tending a fire beneath it. The ayahuasca was being made, he explained, though he cautioned us that it wouldn't be at full potency since the preparation required a full day's attention, then told us to return that evening at eight.

Just before sunset we made our way back to the hut. The going was even slower than it had been earlier. The thought of falling 10 or 12 feet onto riverbed debris—rotting tree trunks, broken branches and such—prevented us from anything more than inch-by-inch progress.

When we arrived, Alphonse was waiting for us. We were invited to join him on the platform floor of his hut. At the rear of the hut his wives and their children were already asleep beneath mosquito netting.

Once we were settled Alphonse asked for an hour of silence while we prepared ourselves. We sat quietly, listening to the occasional rustle of foraging animals and the cries of distant monkeys. Except for the insects, the night was beautiful. Alphonse laughed when he saw us flailing away at them and promised that they would no longer bother us after we drank the ayahuasca.

*"Otro efecto,"* Moises explained. "The ayahuasca keeps the mosquitos away."

When the hour was up Alphonse had us sit in a circle, then retreated to a corner of the platform. In the center of the circle he placed the ayahuasca, a bottle of camphor and garlic in aguardiente, a little bottle of gasoline, a handful of mapachos and a leaf fan.

Alphonse lit one of the cigarettes and blew the smoke into the ayahuasca. Under his breath he began to chant. As he did he filled a small gourd with the brown liquid and passed it to Larry. Larry tipped the gourd to his lips, made a face as though he'd just bitten into a sour fruit, then passed the gourd back to Alphonse. Watching him, it suddenly occurred to me that I knew nothing of these people, of their medicine or its effects. What if something should go wrong? What if we couldn't handle it?

Moises didn't help when he declined to drink. "Someone has to watch out for you guys," he said, "to make sure you don't go off into the jungle." He assured us that was the way it was done.

When the gourd reached me I ignored my fears and drank. The ayahuasca tasted like burnt grapefruit juice infused with dank smoke. It was acrid and awful and almost impossible not to spit out.

Alphonese drank last, then passed the bottle of camphor and the gasoline for us to sniff. They were to protect us from evil spirits, we were told. The mapachos were passed last.

Perhaps 20 minutes after he drank, Alphonse suddenly leaned over the edge of the platform and began to vomit. We'd been warned that we would all vomit, but there was something unusual in the way Alphonse did it. The sound he emitted was unnatural, almost beautiful. From deep within his belly came what sounded like the rush of water over rocks, like a flash flood crashing and tumbling against stone. Louder and louder it grew, boiling up within him with the clarity of a mad spring bursting from a glacier. It was an astonishing sound, moving and powerful.

And then suddenly it came on me and I lunged for the platform's edge. I could feel the toxins in the liquid cramping my stomach, my blood rushed and my head pounded and I heaved into the night.

When I was finished Alphonse was still not through. His rushing river was calming though, the rumbling and boiling in his stomach settling. I looked to Moises, sure I'd imagined the sound. "He's a man of great power," Moises said. "He doesn't do anything in a small way."

Alphonse began chanting and shaking his shacapa. The dry leaves made a noise like wind rushing about the platform, enveloping the haunting and distant sound of his voice.

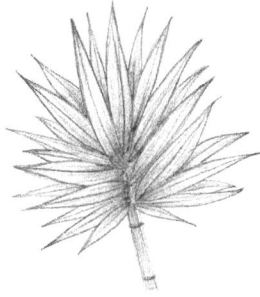

*Shacapa*

The night grew peaceful, the mosquitoes vanished. I lay on my back and closed my eyes. Suddenly a strange image appeared. I saw a bird flying over snow-crested mountains. It was a huge brown bird with long broad wings tipped with white. I was looking at the bird from a great distance and then suddenly felt myself merging with it. I realized I was seeing with the bird's perspective, my sharp eyesight picking out the most minute details of the landscape. I flew over a range of mountains and peered into a stream: I saw fish moving about, the colors of their scales beautiful hues of blue and green. And then, unexpectedly, I tipped off the face of the earth and plummeted toward them. I don't remember any feelings of fear, only that I was hungry and wanted a fish. I split the water with hardly a splash and in an instant was racing skyward again, the fish in my beak. I snapped it in two and the pieces of it entered my stomach unchewed. I remember thinking I didn't generally eat food that way.

The instant I thought of myself apart from the bird I was back in Alphonse's house. I became immensely sad and tried to bring the image back, without success. It was only when I finally stopped trying to fly that the vision returned. I would suddenly be flying, sometimes with the bird, sometimes just below it, looking at the arrangement of the feathers, aware that each feather moved individually to control our flight.

Twice I was able to ask the bird to take me somewhere. First, I wanted to see the woman I lived with, Clare, who was at that time in California. Instantly I was in her room, hovering on the ceiling. For a moment I watched her making love with someone and a wave of nausea washed over me. The moment I got jealous the image disappeared and I was back on the platform in the jungle.

The second image was of our apartment in New York, sublet to friends. They were reading, one in the living room, one in a bedroom, and all was quiet. They had moved the living room furniture around.

The only other vision I can remember from that first time using ayahuasca was of a tree: I stared at it as if I were looking down the wrong end of a telescope, then suddenly found myself next to it, focusing on one of its burls. I saw thousands of ants moving on the bark. I saw them in such detail I could count the hairs on their legs. When I looked across the rings of the burl it was as if I were looking across a vast plane.

And then I heard talking and the others were saying they weren't having much effect; that all they felt was ill. I wanted to stay but was overruled and in a few minutes we started back to our camp.

We'd gotten a good distance from Alphonse's, Chuck and Larry still talking about how little the ayahuasca had affected them, when Moises pointed out that we were walking in the jungle at night, crossing the precarious log bridges, and none of us were using our flashlights.

"Even with no visions it's a good medicine for the jungle," he said. "Night vision is very important here."

The next morning Moises had us take a cold river wash, saying it was necessary after ayahuasca to make us whole again. I did as told and immersed myself in the water.

✤

Chapter Two

# MEETING JULIO

WHEN I returned home to New York, I collected what literature I could find on ayahuasca, hoping I would learn more about this strange and wonderful medicine. In fact, I didn't read any of it. I was afraid that what others had written would influence my next experience and I didn't want any more clutter in my head than I already had.

Much of that clutter involved whether to believe the experience or not. On the one hand I knew it had been real, that I'd glimpsed what it was to be a bird, to be hungry and to eat a fish. On the other I had no way of knowing whether or not I'd invented the entire vision or dream or whatever it was. It was a particularly difficult experience to trust because it was precisely what I wanted to believe. Magic mushrooms and acid had taught me that there was a spirit in everything, that ours was a mysterious world. Ayahuasca not only appeared to verify that, it had allowed me to become viscerally involved with one of those spirits, and that was too fantastic. Was it possible that my ego had really dissolved enough—momentarily—to allow me to interplay with another form, or was my ego so distended that I could dream the vision up and convince myself it was true?

And what of the apparent astral traveling I'd done to California and New York? That my friends would be reading in my apartment was typical enough to have been imagined; equally true that my fears concerning Clare's behavior—we were separated at the time—would surface in the moment I tried to envision her.

There was one odd thing: The furniture in our apartment in New York had indeed been rearranged when I returned. The problem was that I had only noticed it had been moved, I hadn't really paid enough attention to know if it was in the positions I'd seen.

The only undeniable aspects of the experience were the temporarily improved night vision, the temporary disappearance of the mosquitoes, and a sense of connection with the jungle we all shared in the days we spent with Moises following the ayahuasca experience. It felt as though the ayahuasca had indeed made the jungle a more friendly and less alien place than it otherwise would have been. Still, real or imagined, that winter I often dreamt of flying with the bird with the white-tipped wings.

When I returned to Iquitos some months later to spend more time with Moises learning about the jungle, there was no question about my doing ayahuasca again. I wanted to return to Alphonse's, but Moises said he had moved and he didn't know where he was. But he assured me that he knew another *curandero*, Julio Jerena, who would make it for us. He was an old man, Moises said, and respected as a healer.

We traveled by riverboat up the Amazon and then the Ucayali River for nearly 16 hours before we reached the town of Genaro Herrera. There, we ate breakfast and hired a local with a *peque-peque*—an oversized canoe with a small motor outfitted with a long propeller shaft that made it ideal for travel in shallow water—and headed up the tiny Rio Supay to the even tinier Rio Aucayacu. It was a beautiful trip through the forest. Macaws sang in the canopy overhead and pink and gray river dolphins danced in the waters around us.

⁂

Julio's house was set back from the river, a ramshackle, stilted hut surrounded by fruit trees. Old fishing nets dried in the sun next to freshly washed laundry on a patch of lemon grass. A pig and dozens of chickens ran for the safety of the space beneath the hut as we approached.

Julio was sitting on his porch mending a fishing net when we arrived. He was older than I'd imagined, and wiry. He wore a mustache and had widely spaced, dark eyes. Moises introduced us and explained what we wanted. Julio said alright, then told us we could stay in a small hut not far from his.

After we settled in, Moises arranged for me to be taken out on the river in a canoe with a young man named Alberto. Alberto was to let me listen to the jungle, to hear it at night when it came alive. Instead, he shot a cayman, a monkey, a large rodent called a *majas* and wounded an ocelot. When we returned I was furious with Moises. I told him I hadn't paid him to kill animals and if that what the trip was about then we should just cancel it. Moises stood his ground and explained that this was simply life in the jungle. Killing was part of living and if I wanted to learn about the jungle I'd better damned well get used to killing.

⁂

The next morning I woke to the sound of chopping wood and from the porch of the little hut I could see the smoke from Julio's ayahuasca fire. I asked Moises if I should offer to help; he said that making the fire was the curandero's job, but that in any event Julio had an apprentice, a young fellow named Salis Navarro.

As the evening approached I grew anxious, and when it was finally time to take the short walk to Julio's I fairly flew through the underbrush. Moises chided me for acting like a child but I didn't care. I desperately wanted to fly again.

There were a number of men gathered on Julio's porch. Among them was Salis. He was young, strong and bright, with clear eyes and a thick neck. I asked about his being a curandero's apprentice. He told me it was not something he would have chosen to do but the plant spirits had always been friendly with him and urged him to study. When I looked at him questioningly he said that most city people didn't understand. "They can be a persistent bunch of spirits," he laughed.

One of the other men asked what had brought me there. I explained that it was probably the same thing that had brought him: curiosity.

"I'm not here for curiosity," he said. "I'm here for my leg." He pulled up his right trouser leg: His calf was shriveled and purple and the bone looked as though it was covered with only a tissue-thick layer of skin. The flesh was necrotic and gave off a foul odor of rancid meat.

"*Shushupe*," he said, "bushmaster." He explained that he'd been bitten by a bushmaster—the largest venomous snake in the Americas—several weeks earlier while working near Iquitos. He had gone to the hospital there and they had done what they could, but after several days had decided to amputate.

The men gathered around and began to add to the story, describing the size of the snake and mimicking the man as he explained how he left the hospital and made his way by boat to Julio's where he'd been treated with ayahuasca and topical plant medicines. He'd also been given a regimen of exercises to follow, which including walking up and down a three-step device Julio had "seen" while under the influence of ayahuasca, and subsequently built.

"Almost two months now and I still have my leg."

Julio, mostly through Moises, explained that the ayahuasca had cleaned the man's system of toxins and that except for the area in the immediate vicinity of the wound—which was dead—the leg would heal well.

One of the other men said that he too was there for treatment. He said that Julio had recently performed an operation on his stomach, then showed me a scarless stomach to prove it. I asked what had been wrong and Julio said the man had a large tumor in his belly and that he'd had to cut him open, extract the stomach and remove the growth. Afterward he'd washed the stomach in the river, replaced it and sewn the man back up.

I asked when the operation had taken place. He answered that it had been performed two days earlier. "All don Julio's scars heal quickly," the man said.

Everyone laughed at my skeptical look. They said my believing it or not didn't alter the facts. Julio explained that ayahuasca was a powerful ally with many uses but that trying to understand how it worked was difficult. "If you talk with the Shipibo people," he said, "they would tell you things that even I don't know. How is it possible to cut open a stomach and wash it in the river? It isn't. But with ayahuasca it is. How can you work and not leave a scar? You can't. But with ayahuasca you can. I can't explain it to you. You might say it is all a vision. Still, people come to me and with ayahuasca I heal them."

That night, Salis was the primary curandero. He had us make a circle and brought out the necessary things. Once again Moises removed himself, saying he wanted to see that no harm came to me.

We drank the foul tasting ayahuasca, sniffed the camalonga and Agua Florida, put on a touch of Tabu, passed the mapachos. Vomiting came easily, though I was disappointed that neither Salis nor Julio regurgitated with Alphonse's style.

Salis began to chant. His voice was strong and clear, his words a mix of Quechua—from the Andean highlands—local dialect and Spanish. I'd been given permission to tape the songs but all attempts to translate have failed with the exception of little snippets. Among them was this:

*"Dominating the occult science,*
*Dominating the occult spirits.*
*Calling the occult spirits,*
*Calling what moves below the currents,*
*Calling the spirits in these moments.*
*White magic, green magic, red magic, black magic,*
*Vampires and demons, cover us with your shadow.*
*In these moments I want to be granted my desires.*
*Fly, fly little body that was born free.*
*Fly, fly little body that was born free."*

Julio added his voice to Salis' while I waited patiently for the bird to appear. It never did. There were no visions whatsoever that night. Whether that was because I anticipated them or because the ingredients used to make the ayahuasca were different than those used by Alphonse, I'm not sure. Instead, the chanting of the two curanderos began to echo in my head, a resounding noise that seemed to pull me apart, as though a wedge were splitting me in half. I grew terrified of what might happen if I allowed the parts of me to separate. It seemed, on one hand, to make sense: I needed to be pulled apart if I was ever going to become whole. At the same time I didn't know whether I would ever come together again. It was a frightening experience, one I wasn't prepared for. Louder and louder the chants resounded, deeper and deeper went the wedge, until I finally fled the porch for the safety of the river's edge. Moises followed and warned me against going into the water. His voice was like an anchor that pulled me back from the edge of some horrific abyss. I turned to thank him. He was still on the porch.

Suddenly more afraid of the voice than of Julio or Salis, I returned to the circle. This time the chanting was no longer frightening. It was soothing and beautiful and I soon fell asleep. When I awoke, Moises and I returned to our hut.

After a river wash the next morning I asked Moises what had happened and why I hadn't been able to fly. He said that while I was asleep Julio had explained that I needed to be opened up so that some personal things that were holding me back could be removed. That was what Salis and he had done. Moises also said that the magical effects of ayahuasca that I'd experienced the first time were not to be sought or missed. When I needed the bird the bird would guide me. When I needed to become friendly with the jungle, ayahuasca would guide me in a different way. "Ayahuasca gives you what you need," he said, "not what you want." I thought he might have been justifying the ayahuasca's apparent lack of effect, but didn't question him further.

## Chapter Three

# MEETING THE MATSES

THE NEXT morning Moises and I left Julio's to begin my jungle training. We headed up the Aucayacu by canoe for two days, then spent a day making a little camp by the river. We rested there one day, then began a hike into the jungle on a hunting path. It was an exhilarating hike through primary forest. Huge buttressed trees soared 100 feet before branching out into a thick canopy; ancient vines looped among them. There were ant hills several feet tall and just as wide, animal tracks regularly crossed our trail, and a fantastic array of insects in a thousand different colors landed on us and our packs as we walked, probably drawn by our sweat.

All day long Moises pointed things out to me, from medicinal plants to edible plants. At night we hung hammocks covered by cocoon-shaped mosquito nets between trees. For food we had rice and canned sardines, roasted yuca bits called *fariña*, instant coffee and what food we'd gathered during the day.

On the third day, just before sundown, we came to an unexpected—to me—clearing near a little stream, and Moises said that was where my training would begin in earnest. I hung the hammocks while Moises made a fire. He put a pot of water on for coffee, then disappeared with our shotgun. In a few minutes I heard a shot, and a few minutes later he returned with a small monkey. As he tossed it on the fire to burn off its hair, I reminded him that I was not there to kill animals. He said that I'd be very hungry in that case, because we had no more food. When I exploded about that, he said this was survival training, and I'd have to learn to eat what was in the jungle and not depend on having a sack of rice and canned sardines on hand.

"But don't worry," he said. "I brought plenty of coffee for you."

I refused to eat any of the monkey that night and went to sleep hungry.

The next morning he went out to hunt again and brought back a long-necked bird he called a *trumpetero*. He roasted it on a spit over the fire. When I again said I wouldn't eat animals, he went out and collected some wild plants for me.

That day we began to build a jungle hut. Moises showed me which trees were the right ones to use and which to avoid—either because they lacked strength or were filled with ants—and how to use a vine called *tamishi* to lash the frame together. The work was fascinating but tiring, and while the three tubers we collected and boiled for my dinner were filling, they were not what I would have preferred.

❧

The next two days were the same: Moises hunted and ate well; he and I collected edible plants for me. On my fourth day without real food Moises went out hunting early, and by the time I awoke there were a couple of macaws and a large parrot on a spit over the fire. Feathers were everywhere, but Moises was nowhere in sight.

I was starving. I could smell the roasting birds. I tried to ignore them, but finally walked over to the fire, pulled a macaw from the spit and began to eat it. Just then Moises stepped out from where he'd apparently been hiding and announced: "That's the first right thing you've done in the jungle! If you don't eat you will die here. That's the most important lesson."

I was embarrassed, but never again complained about hunting for food.

The next day, about mid-morning, Moises and I were surprised when suddenly, unexpectedly, a young man walked into our little camp. He was dark and wiry. His hair was black. He was barefoot, wore a pair of old shorts, and had two strips of what looked like an inner layer of tree bark wrapped around his chest and stomach. Most unusual, though, was his face: He had a dark blue hash-mark tattoo that circled his mouth and ran across his cheeks nearly to his ears. He also had thin, six-inch splints, like whiskers, in his upper lip. And his forehead was painted burnt orange. He looked very much like a jaguar. I was scared to death.

Moises, however, simply said some words in a language I didn't know—"*Bi-ram-bo! Bi-ram-bo, bu-chi!*"—and the young man returned the greeting. The man then pointed to our shotgun, which was standing against a nearby tree. Moises nodded and made a hand gesture that indicated that it was to be returned. The man nodded and picked up the gun. Moises reached into his pocket and pulled out three shotgun shells. The man took them and disappeared into the forest.

When he was gone, Moises explained that the man was a Matses Indian, though they were often called Mayoruna. While in the military he had led a jungle unit in a ground war against them in the early 1970s in retaliation for a raid they'd made on Genaro Herrera, the town where we'd gotten off the riverboat.

"They stole machetes, shotguns, axe heads," Moises said. "They also took several women captive. Among those taken were two young Franciscan friars who wore long robes and kept their hair long. The friars were later found with their genitals crudely cut off—probably because the Matses discovered they weren't women."

The conflict lasted four days. The Peruvian military won. In its aftermath, the Peruvian military built a small base called Angamos at the confluence of the Yavarí and Gálvez rivers, where most of the Matses camps were, effectively preventing further raids.

Twenty minutes into Moises' story we heard a shotgun blast, and in another few minutes, a second one. Twenty minutes later, the young man walked back into our camp. He carried two large monkeys he'd shot in sacks fashioned from leaves that hung from strips of bark wrapped around his forehead. On his head, clinging to his hair, was a baby monkey. He replaced our shotgun against the tree, then put one of the sacks next to it. Then he turned and started walking in the direction from which he'd originally come.

Moises picked up the gun and a machete and said we should follow. He'd heard a rumor that there was a new Matses camp nearby but had never seen it. We walked quickly through the jungle for perhaps half an hour before coming on a clearing.

The clearing was demarked by posts, on each of which was the skull of a wild boar. At the rear of the clearing, a maloca—a large round hut— was being built; closer to the near side there were three or four very low temporary shelters. There were probably a dozen children milling about as well as several women, two of whom were tending an open fire. The young man handed the sack he had to one of them. She quickly unwrapped the wounded monkey and she and the other woman stretched it over the fire and began burning off its hair. To my horror, the monkey began to scream and thrash about, trying to get out of the flames. The women didn't seem to notice.

While the large monkey screamed, the young man walked over to a young woman who was nursing a baby and handed her the baby monkey. Without hesitation she put it on her free nipple.

In ten seconds I'd witnessed both the cruelest and kindest acts I'd ever seen.

Moments later, an elderly man I later knew as *Papa Viejo*—Old Daddy— came running at us, holding a shotgun. He stopped maybe 15 feet from where Moises and I stood, raised the gun so that it was pointing at Moises' chest, and began shouting. Moises didn't flinch. He simply raised our gun and began shouting back. I thought we were all going to die.

The shouting continued, louder and louder, for maybe half a minute and then both men fell abruptly silent. Moments later they both put their guns on the ground in front of them and began to talk. Some of it was in Spanish, some in Matses, some in hand signals. A few minutes later Moises said it was time to go and we left.

On the way back to camp he explained that the Matses, like most indigenous Amazon peoples, were *bravo*—aggressively brave—and always challenged visitors. If you buckled, they'd have everything you owned. If you didn't, you were generally welcomed. He said he was proud I had stood my ground with him, but that in this case there was not much to fear. "He had no shells for the gun," he laughed.

"How do you know?" I asked.

"If he did his son wouldn't have needed ours."

The incident marked me. If ayahuasca had put the jungle in my blood, then seeing the Matses gave me a destination. I would return to spend time with them.

Chapter Four

# DO YOU BELIEVE IN MAGIC?

THE FOLLOWING year I returned to Amazonia, joined by my brother-in-law, Steve Flores. Moises and I had planned a trip deep into the jungle, to the border region of Brazil. Our plan was to fly in by seaplane, visit a number of indigenous Matses communities and then hike out. During the hike we would be met at a pre-arranged river crossing by Moises' eldest son, Junior, himself an accomplished guide and by then a friend of mine. Junior would have supplies for the last few days of the hike. If things went smoothly we would eventually end up on the Aucayacu Rver and make our way to Julio's home.

One of the keys to the plan's success was our assumption that one of the Matses men would be willing to guide us between their camps and to the Rio Lobo, our meeting point with Junior. Unfortunately, near the end of our month-long stay on the Rio Gálvez, a jaguar killed a 14-year-old Matses boy in a hut we had used just one day earlier. We were one day downriver, at the next camp, when we got word. The killing, for which Steve and I were held responsible because we were the new scent the jaguar had probably followed, meant that the twin villages where it occurred would have to be burned and abandoned. The inhabitants would have to carve out a new village from the jungle somewhere else on the river.

We were shunned for causing the death, and no Matses man would hike with us. However, the headman at the camp we were in, Pablo, who later became a great friend, told one of his young sons to guide us. The son, unfortunately, had no idea of how to get to where we were going, and after four days we decided to backtrack to Pablo's camp. There, we borrowed a peque-

peque and traveled down the river to the military border post of Angamos, where we radioed for a seaplane to come take us out.

We had the plane take us to Genaro Herrera on the Rio Ucayali, and from there made our way to Julio's. We came in from the opposite direction than the one we had been expected to take. Which meant that Junior, who could have known nothing about the change of plan—was still waiting in the jungle for our arrival.

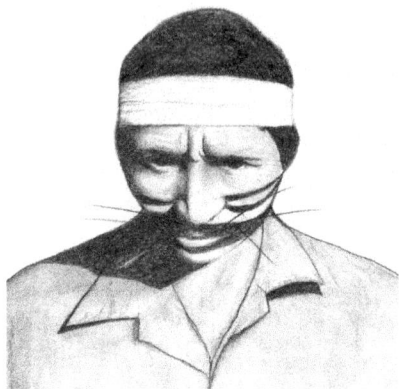

*Pablo*

As soon as we arrived at Julio's, Moises asked him to make ayahuasca. He agreed to do it the following day. I thought Moises was being cavalier about his son—I expected us to set off up the river after him—but he explained the situation.

"*Mi hijo,*" he began, "is at least three days away from here. If he is still waiting for us he will have problems because I know what supplies he had. For us to go after him without additional supplies is unthinkable; that would jeopardize us all. Instead, I'm having Julio make the ayahuasca and you will go and find my son. You'll explain what happened and tell him to leave. That is the only way."

"I'll never find my way. Where will I go?"

"You'll go with the bird. Have the bird tell him."

I couldn't believe what he was asking. I would have had a better chance finding him on foot. I didn't even think the bird would reappear, but even if it did, how would I find someone in a vision? I told Moises that what he was asking was out of the question and that we should set off after his son immediately. But he wouldn't hear of it.

All through the next day he pestered me to concentrate, to meditate on that evening's task; I did as he asked and told him I would try, but still didn't imagine it could be done, at least not by me.

That evening we sat on the porch of the little hut as Julio began the simple ceremony. Salis had helped with the collection of the vine but didn't attend. The only people who were drinking the ayahuasca were Julio, Steve, and myself. As the little cup was handed to me I silently asked for help, then gulped the liquid down.

When we were finished drinking Julio put out the little kerosene lamps and we were enveloped in darkness. It was a beautiful night, full of sounds. There was no moon because clouds covered the sky. Bullfrogs croaked, letting us know that rain was coming.

Not long after Julio began to chant I felt my stomach tighten and lunged for the edge of his platform. I could feel my insides welling up and when I vomited, for the first time I felt some of the swell and motion I'd heard from Alphonse. It was a strange and powerful feeling, a wonderful racking of my system. Over and over the swelling came and I found myself roaring into the night with each heave—though I couldn't imagine what I was heaving as Moises never let me eat after breakfast on days I was drinking ayahuasca. For a moment I imagined myself inhabited by something larger than I was; I'm not quite sure how to describe it except to say that I realized Moises' request was not at all extraordinary.

The visions began soon after my stomach settled and I retook my seat. My mind filled with pictures of demon skulls and hellish faces; a sea of them in corpse-white, a tour of hell. Body parts and wars; hatred and jealousies; famine and pestilence; red serpents and hoards of insects; as though I'd opened a page of my mind from a modern Dante's Inferno.

The visions of horror soon passed and I felt myself rising up from the porch with incredible speed, felt myself hurtling through the clouds and looking down on the whole of the Aucayacu River. In a moment it had become a tiny sliver and the whole of the jungle was beneath me, a blur. In another moment the whole earth was little more than a pinpoint.

I saw skies like I'd never imagined—clear, vast, celestial skies. Deep blues and purples, yellow planets, swirling galaxies. I moved through worlds of green and planets inhabited by forms I didn't recognize.

From somewhere I could hear the shaking of Julio's shacapa and his low, murmuring chant. What a beautiful song it was. I saw the white-tipped wings of the bird I'd traveled with and tried to merge with it. I couldn't.

And then I heard Moises' voice, coaxing me, reminding me to find his son. In an instant I was submerged in cold liquid. It took a moment to orient myself as my vision shifted from a sort of telescopic sight to a kind of macro-vision. Once I'd adjusted I realized I was in the river reeds right in front of Julio's. A snake appeared, yellow and black, with a whitish underbelly, It was long and strong and as thick as my leg. I watched it glide through the reeds. A drip of water hit the surface of the river and the ripples were tactile. I felt them and realized I was with the snake. We swam on the surface around submerged and floating trees, my body moving with powerful contractions.

I remember wondering whether it was all hallucination, whether I was dreaming everything up from my imagination. Just as I did, a bright green tree-frog came into view, sitting on a branch near the water's surface. We— the snake and I—moved silently toward it, and in a flash had eaten it. It felt strange in my throat and stranger still when it jumped in an effort to escape. I was so surprised by the feeling that I separated from the snake for a moment. Re-merging, I felt the muscles in our neck contract to kill it and felt it slide easily into my belly.

Seeing through the snake's eyes, the world was flattened and wide-angled. My peripheral vision was extraordinary. I decided to visit my family and took off with the snake. In a moment we were in New York. I visited Clare at the restaurant where she was working—she'd returned to New York, but we were through—and saw her take an order from some customers, then move to the bar to get their drinks. While she waited she made faces about them. I visited my sister Barbara in her new home. Her husband Paul, a musician, was asking her to listen to a new riff he'd written. I visited an old friend, Gail, in Los Angeles. She was talking on the phone, standing. She held the phone in her right hand and gesticulated with her left.

There were moments when I was with the snake and other moments when I was sort of watching it. It was a kind of seeing, clear and close but just out of reach, the way it feels when someone touches you through a thick coat. The images were all real, I thought, but I still had no way of knowing how real. I wanted to see something that would verify the experience.

I had hardly had the thought when I found myself at my sister Pat's loft in downtown Manhattan. She sat at a desk, drawing. I watched her for a few minutes. Suddenly she stood, walked across the large room and said "Hello," aloud, to both Steve and me. Thinking she could see me I moved about the floor. She didn't notice. I tried to see what she was drawing but with the snake's flattened vision the images meant nothing to me.

I finally decided to visit my own apartment to see if Larry, who was staying there, would be able to see me. In a flash the snake was speeding up Third Avenue in New York, entering my building and gliding up to the second floor. We moved around the landing and up the second flight of stairs to my apartment. Both Chuck and Larry were in the kitchen, sitting at the table, Chuck sat in my usual chair; Larry near the door. Chuck had a bottle of something in his hand. They toasted and I heard Chuck ask when I was due back.

I suddenly found myself back on the porch. My head was throbbing. Julio was already gone. Steve and I spoke for a minute. He hadn't vomited and was feeling ill. We stood and walked to our hammocks. Just as I was getting under the mosquito netting Moises asked whether I'd seen his son. A wave of self-contempt washed over me. I'd been so enthralled with my visions that I hadn't even tried to find Junior, but I didn't dare tell that to Moises. Instead I lied and said I hadn't been able to find him.

I lay in my hammock and closed my eyes. The snake reappeared and I thought of Junior. Instantly we took off up the Aucayacu. We sped through the water, nearly flying past things. I asked the snake if it knew where to turn off the river and into the jungle to begin looking and suddenly we were moving along the forest floor, trees and vines all around us. We came to a small clearing and I recognized the smell of old smoke clinging to the underbrush. Someone had been there recently. I felt silly doing it but forced myself to call out, "Junior! Junior! Come back! We're not there! Come back to Julio's!"

No one answered.

We looked all around the clearing. There was a sensation of death in the air but it didn't feel like human death. Someone had hunted there recently. I asked the snake to keep going deeper into the jungle but it surprised me and returned to the river and began to move back downstream. We moved much more slowly than we had earlier. I felt miserable that I'd have no good news for Moises.

Unexpectedly, because the river was so narrow that far up, I felt motion in the water. It came from both ends of a long, thin object. It occurred to me that the object had to be a canoe being paddled by two people, but that didn't make sense. No one lived that far up the river and we hadn't heard or seen anyone heading in that direction earlier in the day.

The closer we drew to the object the more sure I was that it was a canoe being paddled by two men, but in the darkness and with my snake-vision I couldn't make out their faces. We pulled up alongside the craft and moved downstream with it for a few minutes. I heard talking sounds but couldn't make out what was being said. Suddenly we moved past them. I began to scan the riverbanks for anything recognizable. Within a few minutes I saw the silhouette of the small riverside camp Moises and I had built on my last trip up the Aucayacu. The moment I did I was back in my hammock, the snake gone for good.

I called out to Steve and asked if he was still awake. He was. I told him what I'd seen and asked him what I should do.

"Tell Moises," he said.

"But what if it was just an hallucination?"

"He asked you to do it. He knows the risks."

I woke Moises and told him. He laughed. "My son is safe. Gracias, Pedro."

I cautioned him against false hope. "It was just a shape in the water, Moises. It might not have been a canoe."

"It was a real vision," he assured me.

I asked him how he knew.

"Because you saw two people and I only told you about one."

I laughed too when I realized how he'd tricked me, but still wasn't confident.

"Don't worry," he said. "We'll know soon enough. If they're at the old camp and paddle all night they'll be here at noon."

Moises was so confident that the next morning he had us pack our gear. He wanted to make the riverboat ferry back to Iquitos that afternoon. I spent the morning making notes of the night's visions and when just after noon Junior arrived, no one but me seemed surprised. With Junior was a man I didn't know, a fellow named Mauro.

Moises got on his son for taking so long to get there from the old camp and asked why they left the jungle instead of continuing to wait for us. Junior explained that they'd seen a small plane two days earlier coming from the direction of Brazil toward the Aucayacu and knew it had to be us. But how, he asked, did we know of their return? Moises explained the ayahuasca vision I'd had. Mauro said he and Junior had debated about killing the large boa they'd seen in the river the previous night but before they could decide it disappeared. "Spirit snake," said Junior. "Just disappeared."

It seemed to make sense to everyone but Steve and I. I still wasn't sure it wasn't just luck or a dream. The only way to prove if the ayahuasca had really allowed me to travel with the snake, I thought, was to call the people I'd seen when we returned to Iquitos. There wasn't much to check on, of course; most of what I'd seen was typical activity for the people in the visions. Except for two events: Chuck being at my home on a Sunday evening, a night he normally spent with his girlfriend; and the image of my sister Pat drawing at midnight. Even then, the image of her drawing wasn't significant, as she was a graphics designer at that time—but my feeling that she had been aware of the snake's presence, had even said hello, was.

Steve, her husband, made the first call and shouted for me to join him in the phone booth when she began describing Sunday evening. She'd been working late, she said, trying to finish designing a poster. The drawing she'd done was of a group of jungle animals standing in a thicket. Near midnight she'd stood to stretch and thought of us. She had not, she said, said "Hello" out loud. But while she stretched, the image of a large black and yellow snake had come to her very clearly and she had drawn one into the design of the poster, hiding in the thicket grass.

The call to my home was equally revealing. Chuck's girlfriend had gone out of town that weekend and he had indeed been to my apartment and had a few drinks in my kitchen with Larry on Sunday night.

Looking only at the more astonishing events that occurred while under the influence of ayahuasca could make it appear that the visions were not only the primary event of the medicine, but a primary reason for my frequent visits to the jungle. In fact, they were only one aspect of the ayahuasca experience and that, in turn, was only one aspect of my visits there.

My initial trip was prompted by a desire to glimpse the Amazon before capitalism had completely destroyed it. But that trip had been so potent—and my first ayahuasca experience was one of the reasons for that—that learning about the jungle and its people had become a motivating force for me. I saw it as a place of immense beauty and mystery, a place where growth and decay, living and dying, happened at a fantastic pace. The movement of the rivers, the seasonal changes, the animals and plant life—all of it fascinated me. The whole natural history of the swamps and rainforests cap-tured my imagination. I wanted to walk through it, to taste its wild foods, to meet its people, to sleep out there in the deep green. And the more I traveled there, the more time I wanted to spend there. I'd fallen in love with the cries of the birds and animals, the constant rustle of leaves, the smell of rotting vegetation. And I'd fallen in love with the people who lived along the riverbanks or back in the woods. And learning about all of it was aided by those ayahuasca experiences.

The ayahuasca was just one part of the whole experience, the visions it produced only one of its mysteries. The songs Julio sang—their rhythms were the rhythms of the rivers and the wind. They somehow put the motion of the jungle under my skin, introduced the jungle's spirit to my spirit.

Even the two days it took to get to Julio's from Iquitos were part of the experience, as were the families I'd come to know on the Aucayacu, the day of fasting before we drank the medicine, the meditation time on the porch, and the river wash the next morning. Those things and a hundred others were the rich context in which the visions occurred.

Chapter Five

# MAGIC DARTS AND
# THE WORLD OF THE DEAD

FTER MY experience at Julio's with Steve, I made several trips to the Aucayacu during which I didn't use ayahuasca. Not that part of me didn't want to, it was simply too powerful to use unnecessarily. I still didn't understand the concept of talking with plants or communicating with the spirit world, but I'd lost what remained of my skepticism and knew that it was not something to be played with. When the appropriate time came for me to use it again, I would know it.

That time came in the summer of 1988. I'd taken a long trip with Moises—one that saw us walk across the Peruvian jungle to the Yavari River, the border between Brazil and Peru—that had ended with a three-day ferry ride from Leticia, Colombia, back to Iquitos. Among the people onboard was a Peruvian named Roberto whom I'd known off and on for years. As his game was bilking tourists for phony environmental causes and I was a tourist, we weren't close. Still, we talked occasionally.

"Hello, Peter," he said when we both found ourselves at the ferry's refreshment stand. "Have you done any ayahuasca lately?"

"No."

"There's a fantastic curandero now living in Pevas you should see. I've taken lots of tourists. What visions they have! Much better than that old man you see. Maybe I'll take you."

"Thanks, Roberto. No need."

"Well, then, have you heard about the *ayahuasquero* fight?"

"No."

"You probably don't know anything about them." He went on to explain that many ayahuasqueros used their spirit connections to accumulate personal power or wealth, frequently by making bad things happen to people at the behest of their enemies—what is called *brujeria*. The brujeria needed to be countered by a curandero working for the good, which supposedly led to great battles between good and evil ayahuasqueros. Those battles were said to be fought with invisible arrows called *virotés*, which could inflict great physical harm or even death. I'd heard something about those battles somewhere but had never believed they were taken seriously. Not that the idea of witchcraft seemed improbable, it just seemed more complicated than necessary.

"Well," Roberto said, drinking a beer I'd bought him in exchange for his story. "One ayahuasquero in Santa Clara has been slowly poisoning another in Iquitos. Very well done. By the time the man in Iquitos realized his illness came from virotés it was almost too late. Fortunately, one of his sons has been studying with him and now he too is in the fight. Everyone says that all three of them will be dead before long. Now that's a story, eh?"

While I acted skeptical at the time, when we reached Iquitos I made plans to see Julio to ask him about this aspect of the medicine. I had no real intention of asking him to make ayahuasca for me, but while I was still in Iquitos I had a dream which changed my mind. It was about my father, Tom, who had been dead for nearly 16 years at that time. In the dream he told me that he could no longer see my mother—also dead several years—and asked me to find her and find out why. It was an eerie dream and I decided to use ayahuasca to try to discover what it meant. I don't know what I expected, or whether it was just an excuse to use ayahuasca again, but it made sense to me that that was what I should do.

I brought along a friend from Iquitos who had never been to the Aucayacu, and at the last minute discovered that Moises had found four tourists who would also be going. Junior and Mauro would be accompanying them—Moises did not come—which made our party enormous. Worse, when Moises learned that my friend, Jarli, and I were planning to use ayahasca, he immediately sold the idea to his group.

Despite the size of our party, the time we spent on the little river was glorious. Mauro and Junior took care of Moises' gang, while Jarli and I were left to our own devices. I was saddened to learn that Salis, Julio's apprentice, had been killed in a dispute with a Matses man, one of Papa Viejo's sons. It seems that Salis had been recruited by one of the big tour companies operating out of Iquitos to offer ayahuasca once a week to large groups at a camp just outside the city. It had evidently gone to his head that he was important and when back on the little Aucayacu he took advantage of his position and money to seduce some of the women there. Among them was a young Matses woman, the main wife of a Matses man named Antonio, who, like Salis, had been my friend for a couple of years. The seduction occurred while Antonio was out in the jungle hunting for a few days. When he returned and was told of it he'd put a shotgun to Salis' belly and fired, then headed off with his wives and children to Brazil.

✦✦✦✦

When I raised the subject of the invisible arrows with Julio he was at first reluctant to discuss it. And even when he finally agreed he prefaced his remarks with the comment that I wouldn't really understand what he was talking about.

"This is not something for people to talk about," he said, "so I won't say too much. You ask if there are spirit arrows. Of course. When I was younger and still in Pucallpa there was a brujo there who hated me. At first he used them on my house and chickens. I would come home from fishing and find everything in disarray, or some chickens dead. Healthy chickens he killed with his invisible arrows.

"And then he began to use them on me. One day I could no longer walk. I stood at my table and just fell over."

"What happened?" I asked.

"When I could walk again I went into the woods to talk with the plants. I didn't know what else to do. I really thought he was going to kill me. There I found this." He took out a small stone axe-head. It was very old and perfectly crafted. I'd seen it before but didn't know anything about it. "This is from the Incas, the ancients," he said. "It has a lot of power. It saved me from that brujo."

He stared at me to see if I understood. I didn't.

"I said you wouldn't understand. Look. Ayahuasca is a strong medicine. That is why we call the four colors in our song: red, green, white and black. Each represents a different kind of magic. Some people practice only one or two of them. But if you know four and concentrate only on one there is no balance and the magic can take you over. Some people fall in love with money, or power or women. All different things. But they do not control the magic that brings those things, the magic controls them. *Entiendes?*

55

Understand?"

Again I shook my head.

"*Ah, Pedrito*...Everything has a spirit. This house, these trees, the river, the fish in the river. Ayahuasca helps you reach those spirits. But when people learn to work with those spirits there is a temptation to forget that they are only the doctor, not the medicine, and they lose their balance. They are the ones to watch out for. *Muy peligroso*. Very Dangerous. They are drunk with power."

I'd never heard Julio speak so much, and though I knew I'd missed a great deal of detail with my weak translation, I was thrilled. I still didn't really understand the concept of virotés, but I didn't press him further.

Before I left I asked if he would make ayahuasca the following night. He asked for how many and then why. I told him about my dream.

"You'll have to go to the world of the dead," he said. "*Muy lejos*. Very far. I'll make it strong." He said it plainly, as though it wasn't much different than taking the ferry to Iquitos.

By dawn we could hear the sound of Julio chopping wood for the ayahuasca fire and that evening at eight our whole group set off on the short walk from the small house to Julio's. All but Junior and Mauro sat in the circle around the blue plastic sheeting on the porch. We sat quietly for an hour before Julio brought out the ayahuasca, began to chant, then passed the gourd.

I had spoken to the others about what they might expect but as they drank they were on their own. When the gourd reached me I almost choked getting the ayahuasca down. It was thick and still warm, burnt grapefruit and dank smoke. I knew I would vomit easily and soon.

Julio's chanting was clear and strong, the tunes something I always forgot, until the moment I heard the first notes again. I suddenly leaned for the edge of the platform to retch. Violent empty bursts swelled and pulled deeply from within me. In the back of my head I could hear the words Julio sang, "*Limpia, limpia, cuerpocito, cuerpocito...*" urging my body to cleanse itself. Over and over my stomach contracted tumultuously. The sounds seemed to come from a far place, echoing from across the river, water cascading onto stone. I'd never felt that kind of power course through my body, and though I was utterly helpless I felt fantastically strong.

When my stomach settled I closed my eyes. All around me were insects, visions of marching insects crawling over me, alternately tickling and annoying. As in a movie, the insect wings became the scales on a boa so broad and long I could only see a small portion of it at one time. It was undulating gently, slowly. In the black pitch of its scales glinted a hundred hues of red and blue. I was mesmerized. It turned its head to me and flicked its tongue. Its eyes, almost as large as the scope of my vision, were a fine black and yellow. Its underbelly was strong and white.

In an instant it changed its size to normal dimensions and we moved underwater. Eels and boas swam gracefully amid rocks. I followed their motion and tried to swim with them. I was awkward and ungainly and they ignored me.

The sound of vomiting brought me back to the porch. One of the others, a British fellow named Mark, was leaning over the platform's edge and retching violently. He tried to stand and I reached to calm him. He told me he was about to shit; I tried to help him but could hardly find my own footing and called to Junior to lend a hand. One of the others was beginning to get ill as well.

I closed my eyes again and thought about the dream I'd had. Suddenly I felt myself moving. I wasn't with the snake and I wasn't flying. I don't know how to describe it except to say that perhaps I was still and the world was rushing past me. In moments I was surrounded by darkness. More than that I was hurtling through a kind of vacuum with no body, no sensations. I don't know how long I continued but I suddenly found myself stopping abruptly at a sort of white wall. It wasn't a solid wall, but it wasn't passable either—like a wall of gauze or clouds. I sensed that it was the wall to the world of the dead. Even as I admitted that thought, it seemed preposterous and I began to scratch at it. It fell away like fog in my hands, but however much I tore at it I didn't get through and suspected that I would never get through no matter how long I tried.

I began to call out to my mother while I worked. After some time had passed a figure began to appear on the other side of the wall, just out of reach. Not really on the other side of the wall, but coming together from the stuff of the wall itself, recognizable but as flimsy as the ether. It was my mother. I watched her for a long time, then said hello and told her why I'd come. I expected her to smile but she didn't.

"Hello, Peter," she said, finally. "It's good to see you but you have to stop calling me like this. It's hard to come together in a shape you can recognize as me."

"Where are you?" I asked. "What are you doing?"

"It's not something you could understand. Things are different here. I'm not your mother anymore, but you won't understand until you get to this place."

A feeling of abandonment like I'd never known washed over me. "What place? What do you mean you're not my mother anymore?"

"I'm doing something else now."

"But what about Tom? Why can't he see you anymore?"

"Don't worry about Tom. That was just a dream you had. When it's time for us to be together we will be, but you needn't worry about him. Or me either. Things are good here. Trust me." Her voice began to grow heavy, as if talking was a strain. "Just know that I love you and the gang and I always will. But don't call me. It's just too difficult and I'm doing something else now. If you really need me I'll come, but you can't just call me like this or in your dreams anymore. I love you, kiddo."

She began to disappear back into the gauze and I was back on the porch, crying, wondering whether I'd really seen what I'd seen. In all the reaches of my imagination I couldn't have conceived of her saying what she'd said when she first appeared. But I knew it was crazy to think I'd gone to the world of the dead, if such a place even existed.

I sat on the porch, confused, angry, abandoned, unable to distinguish one reality from the other, the dreams from the visions. And then Julio's song caught me, and I *was* a snake. I was not traveling with a snake. I didn't see a snake. I simply knew I was a snake, or that the snakeness in me had come out for a time. It was fun, sensual. I invited the mosquitoes and other insects to land on me, watched them with flat eyes, then ate them. Mark began to trip up the notched ladder back to the porch, reeling in a spooky windmill motion, his great scarecrow arms and legs nearly disconnected from his body. I had to stop myself from grinning at him like easy prey.

Suddenly everyone was vomiting at once and there was moaning and groaning. It was not good vomiting, it was sick vomiting and I found out later that nearly everyone had ignored my request that they not eat past breakfast. One of the tourists kept saying he couldn't breathe and was going to die. I tried to calm him down, to breathe with him. Two of us had to carry him back to the small house and sit up with him all night.

The next day I washed in the river early, and though I was weak and still upset from my encounter the night before, I knew I was well. I noted that I couldn't find any bites from the insects, though I know I felt them all over me. Either I had just been hallucinating them or I ate more than I remembered.

Later that day I returned to Julio's to thank him. I brought some presents of salt, sugar, batteries and money. He asked if everyone was alright. I assured him they were.

⁂

When we returned to Iquitos two days later, Moises was waiting for us at the top of the steep muddy hill that served as the ferry dock. After he got his group settled back in their hotel, he came to my room.

"The old curandera, Maria, asked me to give you these," he said, handing me a packet of hand-sized, oval leaves wrapped in newspaper. They were *datura* leaves, used for making *toé*, a very powerful medicine, one that I knew a little about but had never used.

"She said to tell you to put one leaf behind your head and one leaf on your forehead just before sleeping. Then crumble a third leaf, make a cigarette and smoke it."

"What for?"

"She says it will help you dream. You will be able to dream who has stolen your things and where they have hidden them."

It was a surprising suggestion and one I didn't give much thought to until I returned to New York some days later to find that my apartment had just been robbed. I called Moises and asked him what else Maria had told him.

"Nothing," he said.

"But why did she give you the leaves for me?"

"I thought you'd asked her for them."

I told him I hadn't and he said he'd ask her when next they met. He called me two weeks later.

"She says she was thinking of you one night while using ayahuasca and saw a house in a big city that was a shambles. She thought it must have been yours and that's why she gave you the leaves. Have you used them yet?"

"No," I answered. I had thought about using them but didn't know what

59

was to be gained. The burglary had happened days earlier and my things had long since been sold. More importantly, the idea of datura frightened me, especially since its use would be unsupervised. It was sometimes called "the wind that blows you over the edge of the world."

"But thank Maria for me," I said. "And tell her the vision was true. Tell her I still have them, in case it happens again."

Thinking about Maria's true vision, and unable to forget what my mother had told me, I began to make a mental list of the things I could have imagined my mom telling me if I met her this many years after she died.

No matter what I came up with, I could not imagine that she would have talked about it being difficult to come together in a shape I could recognize as her. It simply wasn't a thought of mine and it wasn't a thought I could imagine her having. It wasn't something I'd seen in a movie or read in a book, and if I'd had endless paper and endless time and wrote down a list of 10,000 things my mother might say on my meeting her after she died, that would not have been on it. When I realized that I realized I knew the difference between a real vision and an hallucination. I had a workable way to think about it, anyway. If something wasn't on a list of 10,000 possibilities, it was probably a vision.

## Chapter Six

# REBIRTH AND DISSOLUTION

I T WAS nearly two years before I returned to the jungle. A research group at the University of Rome had asked me to get a frog from the Matses whose secretions they used as a medicine. I'd been introduced to it on the trip with my brother-in-law Steve at Pablo's camp. It was a rainy day and I was sitting in Pablo's hut, pointing to things and asking the Matses' word for them. When I pointed to a small plastic bag hanging over the kitchen fire—medicines are traditionally kept high over kitchen fires in the jungle to prevent them molding in the damp air—Pablo said *"sapo,"* toad. (In fact, the "toad" turned out to be a frog, so the word should have been *"rana,"* but Pablo's grasp of Spanish was limited.)

And then he took down the bag, opened it and pulled out a stick that looked like a piece of bamboo that was about the size of a tongue depressor. It was covered in what looked like dried yellow varnish. Pablo spit onto the stick, then used another stick to scrape the spit into the varnish-looking material. In a few moments a bit of the material was moistened and looked like yellowish mustard. Then, unexpectedly, Pablo grabbed my left arm, pulled a small stick from the fire and burned me twice. In a flash he'd scraped off the burned skin, exposing the under-layers. He quickly put the material he'd prepared onto the small burned areas. I looked at Moises and asked what it was. He shrugged and said he'd never seen it before.

*"Sapo, Pedro. Sapo medicina,"* said Pablo. Toad. Toad medicine.

In moments my head began to get warm and my heart started beating faster than normal. A few seconds later and I was burning up from the inside and regretted allowing Pablo to give me a medicine I knew nothing about. I began to sweat. My blood began to race. My head pounded. I became acutely aware of every vein and artery in my body and could feel them opening to allow for the fantastic pulse of my blood. My stomach cramped and I vomited violently. I lost control of my bodily functions and began to urinate and defecate. I fell to the ground. Then, unexpectedly, I found myself growling and moving around on all fours. I felt as though animals were passing through me, trying to express themselves through my body. It was a fantastic feeling, but a fleeting one. When it passed, I could think of nothing but the rushing of my blood, a sensation so intense that I thought my heart would burst.

*Sapo frog*

For perhaps fifteen minutes the rushing got faster and faster. I was in agony. The pain became so great that I wished I would die just to get it over with. But I didn't die. The pounding slowly became steady and rhythmic. I gasped for breath. And when it finally subsided altogether, I was overcome with exhaustion. I slept where I was.

When I woke, I heard voices. But as I came to my senses I realized I was alone. I looked around and saw I had been washed off and put into my hammock. I stood and walked to the edge of the unwalled platform hut's floor and realized that the conversation I was overhearing was between two of Pablo's wives, who were standing nearly 20 yards away. I didn't understand their language but was surprised to even hear them from that distance. I walked to the other side of the platform and looked out into the jungle: Its noises too were more clear than usual.

And it wasn't just my hearing that had been improved. My vision, my sense of smell, everything about me felt larger than life. My body felt immensely strong. The feeling lasted days. I could go whole days without being hungry or thirsty, move through the jungle for hours without tiring. Every sense I possessed was heightened and in tune with the environment. I could see animals before they saw me.

During those days I asked Pablo about sapo's uses. Among hunters it was used both to sharpen the senses and to increase stamina during long hunts. In large doses, the intense sweating it causes could make a Matses hunter "invisible" to poor-sighted but acute-smelling jungle animals by temporarily eliminating the human odor.

As a medicine it was used to eliminate the *grippe*—influenza—still deadly for many indigenous people. It was used on lazy children and on the noses of hunting dogs; it was even used occasionally as an abortive.

I had written about the experience and brought back a stick of the material. Some of it was given to the American Museum of Natural History in New York—to which I also gave a number of throw-away artifacts I collected from the Matses. My articles on the subject eventually reached the attention of a scientist at the University of Rome, Vittorio Erspamer, who asked for some of the material. His initial studies of it showed it to be a complex mix of proteins that were all bio-active—which meant they interacted with the human body as though the body had produced them.

Though I didn't know it at the time, my report was the first ever written of an animal product being put directly into a human blood stream for medicinal purposes, and that, coupled with Erspamer's findings, has opened a whole new branch of study, with scientists now trying to develop human medicines from amphibian skins.

At the time, however, neither Erspamer nor I knew what frog or toad produced the sapo, so Erspamer footed the bill for a trip back to the Matses to collect a living specimen of the amphibian that produced the medicine.

I'd asked Larry to join me as my photographer. He and Moises and I were planning to hike from Genaro Herrera to the Rio Gálvez. Before we set off we made a trip to Julio's and asked him to make us ayahuasca in preparation for the long walk.

On our layover night in Lima I'd had a dream that Pablo had tried to reach me. I couldn't quite remember the dream and didn't know if he was trying to make me come to his river or stay away. I hoped it would become more clear with the help of ayahuasca.

On the day we were going to drink, Larry and I spent much of the time watching Julio prepare it. He was up before dawn cutting the wood for the day-long fire while a new woman he was living with, a beautiful old curandera named Sophia, and Julio's son, Antenor, filled the great pot with water from the Aucayacu. Both Larry and I offered to help with the wood chopping but Julio wouldn't hear of it. As he worked the years fell away from his face. The sinewy muscles on his tiny frame seemed to grow younger and more taut with each stroke of his axe.

By noon, the several gallons of liquid in the pot had been reduced to perhaps a quart. He strained it through an old pair of pantyhose into a funnel placed in a three-liter plastic soda bottle, then refilled the pot and began the process again. He worked quietly, intensely. Now and then he chanted softly or blew mapacho smoke into the pot. At one point he tossed in a whole mapacho cigarette.

*"Muy bueno por los espiritos,"* he said, smiling. Good for the spirits.

When the second pot full of liquid had also been reduced to a quart or so he strained it off again, cleaned the pot, then combined the reductions and cooked them down together. What had been maybe 15 gallons of water at the start was less than a quart when he was done.

I'd asked Sophia whether she would join us that evening. She had said no, ayahuasca was not for her. "It's not a very friendly spirit to me," she said. "But it seems to like Julio quite a lot."

That evening, after Antenor had put away his odd guitar and Julio had answered Larry's question about what his visions were like, Julio stepped into the walled-off bedroom to retrieve the medicine. I was surprised when Moises didn't leave the circle. I reminded him that I'd never seen him use ayahuasca; that he always stayed off to the side to act as a protector.

"I've never done it before," he said.

"You've never done it?" I asked. "But you were the one who suggested we use it on that first trip!"

"Too dangerous," he answered. "But I have a feeling that I should use it tonight."

I resented him for never telling me that he hadn't ever tried it.

"If I start to wander into the river, stop me," he said quietly. I assured him he wouldn't but that if he did, we would.

Julio returned and placed the bottle of ayahuasca on the sheet of plastic near his other things. *"Bueno,"* he smiled. "Ready?"

We all nodded. Julio reached for a mapacho, lit it, then pulled the shriveled piece of corn cob he'd used as a stopper from the bottle. He hunched over, held the bottle neck close to his mouth and began to pray. With his free hand he smoked, blowing short, rapid puffs into the liquid. When he finished the first mapacho he lit a second, then put the bottle down, cleaned out a small plastic cup with smoke, filled it with ayahuasca and began to sing.

The words were clear, the song rich and beautiful. It seemed to echo off the trees around his house and fill the night air. When he finished he handed the cup to Larry, who closed his eyes and drank. The cup came to me next. The ayahuasca was as thick and dank and difficult to get down, as always. Julio repeated the process for Moises, Antenor and finally himself, chanting all the while. What power he possessed! With each song he seemed to grow stronger and more luminous in the light from the little kerosene lamp.

❦

When we'd finished drinking and he'd passed the other things around, he put the bottles to the side of the circle and flicked off the lamp with his shacapa. I closed my eyes and listened to the hissing of Julio's fan as he shook it in time with the songs. In moments, the visions began.

Green points of light appeared in front of me, like a dot matrix. They combined and made the skeleton of an archway and ceiling, a sort of luminous green frame of a cathedral ceiling. I opened my eyes: The lights didn't disappear.

They didn't last long either. In a few minutes I found myself in utter darkness, eyes opened or shut. I saw bright fruit hanging from trees and realized I was in a forest full of trees bearing mangos, papayas and bananas. I reached for one of the bananas. To my surprise it began to peel itself. Instead of a banana it revealed a small beautiful reddish-brown monkey with shining eyes. It began to grin and I felt myself grinning back. But the monkey's grin kept growing wider until it was a hideous, jabbering mouth screaming obscenities that broke off finally into a sort of insane laughter.

I recoiled and opened my eyes. I'd never had such a dream-like vision while using ayahuasca before. But when I closed my eyes the image returned. It laughed at me, and when it did finally disappear it was followed by a series of visions I can only describe as a trip through a funhouse of desires and fears. I was in a place of roller coasters and huge slides. Faces appeared out of the darkness while I rode on the rides. There were demons and beautiful women. There were funhouse mirrors in which I saw a thousand versions of myself. It was a strange voyage, altogether different than what I'd expected or anticipated.

65

The women were cartoonish and sexy, with huge breasts and round hips and dark Peruvian almond-shaped eyes. They called to me. I wanted to be with them. All of them. And then I found myself as a tiny me facing a huge inverted V. It was a luscious vagina seen from below on a giantess of some sort. I began to hurtle towards her. As I grew close she turned and I realized to my horror that it wasn't a woman at all, but a giant man, with a giant penis. I thought of the sexual connotations of the monkey in the banana peel and resigned myself to the homosexual implications of the naked giant. I was disgusted with what I thought was my mind playing a cruel joke on my sensibilities, but as I moved closer I realized I was not titillating myself with a secret urge so much as I was being driven to confront myself. The closer I moved towards it, the more awful the thought of having sex with the giant became; simultaneously I felt I was supposed to embrace it, deal with the implications.

I resigned myself, but just as I got within inches the giant turned around and became the giantess again. She was beautiful, with brown hair and sparkling eyes and she was laughing. She danced above me, tantalizing, a fantastic bronze goddess. I shivered ecstatically and rushed toward her, burying myself in her inviting vagina.

But I didn't stop. I found myself hurtling up the tunnel of her vagina. I grew younger and younger the deeper I went, younger till I was a child, a baby and then in the time before I was born, a kind of amorphous embryo buried in the deepest well-spring of life. I was surprised that I seemed to understand more about the nature of the universe than I'd ever known, as if in that state before birth all things were common knowledge. It was a brilliant state of awareness.

I looked around the space where I'd stopped. It was warm and soft on three sides; on the fourth there were prison-like bars. I was a prisoner of time and the moment of birth, unable to regress further, afraid to come out of the cage. But something was prodding me to leave and I wasn't strong enough to fight it. The bars gave way and I began to emerge. Down the tunnel I slid. There was a light at the end of it. With every moment closer to that light I could feel my knowledge and awareness slipping away. I wanted to stop. It was an awful and cruel joke played on humans by the universe.

The moment I emerged, the moment I was born, I separated from the embryo and watched the baby emerge. All the knowledge I'd had just a moment ago was gone, all the awareness vanished except for the bitterness of knowing that I'd known and didn't know any longer. I could feel immense

66

loneliness coming from the baby's tiny spirit. The baby howled.

The image of the baby gave way to a space filled with beautiful women draped in brilliantly-colored materials. More than colors and material, they were draped in living iridescent light. It was more vibrant and exciting than anything I'd ever seen. I wanted to stay with them forever, but the patterns of light became a light glinting from the scales of a thousand snakes. One in particular seemed to notice me. Its head was triangular and glowing, but though I recognized it as a viper I knew it wouldn't harm me. I tried to travel with it but it reared and wouldn't allow that. I tried harder, and lost the power of movement altogether. I couldn't even open my eyes.

When I finally relaxed, beautiful feelings of warmth washed over me, filling me with joy. I basked in them but in an instant the joy was transformed to something ugly and paranoid. I began to feel meager and weak, cruel and unworthy. Unworthy of the warmth, unworthy of all the chances I'd been given, unworthy of love. I was useless and had always been useless. I was small. I was a waste of the life that had been given to me.

I was sure that the others could see me for what I really was and I wanted to hide. I could hardly live with seeing this, the real me, and certainly couldn't live knowing that Larry and Julio and Moises had seen it as well. It occurred to me that hiding would not protect me from their awareness of my meanness. The only thing to do was to kill them all with my machete. I pictured myself hacking them up and tossing them into the river. I could return to Iquitos and explain that we'd had an accident in the canoes. By the time we returned to look for their bodies the scavengers would have finished them off.

I fought to control the murderous urge, and as I did I felt a warm wind on my face. I opened my eyes. It was Julio, blowing mapacho smoke on me and fanning me with his leaves. He chanted softly.

"You don't have to act on everything you see on ayahuasca, Pedro," he said softly. "Still, I think I'll put the machete away."

A wave of relief shuddered through me and I knew that the wretched moment had passed.

When I closed my eyes again I tried to focus on the dream of Pablo that I hadn't been able to remember clearly. Instantly I was in the jungle. In the distance I could see his village. I began running toward it but the more I ran the further it receded. Suddenly I was surrounded by Matses. I realized I belonged with them, that I wanted to be one of them. They grabbed my arms and began dragging me into the forest. As they did one side of my face began to take on their tattooing and color, so that I was half-Matses, half-me. The half that was Matses had no awareness. The half that was me was being pulled through something I couldn't see, and though I tried to be brave I was terrified and fighting, not because of what they would do with me but because I was afraid of losing me. I knew that if I went with them I would no longer exist. The Matses saw my quandary and stopped pulling. They put me down and began laughing at me as if I were a child who had just failed an important test miserably, then disappeared.

꧁꧂

The sound of Julio's song brought me back to the porch. I was breathing heavily and soaked with sweat. I lit a cigarette and looked around. Larry was walking in the trees nearby; Moises was leaning over the platform, vomiting with great heaves and gusto. Antenor was still sitting by his father's side.

I listened to the music. It was so simple, so soothing and centering. I realized that Julio's voice was the anchor to which I was meant to tether myself.

I wanted to vomit, and left the porch. When I returned I closed my eyes again. I was exhausted. I wanted only simple things: To fly with the bird or travel with the snake. I was tired of the extremes the other visions had produced.

I thought of my friends back home. Chuck, Alberta—the woman I was seeing—my sisters. As each crossed my mind I found myself looking in on them. I didn't feel like I was traveling, I was just there. Chuck's apartment was dark but familiar and I guessed he'd gone to sleep early. Alberta was sleeping as well, but her lights and television were still on. The clock next to her bed read 11:45. I lingered with her for a few moments. She looked so lovely, so peaceful, hidden beneath her great quilt, one of her cats balled up in the crook of her knees. I tried to wake her; she brushed a hand up by her face as if I was a fly that was disturbing her sleep.

Suddenly the image of Clare crossed my mind. I still thought of her sometimes but we hadn't been in touch since she'd gotten married and moved to Florida. That had been nearly four years earlier and I hadn't meant to think of her just then and didn't want to visit her, so I tried to get rid of the thought. It wouldn't leave. Worse, in a moment she unexpectedly appeared. She looked at me long and hard.

"Hello, P," she finally said.

"Hello, Clare," I answered. It felt like I said the words aloud but I don't think anyone else could hear them. "I didn't mean to bring you."

"I know. But I have to tell you something. You have to let me go."

"I already let you go."

"No. I mean you really have to let me go. I'm not coming back to you."

"I know."

"Part of you is holding on, P. But you're holding on to the me that doesn't exist anymore."

An empty feeling welled up in me. "I don't mean to be holding on to you, Clare. I want to let you have whatever life you want."

"Don't you see? It's not your choice to let me have anything. Just let me go."

I started to get angry. I hadn't intended what she thought. I just meant I loved her enough to let her go. "I didn't mean that," I said.

"Yes, you did. That's the problem."

"Okay. Maybe I did. But I'm trying to let you go. It's just hard. Why couldn't you even write one Christmas card just to say hello?"

"I just couldn't. You're not in my life."

"Will I ever see you again, even in the street?"

She thought for a moment. "Not like you think. Not until it doesn't matter whether you do or not."

And then she was gone and I was crying. I suddenly understood what she meant, realized how much I'd been holding on and how all of the visions I'd had that night were about letting go. About desires and fears and how they held me back. The sadness that came with those realizations was deeper than I'd ever known. I felt cut lose from everything that I thought mattered to me. I felt hollow and weak and torn apart.

And then a voice began to speak. "Hello," it said.

There was no one I could see, just a voice, but not one I recognized.

"Hello," it said again.

"Who are you?" I asked, hoping it was just a voice I was inventing.

"You know who I am," it said plainly.

I did. I sensed it was the spirit of ayahuasca. I know that seems crazy, and it seemed crazy to me as well, but I also knew it was true and I began to get terrified. I believed in the spirit of things, and I knew the power of ayahuasca, but I'd never imagined anything like that disembodied voice. It wasn't just a spirit or a vision or anything like talking with Clare or even my mother. This was like being in the presence of something unfathomable.

I opened my eyes, hoping it would go away if I ignored it. It didn't. It was just waiting me out. "What do you want?" I asked finally.

"You're the one who called me," it said. "You're the one who keeps calling me."

"I don't mean to. I just used ayahuasca to get ready for the trip, and to travel and see things…"

The voice said that wasn't true. It said I called because I needed things and I was getting what I needed; my immense sorrow, my confrontation with my desires and fears. The voice said that this was a time for cleansing, for emptying out, not for proving I could visit friends on ayahuasca.

What it said was true, and my initial fear of its presence began to subside. But then it asked me if I would let it enter. It was such a strange request that I was taken aback. The ayahuasca was already inside me, I said. The voice said no, that wasn't what it meant.

Suddenly I saw a snake wrapping itself around my head. I saw my head open and a side view of my brain, as if it had been cut in two and I was looking into it. It looked like the inside of a bee colony, all tunnels. Dozens of snakes appeared and began sliding into the tubes of my brain. At first it felt wonderful, like immense power and motion was sliding into me but then I wasn't sure that I should let them. I thought that maybe I was being fooled, that Julio had warned us that while some of the spirits we might meet were good, others were evil and I was afraid that this might be an evil one. What if it wasn't ayahuasca, or if it was, what if it was some awful and dark part of it?

I asked the voice what the snakes meant, why they had to enter me, but I didn't get an answer. Part of me thought it was a kind of test, but another part of me thought it was a kind of trick, and that if the snakes were allowed to disappear in my brain I would never get them out. I don't know what I thought that would mean but it was terrifying. Whatever it was, I knew it wasn't the right thing, that I shouldn't let those snakes into my brain. I began to pull them out by their tails. They were strong and hard to dislodge and the longer I fought the more I was sure that if it really had been the voice of ayahuasca speaking with me it wouldn't have asked me to let it enter in such a terrifying way. I felt like I was fighting for my life, that if I lost I would be enslaved forever.

The moment I got the last of them out I was no longer sure I'd made the right choice. It was like the vision of the Matses I'd had earlier. The minute they put me down, I felt I might have missed something extraordinary. I asked the voice why it hadn't just talked with me, why everything seemed to be a test designed to make me fight it.

It answered that it had already given me so many gifts that I should have some faith and trust. It said I shouldn't ask for so much without giving anything in return. The voice didn't sound angry or disappointed, it just said those things then disappeared, and I knew my visions were done.

I opened my eyes and stood weakly. The ground was glistening and wet. It had rained at some point but now I stared at a sky full of falling stars and tried to absorb the lessons I'd been given. After a few minutes I stepped off the porch and joined Larry. I wanted to tell him everything I'd seen and heard but was afraid that if I did the voice might come back and I didn't want that to happen. Instead we walked to the river quietly. He told me that he too had experienced the lesson of letting go, though neither of us talked about it in depth.

When we returned to the house both Moises and Antenor were asleep but Julio was waiting up for us. *"Una noche fuerte,"* he said. *"Bastante espiritos."* A strong night, filled with spirits.

He asked us to sit, then sang a song for each of us. While he did, he washed us down with mapacho smoke, then rubbed the camalonga on our hair and torsos. "To see the spirits don't cling to you," he explained. He'd never done that before and it felt intimate and generous. I wondered whether he sensed or saw something of the nature of the experience that night which made him think it was necessary. He didn't say. I remembered the incident with the machete and almost laughed. He'd seen everything. His cleansing was good. The moment he began to blow smoke on us my fears disappeared.

When Julio was finished, he said good night and went to bed. I stayed on the porch for a long time, trying to figure what I'd seen and heard. I thought of what Moises had told me when I first began studying with him: Ayahuasca gives you what you need, not what you want.

I finally gave up thinking and just stared at the sky. I felt alive and liberated. I wanted to embrace the night and the trees and everything in the jungle. Probably an hour or two passed before I grew tired, got into my hammock and went to sleep.

In the morning we bathed in the river, thanked both Julio and Sophia with some presents, then set off for Herrera to start our hike. It wasn't until much later that I realized I'd forgotten to ask Julio about the voice and the snakes, and by then it was too late to return.

✦✦✦✦

The trip to the Matses was unimaginably beautiful. It was a six day hike through the deepest, oldest jungle I'd ever seen. It was first growth, full canopied forest where soaring tree trunks, held in place by giant buttresses, kept the underbrush to a minimum. But it was also the most difficult hike I'd ever done. Every day there were two, three, four dozen, 50-foot, steep, muddy hills to climb. We'd climb one, cross flat surface for a few minutes and then descend an equally steep hill to the streams and creeks at the bottom that had cut those great gouges in the forest. At each we'd have to cut a sapling or two to make a makeshift bridge to cross the water. We all fell into the water regularly, keeping us wet all day. Too, there were swarms of stinging insects that were impossible to avoid, and a number of poisonous snakes that crossed our path. At the top of two of the broadest hills were swamps we had to wade through that looked like such perfect homes for anacondas that we nearly turned back both times.

On the last day, Moises raced on ahead of Larry and me. He wanted to make certain that if there were any Matses hunters nearby they didn't inadvertently kill us. Without Moises, Larry and I had a difficult time following the trail. Our only signposts were the machete notches Moises made in the tree trunks as he walked. But we knew we were getting close to the Galvez River the Matses lived on because the streams at the base of each hill were

72

growing deeper and wider and wilder. At one there was a huge section of a giant fallen tree's branches that spanned the water. We had the option of walking across a high section of it or crossing a lower section that was submerged about a foot in the raging water. I opted for the lower section of branch; Larry took the upper one. We both made it cleanly.

But Moises hadn't. Just on the other side of the water was a puddle of fresh blood, and more fresh blood dotted the leaves along the path. The trail now clearly marked we hurried along and within an hour reached the Galvez. Moises wasn't there but he had a canoe waiting with a young Matses man to takes us to the opposite bank where there was a village.

When we reached it we found Moises in a bad way. His face looked as though it had been sliced with a machete. It was swollen horribly and blood was everywhere. He was in great pain.

We gave him a strong painkiller and after it kicked in, we cleaned him up, As we did he explained that he'd crossed the high branch of the last stream and fallen face first the 15 feet to the submerged portion of the branch.

Once we got his blood cleaned up—though he continued to bleed a lot from his mouth—we looked at the damage. He'd split his upper left lip and the lower section of his nose completely through. Two of his teeth, which he held in his hand, had come out, and a third had been knocked back along the roof of his mouth and was hanging on just by skin. Some of the bone structure of the upper left side of his mouth was smashed.

Larry and I spent half-an-hour trying to figure out what to do. The lip and nose were too torn up to stitch together, and the tooth hanging in his mouth needed an oral surgeon, not us. In the end we decided to use crazy glue to put his face and teeth back together. Larry did the work while I supplied the materials. He removed the shattered bone from Moises' mouth, then glued the hanging tooth and skin back into place. He glued the two teeth back into Moises' mouth as best he could. Then we used duct tape to pull his lip and nose together and packed that whole side of his mouth with sterile cotton, both to keep Moises from trying to talk and to sop up any more blood.

Our trip was, of course, aborted. We decided to begin the two day canoe trip down to the Peruvian military outpost of Angamos the following morning, where we hoped there would be a real doctor or dentist on duty.

To our surprise, Moises looked better than we expected when we woke. The swelling was almost all gone and he no longer looked as though he was in pain, despite the painkiller having worn off.

"I'm going to take the bandages off," he told us. "I was just waiting for you, but I'm better."

"No!" we both said.

"Don't worry. I dreamed that three doctors came and worked on me. The doctors were you two and Julio. You were spirit doctors."

"You can't take the bandages off, Moises," said Larry. "You shouldn't have even taken the cotton out of your mouth. You shouldn't be talking."

"It was ayahuasca. It cleaned me so that I could heal. And then you three worked on me while I slept. Don't worry."

And with that he pulled gently at the duct tape. To our amazement, when it came off, his lip and nose didn't open up. There was just a little swelling and a seam that ran from the bottom of his upper lip to the middle of his nose. We could hardly believe what we were seeing.

"I told you," he said. "I knew I was better when I had that dream. Now I know what ayahuasca can do."

Two hours later he was even able to get some soup down.

By luck, despite our insistence that we cut the trip short, we found Pablo at a village near Angamos, and he collected two specimens of the sapo frog—a *Phylomedusa bicolor*, known as a giant monkey tree frog—for us that we managed to bring out.

✦

Some months later I asked Julio about the voice and the snakes and he slapped his thigh. "*Yah, Pedro*. You missed a wonderful chance to know things. That was a gift."

"What do you mean?"

"Snakes know so much. It was probably the spirit of a snake talking with you, but to you it was a man's voice. If you had let it in it would have lived in you. You would always know who your friends are and who are just pretending to be your friends. You would know who bad people were the minute you met them—sometimes even when you just saw them on the street—and so could avoid bad or troublesome confrontations. You would know many things."

I felt awful. "Will I get another chance?"

"It depends on the spirit."

# PART II

# WHEN AYAHUASCA SPEAKS: AN UNEXPECTED VENTURE INTO HEALING

*Ayahuasca, ayahuasca,*
*Good medicine, strong medicine;*
*Cleanse our bodies,*
*Cleanse our souls,*
*Guide us and protect us,*
*Oh medicine, strong medicine.*

*Ayahuasca, ayahuasca,*
*Good medicine, the best medicine;*
*Cleanse our bodies,*
*Cleanse our souls,*
*Deliver us to the spirits*
*Who can heal us,*
*Oh medicine, the best medicine.*

*—from one of Julio's songs*

## Chapter One

# CHEPA AND THE PIRATES

I T WASN'T until a couple of years later, in early 1993, that a snake came into me, and by that time I had stopped looking for one.

I'd been commissioned to do some medicinal plant collecting by Shaman Pharmaceuticals on the Yavarí and Gálvez rivers. The Gálvez, where Pablo lived, was a second home to me by then; the Yavarí, the border between Brazil and Peru, was another story. Sparsely populated, there were no riverboats or ferries that ran its length and special military permission was needed by non-locals to enter it—permission that Moises was able to secure in Iquitos. Brazil had two small military outposts on its side of the river; Peru had three. Between those posts it was essentially wild territory. I'd been on the river before, but this trip was going to be different because I would be captaining my own boat—a trip I estimated would take a month, most of that in territory where small villages would be one running boat-day apart from one another.

I'd rented a small Brazilian riverboat, the Rey Davíd, a wooden-hulled 40-foot beauty with a 24 horsepower inboard diesel engine. My crew included the owner's son, who would act as motorist, taking care of the engine, a *timonel*—helmsman—who would share the piloting duties with me, and a young woman named Gilma Aguilar Chávez, known as Chepa. She had grown up on the river—her father had owned riverboats—and was recommended to me by her brother-in-law, Joe, a gringo friend of mine. Joe, who owned a large riverboat, urged me to take her, as she was one of the few people in Iquitos who knew the river and the people at the military outposts we'd pass. They were notorious for demanding money and goods in exchange for the right to continue on the river, and Joe thought Chepa could handle them well enough to keep us out of trouble.

But while the scenario was something out of Indiana Jones, the reality was less certain. I'd never had my own boat before, didn't know if my estimates on time, fuel and food would be accurate, and I'd be carrying a pretty woman to the Yavarí—where pirates and smugglers were part and parcel of daily life. I decided to visit Julio and see if I couldn't glimpse anything I should avoid while on the river.

While most of the evening's ayahuasca experience didn't seem noteworthy—much of the river imagery seemed calm—there was one point in the journey when I felt I was being attacked by dozens of ghoulish faces and didn't know how to deflect them. Julio had already taught me that the spirits from the other side couldn't psychically cross the boundary into our world to hurt me, but I was still frightened by them. They were colorful, demonic images that weren't in my sphere of sight as much as they were physically intimidating me. And then suddenly, unexpectedly, a large, thick boa appeared and began to consume them with a terrible ferocity, a bellowing, wild, uncontrolled fierceness that surprised me. The ghoulish visions, those the snake didn't consume, scattered instantly, and in another instant the snake slithered quickly into my mouth, and down into my belly. I didn't fight it. It was just suddenly there. And I knew, though it seemed strange to me, that I would have an ally for the trip.

*The Jacare, one of Gorman's boats*

Once we left Iquitos, perhaps a week after my trip to Julio's, I didn't give much thought—other than occasional amazement—to the idea that a spirit snake was living in my belly. I was more concerned with learning how to pilot the boat and avoiding half-submerged tree trunks that would have sunk us in a flash. Chepa spent hours with me at the wheel, teaching me to go with the river flow, rather than trying to steer through it.

And she proved her worth on our first night out. We'd left Iquitos at about 5 AM and arrived at the little town of Pevas about 12 hours later. Attached to the town was a Peruvian military base and we were required to get papers of passage at each base before continuing on. When we pulled into the tiny port, Chepa was in the pantry. A sergeant on duty saw me and boarded with two soldiers.

"Who are you and where are your papers? Where are you headed?"

I answered his questions and provided the documents he requested, then asked for permission to pass. Instead of giving permission, he pointed to the two lights we were required to have on the boat.

"If you don't have running lights, you can't get permission to continue," he said nonchalantly, then told his men to break them.

I protested. He suggested that he didn't need to break them if his men, who were fed so little, could go through our pantry and gasoline stores and help themselves to whatever they wanted.

That would have ended the trip right there as I'd pretty much used up the funds Shaman Pharmaceuticals had given me and wouldn't be able to replace what they took. Fortunately, while I tried to think of a solution, Chepa came from the stern of the boat. In one hand she carried a quart of rum; in the other a loaf of sweet panettone bread.

"Hello, sergeant!" she smiled. "It must be a while since you've had a good bottle of rum, eh? And sweet panettone?"

He smiled broadly. "Chepita! It's been too long! Come up to the office. Bring your boyfriend."

Twenty minutes later, after agreeing to give the sergeant five gallons of kerosene—the post was out and unable to run their lights until fresh supplies came—in addition to the bread and rum, we had our permission papers and were free to leave at dawn.

It was something she did at every post. When she'd bought the rum and bread I'd been upset, thinking that we were squandering money so that she could give friends gifts. After I saw the magic those gifts worked, I was glad she'd insisted on doing it.

The first four days on the river—the time it took to reach Leticia and the mouth of the Yavarí—were so exhilarating that I didn't give much thought to anything except the sheer excitement of having my own boat and being out on the Amazon. On the fifth day, the day we turned up the Yavarí, I meditated on the idea of what an ally, if I really had such a thing, could do. But it wasn't until the eighth night that I realized its power.

We were four days from nowhere, and hadn't even collected our first plant yet, as we still hadn't reached the first Matses village. It was near midnight and we'd been warned at the last military outpost we'd passed that there was a pirate boat working the river. Because of that potential danger we kept going several hours after we normally would have tied up to a tree at riverside in an effort to reach the Brazilian military post of Peletón. A couple of hours before we estimated arrival, a single spotlight from a boat appeared just after the last bend in the river behind us, maybe a mile back. We didn't think anything of it until the light began gaining—and didn't begin to panic until it wouldn't respond to our signals to it.

The boat, one similar to ours but with a much more powerful engine, took less than an hour to cut the distance between us. And, being weaponless except for machetes and knives, there was little we could do to keep it from approaching. When it reached us, it pulled up directly alongside, tied ropes to our roof posts and cut its engine to idle, forcing us to do the same or burn ours out pulling two boats. There were probably a dozen men on board, all of them drunk. They had two motors in plain view on their deck. I asked my motorman David what we should do.

"They are probably going to kill us," he answered calmly, "then steal our motor and sink the boat."

"So what should we do?" I fairly shouted, absolutely terrified and feeling utterly helpless.

"I am going to go over to their boat and drink with them. I don't know what you are going to do."

"And if I go too?"

"They will probably still kill you."

And with that he and my timonel jumped onto the other boat. The men began to laugh at us, their faces almost cartoonish, ghoulish to me. It occurred to me that those were the faces I'd seen when I'd been at Julio's, and in that moment I silently called on the snake to help me if it were possible.

There was no real time to think. The men were about to come aboard and I knew I couldn't let that happen. I told Chepa to get below deck to the crawl space—I didn't think having a woman in full view would be in our best interests in the face of a dozen drunk pirates without women. Then I grabbed a machete and a knife, and with fear as my guide began to shout to the men in English that the first one to step on my boat would lose his hand. I said it out of complete terror, but it came out of me with a ferocity that surprised them enough to make them hesitate. So I said it again. I knew they didn't understand my English but they seemed to be getting the point. Just then Chepa appeared beside me.

"What the fuck are you doing here?" I screamed. "I told you to hide."

"What do you have?" she said, indicating my weaponry.

"A machete and a knife."

"Well," she said, brandishing a machete, "now we have two machetes."

And with that we both began shouting at them, daring them to step across. Thank god they didn't, but for the next hour it seemed as if they would, until they either grew tired of listening to us or the alcohol exhausted them. In any event none of them boarded us and the scene finally became almost comical, with us—in an effort to get them to leave and knowing that they needed to save face in order to do that—explaining that they were indeed dangerous and could have killed us, but were intelligent enough to know that as a gringo I would have a paper trail and that killing me would certainly lead to their capture and subsequent demise.

When they were finally satisfied that they'd frightened us sufficiently and had regained enough face to leave, they untied from us and put their engine in drive. My two men rejoined us just before they pulled off—I couldn't run the boat without them—congratulating us on the way Chepa and I had handled things. Their congratulations belonged more with the snake than me. I do not believe my initial threat would have been powerful enough to make the pirates hesitate if that ally had not given my voice an extra dimension that masked my fear.

Once we were moving again, I turned to Chepa and told her I had just fallen in love with her. I told her I might marry her. She laughed and told me I was full of it.

The remainder of the trip, which lasted 31 days and covered more than 1,500 river miles, produced no similar experiences, and in the end proved very successful. We collected a number of interesting medicinal plants, including a new subspecies, and I ended up marrying Chepa a year later.

Even before my marriage, Iquitos felt like home to me. I'd spent two or three months a year there—or working in the jungle out of Iquitos—for most of the previous ten years. But after my marriage there was no doubt about it. I adopted Chepa's two young boys from a previous marriage, Italo and Marco, and looked more than ever for work in the Peruvian jungle. I collected plants, I collected artifacts for the American Museum of Natural History, I wrote about the city of Iquitos and the surrounding jungle and its peoples as often as I could. Although Chepa and our two sons moved into my New York apartment after our marriage, my ties to the jungle remained strong and I was able to increase my time to four or five months a year there.

Chapter Two

# AIRPORT JUAN AND ALAN'S MOM

ANOTHER AMERICAN who had actually moved there in 1993 or early 1994 was Alan Shoemaker. Forty years old, bright, good looking and much more a student of ayahuasca than I—someone actually studying it rather than simply using it—he quickly became a good friend. Alan had spent some time in Ecuador studying both ayahuasca and San Pedro—a cactus utilized by the people of the mountains like ayahuasca is used in the jungle—before moving to Iquitos. There he studied and drank with different curanderos than I did, though on occasion he invited me to drink with him at the home of a young ayahuasquero named Juan Tangoa Paima, who lived in a shanty town just outside Iquitos' airport.

One day while I was in town, Alan received the terrible news that his mother had been diagnosed with liver cancer. Her prognosis was not good, and he asked whether I would be willing to drink ayahuasca with him at Juan's to try to take a look at her ailment to see just how severe it was—and, if we were lucky, to seek a cure.

It was a ridiculous proposition on the face of it. I knew nothing about human anatomy, certainly not enough to recognize a liver (and moreover one that was cancerous) during a visionary state, and I had never looked for a cure for anything while under the influence of ayahuasca. Still, it was my friend's mother and he was worried, so I agreed. It was Alan's idea, though I didn't know it till afterward, that we would both look for his mother's ailment, and, if we both happened to see something similar, he would have confidence in what he would later tell her. It was a desperate plan.

The evening we were to drink was clear but moonless. We arrived at Juan's,

83

a two-story plank house that Alan had built for him, just before nine. Juan and his wife and children came out to greet us, along with two neighbors who were going to drink as well. As Juan, whose ceremony was different but as simple as Julio's, was not ready to serve us as yet, I spent a half-hour in his back yard, an overgrown swath of land with an open stream full of raw sewage running through it. I thought about what I'd been asked to do and asked my snake for any help it might be able to give me.

When it was time, Juan called me in and began the ceremony. He offered his prayers and lit his mapachos, served us, then blew out the lights. Within a few minutes the twinkling light show had begun, and half an hour later I stepped outside to vomit. When I returned I began to concentrate on the work at hand. I couldn't. Every time I thought I was on the brink of letting go I had the feeling that I was being watched. But I saw nothing—with my eyes closed—that intimidated or frightened me. Still, I found it impossible to get comfortable and finally decided to open my eyes and reorient myself to the real world.

The moment I did I saw a movement in front of me to my left. I thought it might be Juan—I'd heard him leave to go vomit—but it wasn't. It was more a shadowy, red-brown object that seemed to be moving toward me in stealthy, almost aikido-like slide steps. I kept looking. Closer by another foot. Then another. And then I could make out that it was a crouched man, sliding across the floor to me. I thought my recognition of the spirit would make it disappear, but it kept coming. I didn't like it at all. If Juan had been there I would have asked him to get rid of it, but Juan hadn't returned. And the man kept coming. I had no idea what he wanted, so I silently asked. The answer was a simple and clear, "You."

There was something horrible in the way that simple word was said. And at the same time my fear grew so did my anger at Juan. He was the one who'd made the ayahuasca, after all; he was the one who invited the spirits. He should have been there to ensure that no malevolent spirits entered. He should have been singing his icaros and shaking his shacapa to keep them out. But he was nowhere in the room. There was nothing to do but confront this being, though I had no idea what that meant.

"What do you want from me?"

There was no answer, just another slide-step closer. And then, without asking for help, I felt my mouth open and out came the snake. Its own mouth opened wide and in a moment it had consumed the spirit and reentered my body. I relaxed almost instantly, and just as I did I remembered something that Alan had told me: If you see a spirit you should ask if it is your teacher. If it is, it will say so. If it is not, it will go away. I had never seen a spirit with my eyes open before and don't know if that would have worked, but was angry with myself for having forgotten the lesson.

I remembered it a few minutes later when a young girl and a woman old enough to be her mother began walking across the room, snickering at me. This time I was curious but unafraid, confident that my snake was watching out for me. The women walked slowly in an arc, never coming closer than maybe ten feet, but there was something ominous about them. And as they reached the center of my vision they bent down and began to pick up stones, laughing with each other that they were going to kill me with them. I suddenly blurted out, silently, "Are you my teachers?" Just as I mentally uttered it, their faces contorted to rage and they hurled their stones at me. But the stones turned to tissue as they flew from their hands and fell harmlessly to the floor of the hut. The women, still enraged, stepped away from the arc they had been making and disappeared into the darkness of the room. I said a silent thank you to Alan.

Juan reentered and began to sing. Sure nothing else was going to happen—I felt the lesson was to remember the lesson Alan had taught me—I relaxed and closed my eyes again. There was nothing but deep silence and the far-away sound of Juan's beautiful voice. And then I remembered Alan's mother.

The moment I did, I felt the snake coming out and asked whether it could take me to her. I had no idea of where she lived except that it was somewhere in Kentucky, but that didn't seem to matter. In moments, I felt as though I was zooming through dark space on the back of the snake, and moments later—though I hadn't seen the street or the house or even his mother—I was looking at the insides of a human. Actually, I was looking at what looked like a brown over-stuffed, double-wide hero sandwich. I wasn't sure, but took it to be the liver. And on top of it, almost coming out of it, there was something that looked like a sausage, or several feet of sausage, all red and white and twisted badly. Some part of me (I won't even begin to imagine how to explain it) picked up the sausage and saw that it wasn't really growing on the liver, but rather was a tube into the liver. The sensation I had was that something was blocking the sausage from cleaning itself out. It looked to me—how, I don't know, but I just sensed it—that if she could simply unblock that tube there would be no more cancer. I tried to imagine how she might do that, and very simply the idea of *uña de gato tea*, cat's claw in English—with something else I didn't recognize, came to me.

And then I was back in Juan's home and I heard Alan moving across the floor and leaving by the side entrance. In a moment I heard him begin to shit, and Juan laughed and said it was good that Alan was cleaning himself out—because he often didn't, and so was missing one of the good physical things about ayahuasca. I laughed too and said I was glad that Alan had made it outside, he might have really stunk up the place if he hadn't.

And then Juan asked me to sing an icaro. It was a surprising question, one no one had ever asked me before. I told him I didn't know any. He sighed.

"How many years have you been drinking ayahuasca and you still don't know any icaros?"

"Ayahuasca just never gave me any," I answered.

"I don't believe you," he said. "You're just embarrassed to sing."

"I just don't have a song."

And then, unexpectedly, I found myself sitting up and a few, weak notes came out of my mouth. *Na na na na nana na, na nana na na nana.* I sang them again. And again, stronger each time. There weren't any words, and it wasn't like the beautiful icaros Juan sang; there were only two lines of seven notes each—but they came out of me with power and the strange vibration which marks many icaros. It was amazing to hear myself

"I knew you had a song," Juan laughed when I finally stopped.

"I didn't until now."

"Yes you did, you just didn't let yourself know you knew it."

I felt at once touched and certain that I'd cribbed it from something Julio sang just to please Juan. But I couldn't place it, and it was so simple that I wasn't sure it wasn't a gift.

An hour later the sun was beginning to rise and Alan and I thanked Juan and headed for town. When we got to the main square we sat at a local place and asked for two glasses of water with lemon and garlic—good for a post-ayahuasca cleansing.

Over coffee Alan asked me if I'd seen his mother. I told him what I'd seen and showed him a picture I'd drawn while making notes before we left Juan's. I also told him about the uña de gato and the unrecognizable plant mixed into a tea that I'd seen—but was quick to add that I might have only thought of that because uña de gato was such a good basic medicine.

"That's the same thing I saw," he said, cutting me off. "And do you know what else I saw? I also saw that if she drinks uña de gato with *sacha jergon* she won't even have any cancer in a month."

I didn't believe him, of course, but he believed what we both saw. He called his mother and told her the good news. She went ahead with her Western medicine treatments anyway, but included the medicine Alan sent her in her regimen.

On getting ready to start her second round of Western treatment, however, it was apparent that what Alan had prescribed had had an effect. Her doctors were amazed to find that they could find no trace of the cancer. So clean was her liver that a second set of doctors was brought in and they decided not only that there must have been an error in the first biopsies, but that her X-rays had been confused with those of someone else. Her initial doctors had no explanation but knew that they would not have begun treatment if she hadn't had cancer. Even Alan's mother was herself at a loss. But Alan and I weren't.

"The spirits came through that night," Alan said.

"I know," I answered. "Scary, isn't it?"

And it was, to me at least. I had been raised a Catholic, though it had been years since I'd practiced, so the ideas of spirits and helping guardian angels was something I'd been taught to accept at an early age. And having done a fair amount of hallucinogenic experimentation, I knew the world was not nearly as solid as I'd once thought. Experiences like speaking with my dead mother, astrally traveling to friends, re-living my own birth—while I couldn't grasp their real meaning in this world and on this plane, I could still accept. But the act of seeing a disorder in a human I'd never met and coming up with a cure for it while under the influence of ayahuasca was intimidating as hell because I still couldn't see the whole picture—and didn't even know there was a whole picture to see..

## Chapter Three

# MOMMA LYDIA'S CANCER, MARCO'S FAILED KIDNEYS

IN EARLY July, 1996, Chepa and our two sons left New York for a two-month trip to Iquitos. For Chepa, Italo and Marco, it was a trip home. For me—I left about a week after them—it was a working vacation. I had contracts for two stories—one on the use of San Pedro cactus in Ecuador, the other on the use of ayahuasca in the treatment of severe alcoholism and drug addiction at a clinic in Tarapoto, Peru.

We also thought we would take a few weeks to visit Pablo and his family on the Rio Gálvez, and planned on bringing the kids out with us. I was looking forward to Italo and Marco learning a few things about the rainforest from the Matses children who spend most of their lives beneath its canopy.

Unfortunately, life intervened with hard news. During the week before my arrival, my mother-in-law, Lydia, had been tentatively diagnosed with early-stage cancer of the uterus while undergoing a routine pap smear. I arrived just as my family, Lydia in tow, was getting ready to head to Lima for further tests. We were all sick about Lydia's diagnosis, and were hoping that the more sophisticated medical facilities in Lima would prove it wrong.

I decided to stay behind for a few days to take time to visit Juan, to see if I could learn anything about mom's condition while under the influence of his ayahuasca. I didn't know what that might be, but thought it worth a chance.

I would have preferred to visit Julio but there was no riverboat leaving in that direction for another three days. Alan Shoemaker arranged for the ayahuasca with Juan, and the two of us, along with Alan's wife Mariela, went out to Juan's on the evening of my third night in Iquitos. When we got to his home we saw that there were six other people, all locals, there to drink as well. Juan, dark and handsome, greeted me like an old friend, and introduced the three of us to his other patients who were there for a variety of ailments.

Among the patients Juan was seeing that night was a woman whose husband couldn't stop cheating on her despite promising faithfulness. She concluded that he was under a spell from which he couldn't free himself and wanted Juan to see who had cast it, and how her husband could escape its shackles. Another patient was having inordinately bad luck in all her endeavors and was certain that the cause was someone's jealousy. If Juan could only see who was jealous of her, she was sure she could placate her enemy. The others suffered from physical ailments and needed Juan to see what had caused them and what plant medicines they should take to effect a cure.

As always, the ayahuasca experience was not what I expected: I spent most of the evening in deep meditation about the first two years of fatherhood I'd just been through. I questioned the choices I'd made for and with Italo and Marco, and alternately felt good and awful about the job I'd done.

When Lydia and her cancer finally took over my thoughts, I found myself moving up through a sort of tunnel, at the end of which was a place called Joe's Café. It was the only recurring vision I ever had that looked like normal reality. It was a nondescript soda shop I'd visited a couple of times during ayahuasca dreams, where the proprietor, Joe, served unusual fare. When I entered the cafe that night, it was particularly quiet and Joe told me to think carefully about what seat to take at the counter. After I did, he said to deliberate well about what to order.

I ordered chocolate cake from a plastic-covered silver stand and he served a piece on a platter. Then he heated it with something like a blowtorch and the cake melted into a large, thin square that filled the tray. I looked into the now-reflective icing and saw Lydia. I tried to look into her uterus and saw what looked like a small red spot: the cancer. It wasn't very big at all, but it was there. And then I saw Lydia dead. I saw a death mask and skull. I didn't want that to be the answer to the question about whether she was going to be alright. Then suddenly the death mask smiled and she was alive. And I realized that whether she lived or died—both were possible. But to live she must choose to live and then fight for it.

I looked for her in the vision within the vision and told her what I saw. She was non-committal. I said a mental "sorry, mom" to her and then started to slap her. Not really her, but the air around her head, hoping the concussion of the wind I caused would wake her up and she'd realize we all loved her and didn't want her to die, but that it was in her hands. I explained that we hadn't abandoned her, we'd just gone to New York.

She didn't respond, so I tried to really slap her—but my hands passed right through her head. I got so angry that I pushed her into a large green garbage container. At that she came out swinging. I told her that since she showed that she didn't want to die in a carting container of trash, she should not let cancer kill her either. But the choice was hers, she had to do it herself. She said she'd fight.

To ensure the message got through I put one hand on her forehead and one hand behind her head and tried to push the message deep inside her— deep inside that part of her spirit I seemed to have contacted, provided I hadn't invented the whole vision.

Joe's Cafe. An excellent joint.

I left Iquitos for Lima two days later. Chepa, the kids and Momma Lydia were staying at Chepa's sister Amelia's house and I joined them there. Lydia had been to Lima's renowned cancer clinic for a biopsy and was awaiting results. She looked fine and joked that I shouldn't slap her so hard in her dreams. I was surprised, as always, that she was aware that I'd tried to visit her spirit while under the influence—or better, with the help—of ayahuasca. I shouldn't have been. Lydia was only two generations removed from tribal life, and her ancestors were a group that utilized not only ayahuasca but several other types of unusual medicines as well. Her little house in Iquitos was always busy with friends and among them could often be found ayahuasqueros, healers who worked with smoke, rocks, chicken eggs and a host of other things. She herself had been initiated into drinking ayahuasca at age 12, and continued to attend ceremonies weekly.

The only thing that seemed amiss with the family when I arrived was that Marco's eyes were puffy. Chepa thought it might be a result of a bad fall he'd taken on some rocks a day earlier while he was playing with Italo. "He really whacked the back of his head," she said, but since there was no blood and the swelling on his head was already almost gone, we didn't think much of it.

However, the following day, when his eyes were little slits and his cheeks were a little puffy as well, we began to take notice. By the third day, when nothing changed and the swelling didn't go down, Chepa decided to take him to a doctor.

When she returned she reported that the doctor had said he was fine, just a little *enchado*, swollen, probably from a parasite or spider bite, and it was nothing to worry about. But an hour later Chepa was in tears and tearing out of the house, headed back to the doctor's with Marco.

"What's wrong, Chepa?" I asked.

"Look at this!" she said, pulling down Marco's pants: his scrotum had swelled to the size of a grapefruit and his penis was as long as his forearm. It looked like a water balloon ready to burst. "He came into the bathroom to pee when I was brushing my hair and showed it to me," she said through her tears.

"Go, Chepa," I said, "but don't get too frantic. The doctor's probably right. It's just a reaction to a spider bite. I had something similar from a bee sting when I was a boy..."

She was gone before I could finish.

When she returned she was distraught. The doctor, she said, had apologized for an inadequate checkup and told her to get to the emergency room of a nearby hospital right away.

We took off in a taxi—Marco, Chepa, Amelia and myself—for the hospital. There, Chepa insisted on Marco being seen quickly, and the doctors, after drawing blood and urine, told us Marco was suffering from a renal failure. If he lived, they said, he was in for at least six months of treatment beginning with several weeks in the hospital. But as he might not, we might consider calling a priest.

It is impossible to even begin to explain the overwhelming feelings of fear, helplessness, hopelessness, anger and grief that overcome a parent at a moment like that. You cry, shout at the doctors and curse whatever god you believe in all at the same time. You want to run away, set back the clock, trade places with your kid. You demand new doctors, new tests, a new hospital, anything that might produce something different than what you've just been told.

I had only been a father for two years, had only had Marco and Italo in New York with us for 15 months, and neither of them had ever really been sick in that time. To suddenly hear a doctor talking about one of my kids and saying "He might not live through the night," was devastating.

The doctors assured us they would do everything they could, including bringing in Lima's child-kidney specialist, who had already been called. There was nothing we could do but sit with Marco—who didn't feel sick a bit and thought his gargantuan penis was terrific.

The specialist, Dr. Rivas, arrived shortly and gave Marco a battery of new tests. When he finished he said our best bet was to try to stabilize Marco with steroids. There was nothing else we could do.

Later that evening I was told I had to leave as only mothers were permitted to stay overnight. I pushed until the hospital staff threatened to call the police, and then finally left. There was nothing I could do except anger the doctors.

Marco survived the night, and early the next morning we discussed taking him to the States for treatment, but decided against it. We had the number one children's kidney specialist in Lima working on him and I was afraid that if the illness were brought on by a parasite from Iquitos, stateside doctors would have less of a chance of knowing how to handle it than physicians in Peru.

We spoke with Dr. Rivas in the morning. He was a young man who'd been trained in the United States. He diagnosed the condition as nephrosis of the kidneys, explaining that the kidneys were eliminating all of the protein in the blood along with the toxins they were meant to eliminate. He reassuringly told us that children generally grew out of it after prolonged treatment with the steroid Prednisone, and a diet that excluded salt, sugar, fat and gas. No soda, chocolate, cheese, nuts, sweets, fried food; the list was long and needed to be constantly checked.

Dr. Rivas took personal charge of Marco's case. Marco responded to the Prednisone by immediately blowing up like a beach ball in his stomach, chest and face. It was not only frightening to have him so sick, it was also eerie to see him swelling up like that since I'd had rheumatoid arthritis at his age and been a treated with large doses of cortisone and had blown up similarly.

But our concern was less with his looks than with his original swelling. When it didn't immediately respond to the medication—in fact his scrotum and penis continued to swell until we could see through the taut skin— Dr. Rivas shot him up with Lasix. I'd only ever heard of it as something trainers gave race horses to make them piss their weight off to get an illegal edge. But it worked. Within a day the swelling had subsided considerably.

According to Rivas, about 90 percent of the kids got better in six months. The others? He begrudgingly told us they needed new kidneys because if the kidney didn't repair itself the nephrotic condition would become a necrotic one The kidney would simply begin to die.

But he tried to reassure us that even in that event nothing would be fast or drastic. We'd have a wide window of opportunity to get a transplant, if necessary.

As to what caused the illness, he didn't know. He said it appeared most often in two- and three-year olds, only rarely in kids of seven or eight. Marco was seven. When we pushed him to come up with an explanation for why our healthy, baseball-playing boy had come down with renal failure he shrugged and asked if we believed in black magic. Before I even knew what I believed, I said that while in Peru, where black magic is taken as something real, I did. In the States, where we don't believe in it, I didn't. He said not to take him literally, all he meant was that there was no parasite, no insect or spider bite, no bacteria, no virus, no infection that caused the body to start throwing off its protein. It was not yet figured out. It was his thought that the nephrotic condition was the result of a former condition, perhaps a viral infection that had been dormant for several years, and then became active and fixed on the kidneys, causing the nephrosis. He said Marco had a considerably better chance than when similarly re-activated viruses fixed on either the heart or bone marrow—those often resulted in the child's death.

His reassurances didn't prevent us from crying ourselves to sleep for several nights, even as Marco began to stabilize. I pestered Dr. Rivas day and night and visited Marco with Momma Lydia daily for hours. Chepa slept in the hospital most nights. Finally, after nine days, Dr. Rivas announced that things were proceeding apace and Marco would be released within a couple of days. He pleaded with me—for his sanity as well as mine—to return to Iquitos and let Marco alone. Chepa concurred, saying she could no longer bear to see me feeling so helpless. "Don't worry, baby," she said. "Marco is getting better and you still have your stories to write. It will be better if you get back and begin to make your arrangements." I waited another two days before I was confident that Marco was indeed on the mend before I finally agreed to leave.

I thought I would go to Tarapoto, where I had the ayahuasca-as-addiction-therapy story to do, the day following my return. But when I called Chepa and she said that as soon as I had gone Dr. Rivas had decided to keep Marco another couple of days, I simply couldn't leave. So I hung around Iquitos, waiting impatiently for them. They finally returned a week later. Marco had spent 17 nights and 16 days in the hospital.

I met them at the airport. We ran into each other's arms, but the boys were cold to me. As they saw it, I'd abandoned Marco in a hospital, and Italo in Lima without his brother to hang around with. I explained as best I could but it took a little while to get things squared away with them.

Marco looked bleached of color except for his bright red cheeks, and he was enormous. Beyond the Prednisone swelling, he still wasn't pissing regularly, but Dr. Rivas had said that would subside in time. The only really good news was that Lydia's biopsy had come back indicating a small tumor that looked as though it could be removed with a hysterectomy.

I wasn't convinced at all that Marco was en route to getting better and so decided to catch a boat to go to see Julio. I thought that if I drank ayahuasca with him maybe he could "see" what was really wrong with Marco and what was needed to cure him. I respected Dr. Rivas, but neither he nor any of the other doctors who'd seen Marco knew why his kidneys were malfunctioning or how to cure him. But I trusted Julio's ability to see things that a western-trained doctor might either not see or dismiss out of hand as magical.

Chepa encouraged the trip, though she was not joining me; she was afraid that if something happened while we were out there there'd be no way to get Marco to a hospital quickly. Italo decided to stay as well, as being in the jungle wasn't fun if Marco wasn't with him.

So the following evening I caught the *Madre de Selva*, a huge old riverboat packed with cargo and passengers headed to Pucallpa, and booked overnight passage to Genaro Herrera. In preparation for the trip I'd bought food, mapachos, batteries, matches, machetes—gifts for my friends on the Aucayacu—as well as gasoline for the motorboat from Herrera to the Aucayacu and back. I also carried a good supply of *chacruna* leaves, a key ingredient for the ayahuasca that was no longer plentiful in Julio's part of the jungle.

We arrived in Genaro Herrera at noon the following day. I met my friend Fernando, who owned one of the town's three peque-peques and he agreed to take me to Julio's house.

A couple of hours later we shoved off and began moving up the broad Ucayalí. An hour later we'd reached the mouth of the Supay River and turned into that. The Supay was as beautiful as always; pairs of gold and blue macaws flew overhead, the sun blazed. I saw again the color green in a thousand shades and hues, each more beautiful than the last.

In an hour we'd reached Supay Lake, a beautiful and serene jungle lagoon where pink and gray river dolphins played. As we entered the lake it started to pour—a thunderous, monstrous jungle rain that soaked us through and didn't let up until we'd crossed it and began to make our way up the Aucayacu.

Because it was low-water time of the year, Don Fernando's boat could only make it up the narrow river as far as Aucayacu pueblo, a tiny river community of mestizos and Matses Indians. I climbed the steep muddy bank to the village, said hello to several friends and asked for help to carry my things the 30 minutes through the jungle to Julio's house. Fernando agreed to pick me up in two days.

# Chapter Four

# INTO THE HEAT OF BATTLE

B Y LUCK Julio was home when I arrived, rather than off somewhere, and we greeted each other warmly. Surprisingly, none of his children were around; he said they were all off at a fiesta at a nearby village.

After we'd visited a while I explained the purpose of my visit and asked if he had time to make ayahuasca for me. As a rule he would explain that he didn't have time, that he was mending his roof or needed to tend his crops. I would then volunteer to help with his work for a couple of days, after which he would make time for me. But this time, when I explained that I wanted to know what was making my son so sick and was hoping he could see the cause, he didn't hesitate. He would make it in the morning and we would drink tomorrow night.

Over a dinner of boiled river fish and plantains I asked Julio about the use of ayahuasca in the treatment of cancer. He shook his head and said ayahuasca didn't cure cancer because it is hot, and cancer is cold. "Cancer needs to be cured by something frio, cold, like it is," he said.

I later told him about the voice that had been coming to me. I'd never mentioned it before. He told me not to be afraid of it, that I could ask it things. "That's why it comes. Ask for medicines or a song. Ask anything you need to ask."

That night I had a horrible dream in which Marco's scrotum had begun to swell up again.

The following morning we both woke early. While I went to the river to get the cooking water, Julio walked into the jungle alone to cut the ayahuasca. He returned within an hour with a dozen eight-to-ten-inch lengths of the vine, and a white two-pronged stick from which he'd cleaned the bark to use as a stirrer. Then he grabbed a machete and cleared a small patch of ground about 30 yards from his home. When I asked why he wasn't going to use the spot he normally used for cooking, he said he thought it would rain later and the area was well-shielded by fruit trees.

*Marco ill, held by Chepa*

The area cleared, I began cutting firewood and started a fire while Julio pounded the pieces of vine with a hardwood mallet, to crack them into slivers. When he was done he "cleaned" his old ayahuasca cooking pot with smoke from the mapachos I'd brought. He put a layer of the crushed vine on the bottom, then a layer of the leaves I'd brought, then another layer of vine, and so forth until the pot was full. He added some small tree bark sections as well, but I didn't ask from which trees they'd come.

By the time he was done and we'd filled the pot with water, the fire was raging between two stout meter-long sections of *pumasacha*—a tree with bark that has a puma's coloration—and we set the pot on them.

When the liquid began to boil he removed some of the burning wood from the fire to keep the medicine from boiling over. He monitored the fire for several hours as the ayahuasca cooked down. He chain-smoked the mapachos while he worked, blowing the tobacco smoke into the liquid. He chanted quietly.

By noon the rain he'd promised arrived, a jungle wall of rain that sounded like thunder as it approached; rolling thunder that grew louder and louder until it was suddenly on us. I thought perhaps we were done for, but Julio laughed and said we'd just move the fire and finish the ayahuasca in his kitchen if it didn't abate.

When it didn't, he carried the pot into the kitchen area of his platform hut. I followed after with firewood and arranged it on his *tushpa*, a large raised square cooking area made from a wooden shell filled with clay. When the liquid had been reduced to about a quart he strained it off into a plastic bucket through an old tee-shirt and set it aside. He filled the pot a second time and began to cook that down as well.

By six, the second pot of water was strained into what remained from the first. Julio threw the vine and leaves behind a nearby tree, cleaned the pot, poured in the ayahuasca and began to cook it down again. By seven, when a little less than a quart remained, he took the pot off the fire to let it cool. A few minutes later, he poured it through a funnel into an old beer bottle he'd cleaned with mapacho smoke, capped it with a corn cob stopper and set it aside.

Julio started the ceremony at about nine. There was a quarter moon smiling down and a partially starry sky that was later blanketed with clouds.

As always, Julio spread a sheet of plastic on the floor in front of his little bench, then placed his things on it.

He sat and cleared the air with tobacco smoke. Then he made his *arcana*, an invisible barrier that would prevent any spirits entering the space whom he had not invited. He spoke of saints and demons, angels and Lucifer. He invoked them all to come and visit us tonight; to come with calm and good intent into the little circle we made—I sat on the floor opposite him—to come and teach us red magic, green magic, white magic and black magic. "We call on you to come oh Saint Sebastian, Saint Cypriano..."

Then he said a quiet incantation for me, poured the medicine and passed it to me. I drank. Six gulps, and on the last I felt my stomach clench and had to fight to keep it down.

Julio drank next, put out the kerosene lamp, and began to chant.

In a little while I felt a sudden rush to my head, a sort of lift-off of immense and sudden certainty. I reminded myself that it was only a few hours, it wouldn't kill me, I was with Julio, doing what I'd come to do, and should focus on Marco rather than my evaporating ego.

In front of me, eyes open or closed, patterns appeared; moving geometric shapes, cathedral ceilings, lots of green crystals—beautiful.

I was really high and lay down to center myself, enjoying the rhythms of the color and motion and thinking that something strong could happen.

And then a voice very clearly asked: "What's the matter? Are you afraid to sit up and face what you've got coming?"

And I thought, "No", so I sat up. In front of Julio's house, just on the other side of the platform where we sat, the trees had become huge mantises ready to march. They were emerald green and glistening despite the absolute pitch of the night. They were full of spirit.

Surprisingly, the colors and motion and patterns which normally dissipated after a few minutes, didn't. Rather, they intensified. I saw lines of light, thin as lasers, connect my fingers, connect boards in the floor, connect ceiling beams. I tried to shake them off—they were like spider webs and slightly terrifying—but they were sticky and wouldn't shake free. Then I realized they were coming from on top of my head— not the top, but from above my head, as if there were a tube coming out of my head eight or 12 inches high and these lines of light were coming from that. I didn't have control over how to shoot them out of me but I knew they came from me, like I was seeing the lines of energy around me in a way that was clearer than I'd ever seen them before.

I thought Julio was wonderful; sitting in darkness, a shape, a mass of sorts, in utter black. I knew where he was sitting but couldn't make him out. I knew the singing in the air was his voice but it didn't come from him in any way I could identify. It was just sort of everywhere. Not loud, but thick, like a blanket that covered everything, or protected everything.

I started thinking about Marco, was aware that I was in touch with the voice but wasn't in control at all, or calm enough to get past the images and patterns, the extraordinary lines of light.

And then, out of the blue, I felt my stomach clench. I leaned forward and crawled the two meters to the edge of the floor to throw up. The vomit came out of me like cannon fire, thick and hot, and blew into the night.

Then again. And again, four times, five times, 10 times, until I was empty and tearing and snot was pouring out of my nose. I was spent and it was all I could do to lean against one of the house posts while on my knees and stare at my vomit down below the house. I thought I might see things in it, like a mirror, but all I saw was the dark, shimmering fan-like shape the liquid made on the ground below.

I gathered myself up and returned to my seat, my mind empty except for laughing at myself for getting so beat up by a little puking session.

I began to think about Marco again, about what made him ill and how to make him better. The snake in my stomach writhed a little and I said hello to it.

Suddenly, all around me the patterns converged and lost much of their color. It seemed that I was looking at, and being in, a sort of rolling mud slide, only the mud wasn't sliding, it was just swirling slowly, everywhere I looked, in all directions.

I realized it was the motion of the muscles of a snake, a huge snake I couldn't dream of seeing in its entirety—it was like the snake mother, the same snake prayed to by the Hindus, the Naga, or one of them. Or if not a Naga, still the spirit of ayahuasca. Julio had once told me that if you see it you can ask it anything, so I asked, from within the muscles of the beast, to tell me what was wrong with Marco and how to cure him.

Almost instantly I saw Marco in the writhing muscles of the snake, in the folds of the muscles, and a voice told me to get him, to take him out of where he was.

I asked what that meant and was told I had to save him, that time was running out. I called to Marco and he answered. I saw where he was and went to get him; the folds of the snake's muscles shifted and he wasn't where I saw him anymore.

The voice said to take this all very seriously, that I was to save Marco or lose him.

I said I didn't know how, that spiritual battles were for Julio, who knew those things, not me.

But I was told just to do it or lose Marco. He was, I somehow knew, though it was a new idea for me, in someone's power, whatever that might mean. I told the voice that I didn't know how to save Marco, and it answered that I should use everything I had.

I said I didn't have anything for this sort of fight. It said it had given me everything I needed.

Suddenly, I remembered my song and my snake and I thought about those thin white lines of light coming from my head and fingers and knew I had those things at least, and it seemed reasonable that they might be powerful in this setting for this fight.

So I called to Marco again in the shifting mud or muscles and Marco answered and I went for him; when I got to where I thought he'd be he was gone again, in a flash. I heard him and pushed through the folds to reach him. The thing we were in moved again and he was gone. He was being moved and held. He had his voice but not the strength to come to me.

I wondered whether I wasn't deluding myself, that it wasn't Marco at all but just my arrogance leading me to believe I was in some sort of battle for him.

Marco called to me in English suddenly, asking me something. I forget the phrase now, but it was something like "Hurry dad, I don't like it here."

And then I knew that it was all real, or real on some level. His voice was so unexpected, so chilling, something I didn't and couldn't have expected him to say. So I went after him again. Each time I did, the great snake writhed. It was so huge that a slight shift would move Marco.

I opened my mouth and sent my own snake out—not really sent it out, just asked if it could help, but it seemed to know what to do before I even thought anything. Just after it left I began to sing: *Na na na na nana na, na nana nana na na*...and singing seemed to open the coils so I could see Marco clearly, finally.

But whatever was holding Marco was strong. It would rather let him die than come to me.

I had to fight hard, to will him to come. For five minutes or two years I searched for him, found him 50 times and 50 times he disappeared.

Once I almost reached him, in a fold to my left, and he said something like, "C'mon, dad" and then when I almost had him he was gone again. I couldn't hear him or see him for a long time and the voice told me to keep looking, to take this seriously, and I did. When I found him again, I heard him crying for me to help him, that he didn't like it and couldn't move. And then there were the lines, the lines of light. I tried to make a lot of them to shoot to him but I couldn't. But a few did come out and must have grabbed him because he was suddenly near, and I reached for him and was able to grab his hand.

But then, as I did and was pulling him across some line, or out of the snake's coils or out of the grip of whatever had him, a kind of chasm opened up and I wasn't holding him tight enough and he slipped and began to fall.

And the voice said not to lose him now, so I sent my snake, or my snake went, and I sang and some light lines reached out for him and the snake and the song and the lines grabbed him, but something wasn't letting us just take him. Something was keeping him from me.

I opened my eyes.

The voice told me Marco would die if I didn't get him now. So I went back to the battle and told him to reach for me, to grab the snake and the lines, to get free.

The more I sang, the more the void, or chasm—which was not moving like the snake all around it—seemed to give him up a little and so I sang and sang and reached with the lines until finally I had him in my arms. And I held him tight. Not really him, but the spirit of him, and I knew he was free and I had somehow won, though I didn't know how I'd known what to do.

But then the voice told me I hadn't done anything yet, that I had to protect him or they would take him back. So I tried to make light lines to wrap him up, lines that would act as a barrier against anything trying to grab him. A web began to spin around him while he was in my arms—fine, thin, strong coils of light, bright light, wrapping him like a mummy.

And I thought, good, now he's protected.

But the voice said no, I didn't have the power to protect him. Only Julio could do that and I'd better have Julio do it because the other people, the other force, was about to take Marco away in a rush, was about to attack.

And I knew I'd better have Julio sing a song to protect him, so I spoke out loud and asked Julio "Can you sing a song to protect my son?"

Julio asked me "What?"

I don't know if I spoke in English or Spanish, my own voice sounded strange, broken.

But I knew I needed protection for Marco. Julio asked how could he sing for my son? And I said, "Just sing a song to protect him."

He asked me his name. I said Marco. He asked me his age, I said seven. I told Julio that I'd been told to ask him to sing, and then he did. A beautiful song. And I could feel Marco getting protected, and when he finished I felt like Marco was saved.

I opened my eyes. I was exhausted and sweating and I felt stone-cold straight, like I'd used everything I had up and was empty.

Suddenly Joe of Joe's Cafe appeared and said, "You did good, kid," with a sort of wink. And my snake came back into my mouth, or actually I opened my mouth to let the snake back in and a snake started to come, but it wasn't my snake and so I grabbed it. I realized I was very vulnerable now, and some bad spirits were willing to take advantage of my state of mind or exhaustion.

All sorts of snakes tried to come in, while my own snake was still outside. It finally came in and slid down my belly easily. And I thanked it for helping and it sort of smiled.

⁂

I was proud and thankful and absolutely bewildered over the idea that I'd been in such a fight. Of course, now that I had, there'd be a price to pay. I might have to help people who needed it. I didn't mind the idea, it was a responsibility I was willing to assume, if called on. It's just that I had no idea if I could do it again, or if I was just another jerk who thought he'd glimpsed something special.

⁂

A little while later I began to wonder who it was that might have put a spell on Marco, and I thought of his birth-father. But then I thought past him and thought of his mother, Marco's grandmother—I didn't know if she was alive as I'd never met her. But I thought maybe she was angry that we hadn't brought Marco to see her since I married Chepa, and maybe it wasn't brujeria, or black magic that had made him sick. Maybe it was a sort of misguided love that had grabbed him. Maybe Marco's grandmother had grabbed hold of him in the moment of his fall.

Suddenly I saw Marco's head and without thinking I bent down and sucked out a red, wet, fleshy lump. It came out easily, and I was going to spit it out. But I remembered what Bertha of the Southern Utes had said: "You can't just suck out bad things and throw them away or they will land on someone else—negative things have a life of their own." So instead, I imagined putting it in a rock and sending it to space and burying it in a barren place where such things were put.

The sucking out was so simple and clean that it was amazing. The sensations were real, the fleshiness an absolute surprise. And I felt I'd done something good. Not with arrogance, just that I knew how to do it now.

I kept reminding myself that I shouldn't be prideful; that whatever was going on was happening with the help of benevolent spirits. I tried to realize my position honestly. Julio was a good teacher, strong and kind, and that he had helped me access helping spirits.

I thanked the spirits and tried to see Marco. I saw him in bed with Chepa and Momma Lydia and he'd gotten better and Momma Lydia was laughing and she covered her face with her hands and Chepa was crying and Marco

103

was saying: "I'm better, okay? I'm not sick anymore."

And I was happy. Exhausted but happy. What an extraordinary night.

There was just one more thing. I'm not sure when it occurred, but it was sometime after the battle and before I went to sleep. I was thinking about Marco and how he was saved and how Chepa and Momma Lydia were happy he was better, and then the voice said: "You've saved him. But that doesn't mean he's physically better. The physical effects of the misguided love that clutched him are real. He'll still have to get better from those." Something like that. A bringer-back to earth if ever there was one.

The following morning I returned with Fernando to Genaro Herrera. When I reached Iquitos the next day I raced to our little house, hoping that the last thing the voice had told me was something I'd invented. It wasn't. Marco looked the same as he had in Lima: all swollen from the steroids. So while I felt he was better, that the battle had been real on some level, I had no way of knowing for sure. I did gain a measure of confidence when Marco asked me, later on during the day of my return, whether that was me who'd come to him in his dream and was wrapping him up in light. I told him it was and he said good, because he'd been having a scary dream about being lost. "I can't remember all of it but I didn't like that place," he said. I hugged him.

We returned to New York two weeks later. The doctors at the Cornell Medical facility there continued his treatment of Prednisone but, like Dr. Rivas, had no explanation for the condition. Six months later Marco was finally able to get off the steroid without his kidneys throwing off protein. And with the exception of a one-month relapse a short time later, he's been fine ever since.

PART III

# RED MAGIC

# AN INTRODUCTION TO AYAHUASCA HEALING

*Red magic that moves within our blood,*
*Green magic that moves beneath the sea and through all the firmament,*
*White magic that fills the sky,*
*Black magic that dwells within the earth,*
*Protect us from all evil spirits,*
*Guide us to the other realms,*
*Teach us of the things that live on the other side.*

*—from One of Julio's Songs*

Chapter One

# GUESTS AND
# THE COLD BEER BLUES BAR

IN 1998, two years after Marco got sick, Chepa and I decided it was time to move to Iquitos for a while. Chepa and I had, by that time, a baby girl, Madeleina Lydia, so we were quite a group. Never having had to support us there for more than a few months at a time, I rented a building across the street from a port in a tough part of town and we built and opened the Cold Beer Blues Bar/Restaurant Madeleina, within weeks of arriving. It quickly became a hangout for the couple of dozen ex-pats in town as it was one of only two gringo-owned bars in Iquitos. I also had an agreement with an agency that set up tours to take occasional groups into the jungle for two weeks on what I called an Amazon Jaunt. I'd never done anything like that before, and spent weeks before arriving in Peru feeling guilty about the thought of exploiting ayahuasca for money. I'd refused several offers to lead ayahuasca trips over the years, and always felt good about that. But knowing that I wouldn't have enough money to support my family for very long without an income—and also knowing that the bar was going to take a long time just to pay back the investment, much less make any money—I finally decided I could live with my guilt in exchange for feeding my family. I didn't know why I felt so guilty. The medicine had been a wonderful teacher for me; why wouldn't it be wonderful for other people? It must have been the money element.

Once I decided to do the trips, I made up an itinerary of things I would enjoy sharing with people. Using Iquitos and our bar as the trip's hub, we would go out into the jungle three times, each of those ending with an ayahuasca experience. For the first leg we'd travel to Julio. The second would involve a several day hike led by Moises that would end with a visit to Don José, an old curandero on a small crystal-clear, black-water river with whom I had drunk ayahuasca a few times. The third leg would be a two-day stay at the botanical reserve of Sachamama—a short distance past Iquitos' airport—where we'd drink with the reserve's owner, Francisco Montes, and a curandero he worked with, Don Ramón.

The trip would be difficult. My guests would have to help carry the gear, and we'd be sleeping either in the jungle itself or on the floors of platform huts. I didn't know how many people would want that kind of tour—absolute Amazon reality, you might call it—but I was hoping there would be enough to make ends meet.

My first group was set up to arrive just a couple of months after Chepa and the kids and I did. To help organize things I asked Larry to join me. He said he would, but asked if a friend of his, Duke, could be included as well. I wasn't thrilled with the idea. I had met Duke a couple of years earlier in Iquitos. He was a Vietnam vet who still seemed wound up from the experience. His tightness showed itself in an aggressive streak I didn't like. But Larry insisted and I relented.

In the weeks before the groups arrived, Larry, Duke and I spent a good deal of that time running around Iquitos buying hammocks, mosquito nets, boots, pots and pans, and the thousand and one other things the trip and the bar required. As the day of my small group's arrival approached, I grew more and more nervous: What if the trip stunk? What if they hated me? What if nobody got the ayahuasca experience to the full extent? What if all they got was bitten by insects?

Larry was great. He worked at keeping me calm and focused as much as helping me compile and execute my shopping lists. Duke, on the other hand, proved to be difficult at times. At the crowded markets he would sometimes announce that people were jostling him on purpose and he would just start bumping the old ladies and children in his way. More than once Larry had to pull him out of the crowds to avoid angry confrontations with the locals.

In addition to my nervousness about the trip itself, I was a wreck about having the guests in my care drink ayahuasca. I knew they'd be taken care of—by Julio's children at Julio's, by Moises, Junior and Mauro at Don José's, and by Francisco at Sachamama—but I was still nervous.

Alan Shoemaker, over coffee one day, came to my rescue on that point. "Listen, Pete, just stay calm about the ayahuasca end of things. Nobody's going to die. You'll handle it just fine, especially with all the help you'll have. Just remember to tell your guests that if they see anything they don't like, they should just use their breath and blow it away, change the television channel."

"Does that work?" I asked, surprised.

"You don't know that? Of course it works. Just blow it away."

"I never heard that before."

"My god, Pete, you mean all this time you've been stuck looking at the bad stuff?"

"I guess so. I mean, I had no idea you could get rid of a bad vision that way."

"That's one of the problems you have with refusing to read about other people's ayahuasca experiences. You miss a lot."

"I guess so. On the other hand, whatever I see I know wasn't put there by someone else."

"That's the tradeoff. But don't forget the breath. Use it just the same way Julio and the other ayahuasqueros use it when they're breath-whistling their icaros. Purse your lips and direct a small stream."

I knew breathing was important, and the control of breath vital for some of the healing I'd seen curanderos do, but I'd honestly never heard that you could change what you were seeing with it. I determined to try it as soon as I had the chance.

A few days later my group arrived—two men, two women. The younger man and woman, Mike and Rochelle, were a former couple, it turned out, trying to work through some things. The other man, Addison, was a Texas lawyer going through a mid-life crisis, and the other woman, Jane, heir to a sizeable working farm in the Midwest, was an adventure buff.

Over beers at one of my favorite bars, a wooden shack built on an over-hang overlooking Iquitos' floating raft slum, we got to know each other a little. For the first time I found myself explaining the ayahuasca experience to people who had never had it but were looking forward to it. Other than my friend Jarli, and my wife and kids (Marco and Italo only got a taste), I'd never been the one to introduce someone to it. The reality was that despite the number of times I'd done it, I really knew very little about it. I explained how it was made, that it was used by almost everyone in Iquitos periodically, that ayahuasqueros saw illness—physical, emotional and spir-itual—as the symptoms of disturbances on some other level, and so tried to access those other levels in order to effect a cure. I suggested that on the first time out—which I told them would not be a full dose—they might try to record anything they saw in a notebook immediately after the experience so that they could check it later. At the same time I didn't want to tell them what I saw under its influence, because I didn't want them looking for something that would prevent them from experiencing their own visions.

Of course they pressed me, and I explained that my early ayahuasca journeys frequently involved the ability to associate and travel with animals. I told them there were lots of hallucinations: monkeys peeling themselves out of bananas and turning into women beautiful beyond description; huge, glistening snakes whose scales were made of the colorful twinkling lights, and so forth. And I told them that when I was sent to the funhouse of desires and fears, I felt I was tapping my real desires and fears, some of them buried so deeply I needed a funhouse atmosphere to face them.

✪

## Chapter Two

# JULIO'S BICYCLE AND
# THE WIND OF THE WORLD

THREE DAYS later we were at Julio's, ready to drink. The circle included my four guests, Larry, Chepa, Julio and myself. Duke, who was
very familiar with ayahuasca, wasn't drinking as he'd agreed to act as guide
for anyone who needed to vomit or shit—a very generous gesture. He was
joined in watching out for the guests by Julio's oldest son, Jérnan, along
with Jairo and Antenor, as well as one of Julio's daughters, MaBel.

Julio served half portions for those who'd never had it, and full portions
for Chepa, Larry and myself. The ayahuasca was thick and awful, the familiar foul taste both comforting and appalling.

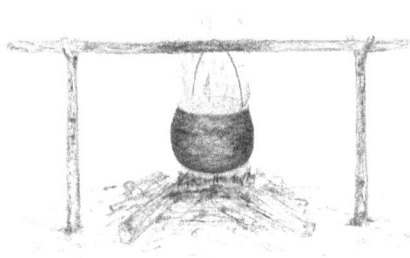

*Ayahuasca cooking*

When all were served, Julio blew out the kerosene lamps with a flick of his
shacapa.

It couldn't have been thirty seconds later when I felt myself begin to pulse
and the little dots of green light, sharp, precise, exhilarating, began to
twinkle in the darkness. Moments later they began to multiply and form
connecting beams that soon became the fantastic green-domed cathedral

ceiling of the universe. The speed with which the pulsing iridescent green geometric pattern formed surprised me, and I opened my eyes to see if I weren't dreaming.

To my left, Addison had broken into a green geometric energy pattern. To my right Larry was cracking into shards of green crystal, and everywhere else the pattern was invading all shapes until the whole world was breaking into the fine green crystalline shapes.

The voice of Julio in the background, his simple icaros coupled with the chic-chic-chic of his shacapa, was a reassuring heartbeat. I turned to Larry and whispered, as best I could: "Julio can really cook!" Then I took one more look at Addison, who had dissolved into pieces of green glass, and asked if he was alright. He said he was fine so I closed my eyes and let the ride begin.

Or rather, I should say I was blown onto my back by the medicine. The moment I lay down, the patterns of the cathedral ceiling gave way to shapes that quickly became a glorious ride in the funhouse, replete with roller-coaster ups and downs, faces out of nowhere, funny and scary images coming at me like I was in some dark part of Coney Island. At some point I found myself in the place of funny mirrors, me in each one, sometimes long and skinny, sometimes short and fat, sometimes impossibly stupid, sometimes intelligent. And sometimes the mirrors reflected parts of my soul, both good and bad: the frightened, small person; the arrogant ass; the phony, the drinker—all of my bad qualities magnified in the mirror veritas. I managed to let them pass, appreciating them but not letting them crumble me into catatonia.

After the funny mirror room, the world began to turn into a vast array of DNA code strands. They glistened and held the secrets of the universe. They were vertical at first, then went horizontal. Thousands combined to become just a few. They joined and began to turn slowly, becoming the true twisted strand of DNA. And then the back wall of the universe opened and I realized they weren't just twisted strands of DNA, they were the spinning wings of a bicycle bi-plane being ridden by a laughing and joyous Julio— Julio as he is on the other side, old but huge, a force capable of riding the bicycle that propels the universe, rocking back and forth in time to his earthly icaros, wearing an open and generous grin, his eyes sparkling and shooting out lines of warm and comforting light.

I found myself laughing in awe and admiration. All of the motion of that world was being powered at that moment by Julio pedaling the pedals that spun the wheels that moved the wings of the green fractal bi-plane. It was the first time I'd seen him on the other side, and with the image my confidence elevated enormously and I felt I was in the arms of warmth and tickled by a kind of love I'd never felt before.

Julio disappeared and a huge vase filled with thin, deep red, almost purple flower stems appeared. Their tulip-shaped flowers were dripping with the same deep red juice of the stems, and a voice asked if I wanted to drink. It was the sort of thing I'd said no to in the past, but with Julio running the universe I couldn't resist, despite my fears, and a stem was given to me. I took a few drops of the nectar and wondered what would happen or what I was being invited to be a part of. In moments, a terrible wind began to blow. A wind that started at the beginning or end of the universe, and the world blew away and suddenly I was alone in a sort of void, ungrounded, feeling that I was at the place where all things are born and all things die. The winds rushed through me and I felt as though I were going to be blown away by them. The only thing I saw to clutch onto was the bottom of a piece of material—so large I couldn't see what it was—that was flapping ferociously.

I reached for it and grabbed hold as the wind became the four winds of creation and rushed through me in all directions. I might have been holding onto the sail that directs the universe, or the bag that holds it, or the coattail of the spirit that holds the coattail of creation. The winds almost tore me apart, and I was small, so small that I couldn't even be afraid. I was in the land of awe, the place where my mother is and which she said she couldn't explain to me. I knew now why: It was incomprehensible. It was the beginning and end and beginning again of all things. It was the place of places and I knew it was a place where all I had to do was ask and I would know. But even as I thought that, I knew I couldn't ask anything of those terrible winds or of the place or its beings: I could do nothing but hold on. It was not somewhere I'd seen in a dream or vision. It was the "is-ness," the being, I was in the presence of, and it was terrible and brilliant and cold. I laughed quietly and heard Julio singing in the background. It was almost more than I could bear.

A howler monkey began to wail in the jungle outside the hut, adding its ferocious howl to the noise of the wind. And then a wind that I will hear coming for me when it is time to go to that place for real began to scream. The message was clear and simple: When that wind blows, it will be time. The rapture was broken when an enormous man appeared in the crack between the universes. He berated me for calling on him when I was drunk and I instantly remembered two occasions when I drank ayahuasca while drunk in my apartment in New York.

"You dare to call me when drunk?" he bellowed. "You dare to call me when drunk?" Over and over he shouted at me, his voice becoming the wind around me, through me.

I couldn't have voiced an apology if I tried. I had no voice. I was being permitted to witness something extraordinary, something I could not and cannot aptly describe, a place beyond human description because it is not a place where humans go. It was a glimpse of unimaginable fury and beauty, the first and last, the word, the wind.

At some point Julio sang a deep, deep-pitched song, notes that cut through all things and grabbed me back to the floor of the hut where we sat. I laughed again and I was calm, exhausted, rich. Then I stood, walked outside and threw up the bile.

Chepa joined me. "I'm having a hard time," she said. "Walk with me."

I reached out for her arm but she pulled it away.

"Don't touch me. Just walk with me."

She started to walk across an open space on limp legs. Each step was high and unsteady, as though she were walking on stones. "Don't let me fall into the holes where the snakes are," she said. "There are so many I can hardly walk."

I told her there were no holes, but in her world there were, and she was frightened by them. We walked back and forth for what seemed like hours, her never letting me help her, until she finally said she thought she was whole enough to return to the ceremony.

As we stepped into the little circle she sighed. "I love Julio's voice. There are no snakes allowed here."

I smiled and took my place, then turned to check on everyone. They all seemed to be doing okay so I lay back down to try to recapture just a glimpse of that place I'd been.

Almost immediately the giant vase with red-purple flowers appeared again and one of the flowers bent forward and asked me if I'd like to drink. I reached out to it and took a sip of its nectar. This time the winds did not begin to howl. This time the world began to change color—everything began to be infused with reds. Light reds, dark reds, purple reds, iridescent reds. I opened my eyes and looked to my right. Larry, who'd been crystal-line green earlier in the night was now deep, deep red. To my left, Addison, who was now standing and slowly dancing in rhythm to Julio's voice, was a mountain of reds. The roof of the hut, the jungle outside, the moon and even the air itself were infused with red. I closed my eyes again and one of the flowers was high above me, dripping its purplish nectar down over me; it was sticky and sickly sweet, like thick blood.

The moment I thought of the word "blood" I found myself in a tube of red liquid. It was moving very quickly, pulsing, and I found myself moving in it, not swimming, but being carried along at an amazing pace. As I moved the pulsing intensified, like a drumbeat—but rather than a sound it was the feel of a drumbeat, throbbing—and I suddenly realized I was inside my own body. Somehow I was in my bloodstream and racing toward my heart. I began to look around, taking notice of the bloodstream I was in: It wasn't really all liquid at all, more like millions of little balloons filled with red liquid travelling in a gelatinous goop. They were soft to the touch.

Suddenly the throbbing intensified a thousand times and I passed through a fleshy portal that nearly closed on my legs and I was spun around and around, as though I were in a whirlpool, bouncing off the fleshy walls of the place. It occurred to me that I had entered my heart, that I was in the place where the beating began. There was nothing to see except the balloons and the goop, but the throbbing seemed as though it would split me in two.

Just as suddenly I found myself back at Julio's and he was shaking his shacapa at me and chuckling.

"Ah, Pedrito," he said, "todo bien?" Everything good?

"Todo bien, Julio."

I looked around at the others: everyone was coming out of their reverie to some degree. I asked if all were alright, and was assured it had been a good night, and that they'd been well taken care of by Duke and the others. And, of course, by Julio.

## Chapter Three

# MEETING THE DOCTORS

WHEN THE first trip ended, Larry returned to the States. Duke wanted to stay on as an assistant, but I couldn't let him. Near the end of the first trip he'd gotten into an altercation with one of the guests and punched him hard in the chest. He'd promised it wouldn't happen again, but I couldn't take the chance.

For me, the next several sessions, with that first group and the next few, were each infused with red. The green cathedral ceiling was now a red cathedral ceiling. The DNA strands became part of each experience as well, and going into the bloodstream became commonplace. I didn't know what to make of it. Some nights I spent nearly the entire experience being flat on my back while the purplish flowers dripped their thick nectar all over me. Others I spent as if in any other ayahuasca experience—part visionary, part hallucinogenic—with the exception that the world was always red. It didn't bother me, I just didn't know what it meant or if it meant anything at all.

On the home front things were not going well. The stress of opening a bar/restaurant and the long hours necessary to build a clientele were wearing on me. I was drinking too much, too regularly, and Chepa got tired of it and began working less. In response, I became something of a bully when I was drunk, letting my rage at having to work so hard, and so often alone, surface—which in turn pushed her further away. None of it was good for our kids, who saw a perfectly rational and good man in the morning and afternoon and either a funny or howlingly angry drunk at night. Chepa and I had been married for nearly six years when suddenly, our family began to fall apart.

It was a side of me the tourists were probably aware of but I hoped didn't actually get to see too often. With them I was a workhorse, and a surprisingly large number of them got unexpected healings through the ayahuasca.

I began to joke to my regular clients at the bar, all of whom were friends, that while my tourists were all getting healed, it was I who needed to be worked on. Part of me was serious.

A week or two after I began to make my joke, I had a private tour for just two people, a couple who had asked that I arrange for them to be introduced to several of the different types of healing done in Peru. The purpose of their trip was to seek alternative medicines and curing practices that would help allow the wife—who had a deteriorating spinal illness which was then in remission—to keep the illness at bay.

Unfortunately, the husband arrived sick with what appeared to be the flu, and so the healing attention turned to him, rather than his wife. He spent two days being worked on by an egg-healer, a curandero who used an egg as an absorptive to remove physical ailments. But after the second day the curandero told my client that while his flu was gone, he had another illness that was deeper than he was capable of working on.

I had also arranged for a San Pedro curandero who I trusted to fly from the high Andes to Iquitos for a San Pedro ceremony. The curandero, Victor Estrada, arrived within a day or so of my clients, and when the egg-healer said he couldn't continue the work, Victor suggested that he would focus on it during the ceremony.

I knew Victor as a capable healer, a man filled with deep love and commitment to his work. I drank with him whenever I was in the mountains.

During the ceremony, Victor spent several hours rubbing a rounded stone over the man's face and body. But under the shape-shifting influence of San Pedro, what I saw was that the stone had become a scalpel, and he was cutting the man's sinus cavities open, then the chest cavity open, then cleaning out his organs one by one, replacing them and finally stitching him up. It was replete with blood and guts everywhere, though an outsider wouldn't have seen it.

Watching the curing reminded me of that visit to Julio, when one of the men at his place told me that Julio had removed his stomach and cleaned it, then sewed him up, leaving no scar. I didn't realize then what the man was talking about, and had never witnessed such an operation until I saw Victor work.

And the client, who had never told me about any physical condition he suffered from, told me the next day that something he'd suffered from since childhood had been cured that night. He asked what Victor had done. When I told him that he'd become a surgeon and his stone a scalpel, the man thought I was a little crazy. When I told him about the blood that flowed everywhere, he thought I was really crazy. When I told him I saw the whole operation—was graced with having been allowed to shift my vision to see the whole operation—he thought I was just full of it.

Regardless, he was happy to be rid of it.

A few days later I was with the same clients at Julio's, and the man commented to me early in the ceremony that Julio was just sitting on a low stool, not making any effort to work with his body as the first two curanderos had. I told him that each curandero worked differently, and that he couldn't really compare styles. Later that night, after another visit to the red world—during which the voice, in answer to my question of how to heal my family, had simply told me "You know that; drink less"—I asked my client how his experience had been.

"Well," he said, "after the egg healer and Victor, I was determined that the ayahuasca-work focus on my wife, not me. So I was just lying down at one point early on, feeling that the ceremony would be interesting but inconsequential for me. My legs were crossed on the ground in front of me. And then I heard Julio say to the man next to him in clear English—although I know he doesn't speak any: 'You know, I'm not going to be able to work on him with his legs in that position.' And then suddenly I felt Julio waving his fan towards me and my legs simply uncrossed without me doing it, and I heard Julio say, 'That's better.' After that I decided not to question his methods anymore. Let's just say it was an amazing evening, and Julio is a remarkable healer."

I didn't want to tell him that there was no one sitting next to Julio; he wouldn't have believed me.

A few days later I was taking the same two clients to Sachamama, the botanical reserve outside of Iquitos. Set in high, canopied second-growth jungle, the space was tranquil and physically beautiful. After the rigors of the trip to Julio's and the difficult jungle hiking I put my guests through, I enjoyed taking them to a place that was not physically demanding.

My son Italo asked if he could tag along, and said he was thinking it might be good for him to drink ayahuasca. With permission from Chepa and my clients, I said okay both to his coming and drinking if he liked. He was nearly 14, and though he'd never been given a full dose, he'd had a sip of ayahuasca on several occasions at Julio's. I don't think I would have said okay if he had been born in the States, but as it was part of his cultural heritage and something he'd been around with both me and his grandmother, Lydia, his whole life, it seemed like an appropriate thing to do.

While my clients were perfectly at ease after the several curanderos they'd visited in the previous ten days, I was edgy. I didn't know whether it was the presence of Italo or that I was never as comfortable drinking with other curanderos as I was with Julio, or that Francisco never allowed me to bring extra people to watch out for the guests, but all day I couldn't shake the feeling that something was in the air. There were low rain clouds gathering as well, and the static electricity from the pending storm was palpable.

The evening began calmly enough, with Ramón and Francisco offering prayers and mapacho smoke, then calling each of us in turn to drink. My clients went first and second, I was third, and Italo was last. Minutes later, after Ramón and Francisco drank, the kerosene lamps were blown out and the ceremonial space became utterly dark.

A few minutes later the twinkling of lights began, the greens quickly giving way to the reds, and the red lights quickly forming strands that in turn joined to make a huge double helix DNA. I watched with wonder as the light show progressed, then with apprehension as I found myself face to face with a grotesquely grinning clown's face that had appeared quite suddenly.

There was something wretched about it, and I decided to try Alan's trick of using my breath to change the screen: To my surprise the clown face simply dissolved the moment I blew on it. In its place the steep metal tracks of a roller-coaster hill that I was about to fly down appeared. Woooooosh! And down I went, down an impossibly long and steep hill. It was thrilling. At the bottom the car I was in made a sharp right around a hairpin turn, then began a long slow climb to the top of another hill. Halfway up, the car slipped and began sliding backward. Faster and faster—until we were moving much too fast to make the turn in reverse; the car jumped the tracks and began tumbling into the pitch black of an abyss. I blew my breath again and the abyss dissolved and I found myself staring at Chepa.

Grief passed through every part of me. How sad I was that I had not been able to keep such love from fading! How lost I felt without her! I started to cry, deep, deep sobs.

I heard Italo call out, "Dad? Dad? Are you there?" and I was pulled back to the reality of the ceremonial hut.

"Italo?" I called softly, and when he answered I slid across the few feet of dirt floor that separated us and put my hand on his arm.

"It's really weird, Dad."

"I know. It's strong. But it can't hurt you, and I'm right here. Just remember to breathe if you see something you don't like and it will go away. Are you okay?"

"Yeah. But don't go away."

"I won't. I'm right here."

I lay back down and closed my eyes again. In moments I was engulfed in my sadness again, and glad for the human contact with my son.

"You keep trying to do things that make her happy," a voice suddenly said.

"I know," I answered to the bodiless presence, thinking that yes, I did always try to make Chepa happy. I was good. A good man.

"It doesn't make her happy."

"Why not?" I asked, another wave of grief washing over me.

"Because you're trying to make her happy by doing things you think will make her happy."

"What else can I do? What does she want?"

"She doesn't know. You thought you were making her happy all those years, just like you think you're loving your baby now, but your baby isn't happy either."

Telling me my baby Madeleina wasn't happy just added to my misery.

"How can I fix things?"

"You will never make them happy until you can be them. That's when you'll learn to see how they feel and what they want."

"Can't she just tell me?"

"No. But she's been trying. She doesn't know how to say it. She is not being you either. But you're the one who has to fix it now. You have to become them to understand what they need from you. Giving them what you want to make them happy just doesn't work. You are losing them."

"How can I become them?"

There was a pause and in the silence I could hear Ramón and Francisco chanting somewhere in the distance. I squeezed Italo's arm and tried to imagine being Chepa and Madeleina. I could see them, I could see me trying to enter them, but I didn't feel at all as if I was them. I understood, on some level, what the voice told me, and knew it was true, but didn't know how to do what it asked.

I began to hear a rushing sound, like wind blowing through reeds. It came closer and closer and began to frighten me. I decided to blow it away, but blowing didn't work. The rushing began to change and I could hear a kind of gibberish, as though dozens of small people were all around me talking very quickly in a language I'd never heard. The gibberish and the rushing grew to a fever pitch and then suddenly stopped.

"We heard you," said a voice that was new to me. "We heard you say you were the one who needed healing. We've decided it's your turn to be healed."

"Who are you?" I asked, suddenly very intimidated.

"We are the doctors you called at your bar to heal you. We're going to fix your heart."

"Wait a minute. I was only kidding with some customers...."

"Don't be silly. And don't be afraid. It will hurt, but we need to fix your heart."

I was very afraid. I could feel someone or something grabbing at my heart—not my physical heart, but my soul heart. "Wait a minute. What are you going to do?" I fairly shouted.

"We're going to work with your heart. We have to get rid of some things in here and we have to open some things where you're stuck. We have to change you."

I could feel a dozen of what might have been hands begin to pull at my heart. Every time they touched it I was given a kind of electroshock of memory and pain: images of my mother, my father, fights I'd chickened out of as a boy, pointless arguments with Clare and others, drunken screaming at Chepa—a thousand bolts of electricity and anguish were running through me.

"Wait!" I shouted. "Wait a minute! I'm not ready!"

"Of course you are. You're just afraid you're going to die."

I was more than afraid; I was terrified. I couldn't breathe, I couldn't think. I just wanted no part of it.

"You have to trust us. We can't do the work unless you let us."

121

I tried to catch my breath. I felt for the reassurance of Italo, then said, "Okay, I'm ready."

But the minute they began to work I panicked. "No wait!"

"You have to trust us. You can't fix the things you want to fix until we work on you. Just let us work."

I knew they were right. I knew I needed fixing but I wasn't prepared for this. I had no perspective. I had no idea if they meant me good or evil. I just knew that when they touched me I was deathly afraid of changing forever and I was desperately clinging to what I already was. The dissolution of the ego during ayahuasca was difficult enough to handle; this was the death of me as I knew me—perhaps even real death—and I could not bear it, did not have the courage to face such an unknown.

"Can't you work without me letting go as much as you are asking me to let go?"

"No. You have to let yourself go into forever to get healed. You have to trust us."

The battle within myself waged for eternity. My fear reached depths I had never encountered. Over and over the doctors cajoled me to let them work. They jeered me, they laughed at my gutlessness. They ordered me to let them do their job. They threatened me with not helping me if I wouldn't let them. They told me I could not be Chepa or Madeleina if I didn't let them heal me. I tried to let them work, but each time I was more frightened than the last, until, finally, in desperation, I asked them again if they couldn't work on me without me having to let go and fall into the abyss. The voice repeated that they couldn't, that they needed my approval. And when finally I said, out of exhaustion as much as anything else, "Okay," one last time, they said they didn't believe me. That I would have to shout "Please heal me" to give them the freedom to access the depths they needed to access.

I couldn't do it. I knew I was gutless, pathetic, and knew they knew it too, but I simply could not let go the way they said they needed me to—even though part of me thought that I might very well come out much better on the other side of my fear. If only I had the courage to make that leap.

"We'll try it next time," the voice said at some point, and just as he did the rushing of the wind through the reeds began again, this time moving away from me.

"Wait, come back! I want you to heal me!" I called after them, but they and I both knew I couldn't do it that night, and they didn't return.

Exhausted, I got to my feet, told Italo that I was going outside to vomit and left the hut. Outside, the trees in the light of my flashlight were iridescent, the leaves dripping with new rain. I hadn't noticed the rain. I vomited the bile of my cowardice, then made my way back inside to Italo, who was rolling restlessly on the dirt floor. "It's hard, Dad," he said. "There's ghosts here."

I gave him a piece of hard candy then put my arms around him. "It will be over soon. It's very powerful tonight."

"Just don't go anywhere again."

"Okay."

I looked over to where I thought my guests should be and in a few moments my eyes adjusted to the darkness enough to make out the shapes of Don Ramón and Francisco kneeling near them, working on them. A few minutes later, confident that Italo was calming down, I lay down next to him and closed my eyes.

✦

I began to fall. A long, long fall, but I wasn't afraid without the doctors around. I said a silent apology to them for my own failure and promised to be more brave next time, hoping they would come back. It was just that they had been so unexpected, so demanding and so utterly real, even though, thinking about it, I realized I'd never seen them.

I landed with a thud on what felt like soft earth, bounced high in the air and fell again. When I caught my breath I looked around and realized I was in a huge red cavern. A monstrously large red cavernous space with hills of reddish dirt, or goop, scattered all around it. It wasn't dirt, though, or goop, it was as if the material was the tangible element of pain and suffering, and the entire place was filled with it. The whole place was infused with anguish and there was activity everywhere, though there weren't any people. Movement was more like it, and thunderous booming sounds, violent vomiting sounds. And smells of something putrid—not a dead smell, but living, wretched smells that nearly choked me. I didn't understand what was happening, what the motion was, or where the smells came from: everything seemed to come from everywhere. Near me, though I couldn't see him, I felt Italo's presence in the same cavern.

I heard the vomiting again from somewhere far away and turned my eyes in the direction of the sound. On a hill to my right shapeless globs of red material fell in time with the vomiting. In that same moment I realized I was hearing the sounds of hundreds, thousands of people vomiting, and thousands of others crying and wailing, and I wondered for a moment if I wasn't in some sort of hell, so filled was the place with human suffering. But even as the piles grew, hands I couldn't see were scooping the goop and fashioning things out of it, and it dawned on me—or rather, a radiant awareness shot through me in an instant the way ayahuasca awareness often does—where we were.

"Italo!" I called out, though I don't know if I used my voice or not. "This is the place where the healing happens! This is the place where everything we throw up on ayahuasca comes!"

I was laughing. "This is the room where all the rotten stuff comes and the healing is done with that stuff!"

Suddenly all of the color red I'd been seeing for the past two years, the trips up my bloodstream and the DNA all made sense to me. This was the place of red magic! This was the healing magic. It was in Julio's song all along: "Red magic that moves within our blood." I'd heard it a hundred times, I'd just never seen it before, but now, in that room, sharing that space with Italo, I was in awe as much as I'd been when I felt the winds rush through me. I just laughed and laughed and grabbed Italo tight. Why we were being shown this place I didn't question. Just being there was enormously healing. I felt I was being shown something very special. The realization of the pain and suffering that was being retched by all those unseen humans into that space, and the knowledge that that same bile could be used by healers to heal struck me as almost impossible to comprehend. There was an enormity to it I couldn't fathom.

In a few minutes or a year, I was brought back to the floor of the hut by Italo's voice. "Dad, you're squeezing my arm too tight."

I loosened my grip. "Did you see it, Italo?"

"What was that place, Dad?"

"The red room. The place where the healing happens," I said, thrilled to find he'd been there as well.

"What was all that stuff?"

"Pain and suffering."

"It stunk."

"It always does," I laughed, hugging him.

The next day while I was back at the bar waiting for my guests to arrive for lunch, I couldn't stop thinking about the previous night. I felt awful that I'd been unable to let the doctors work more easily on me, and kicked myself for not remembering to ask them the simple question: "Are you my teachers?" If they'd said yes, my fear might have diminished enough to allow them to do what they wanted. If they had meant me ill they would have just disappeared. But I already knew they—if they existed at all—didn't mean me harm. That was why they'd shown me the cavern and how they transformed pain and suffering into healing material. It was why they let me glimpse what red magic was. I wondered if they would ever come back, and, if they did, whether I would have the courage to let go.

Chapter Four

# THE DOCTORS SAY
# IT'S TIME TO WORK

ABOUT A MONTH later I had another small group, most of whom had been with me a year earlier on a trip to Machu Picchu, during which they'd done San Pedro with Victor in the ruins of Sacsayhuamán outside of Cuzco. This time around, the group leader, Maryanne C., or Mac as she preferred, had asked to spend a week in the jungle before heading to Machu Picchu and then Lake Titicaca in southern Peru.

We'd intended to travel to Julio's, but after a day or two acclimating in Iquitos, the group opted to do a few smaller trips rather than one big one. We took day trips on the Amazon, spent time at Iquitos' markets and ports, and finally took two days at Sachamama.

Of the group of seven, all but two had experienced San Pedro the previous year, and most had tried ayahuasca back in the states, so I had no hesitation in sending word a couple of days before the ceremony asking Francisco to have Don Ramón make a strong brew.

On the day we arrived, Don Francisco was waiting for us, having spent the morning preparing a flower bath for my guests, a sort of aura-cleansing done with flower essences extracted into clean river water. After bathing, the group spent the afternoon walking the intricate jungle trails of the botanical garden, and when night fell, all were anticipating the commencement of the ceremony.

By eight o'clock or so Francisco led us to the simple framed doorway of the ceremonial hut, then *sopla'd*—blew—each of us with mapacho smoke to clean us of unnecessary emotional baggage before we entered. The hut, a leaf-roof on posts, had crude benches along the outside walls, an open dirt floor in the center, and a simple makeshift altar at the far end. On the altar were the things Don Ramón and Francisco considered necessary for the ceremony: candles and kerosene lanterns, the bottle of ayahuasca, shacapas, bottles of Agua Florida and perfumes, a few talismans, and a good supply of mapachos and matches. Most of my crew, in their late forties and fifties, took seats along the benches, while I opted for a space on the floor.

When everyone was settled, Don Francisco blew out all the kerosene lamps, leaving the room lit by a single candle on the altar near Don Ramón. Outside the sky was thick with cloud cover. If there was a moon it wasn't visible. Don Ramón lit a mapacho, and by the light of his match Steven K., a young man who was traveling with his mother, saw a movement on the ground. He asked me to shine a flash on it. I did, and there, sitting on a slightly raised mound of earth directly in front of the simple altar, was an immense tarantula. It didn't recoil from the light, simply looked as though it were staring straight ahead at both Don Ramón and Don Francisco. It didn't move, in fact, until Francisco brushed it out of the hut with a cedar branch. The seven of us all laughed once it was gone and took it as a good omen.

Some minutes later, Ramón began calling the participants to the altar. All but Steven's mother planned on drinking, and as each approached he sang an icaro, then served the foul tasting ayahuasca. When it was Steven's turn he found he could not keep the liquid down. He tried several times but could not do it. As he came back to his seat, head down, he asked if I was disappointed in him. I was surprised at his question and told him no, that power plants were like that—they made themselves so odious that you had to be really sure you wanted to ingest them in order to physically do it, and this was not the right time for him.

I was the last to drink apart from the curanderos, and could hardly keep it down myself. Once I did, I put the bottle of aguardiente to my nose, then poured a small amount of Agua Florida into my hands and rubbed it vigorously into my face and scalp.

I returned from the altar, sat on the dry earth floor of the hut, and closed my eyes, waiting for Francisco and Ramón to drink. Then the candle was extinguished and the hut thrown into complete darkness. Within fifteen or twenty minutes the first of the ayahuasca twinkle-lights appeared behind my eyelids: yellow, green, silver dots of light beginning to connect in their familiar patterns. Moments later came the reds, and I suddenly felt an enormous fear well up within me. I opened my eyes but they didn't disappear. Instead, my whole field of vision, eyes open or closed, became filled with rapidly connecting red points of light that quickly formed themselves into a huge, swirling double-helix DNA thread that turned itself on its side and began rolling towards me. My dread increased. The doctors were coming to visit and I wasn't ready for them. Wasn't ready to die that little death again. Wasn't ready to be worked on again. I wanted to stop right then, come down and save it for another night when I was better prepared. "Oh god," I thought, "I can't do this again."

It was no use, of course. I knew no antidote to ayahuasca. Worse, I felt my lips beginning to go numb, an indication that one of the admixes that had been included in making the ayahuasca was *chiric sanango—Brunfelsia grandiflora*—a plant closely related to datura or toé. Adding that meant the experience was not going to last the normal two hours or so, but could well last the entire night or even into the morning.

I realized my group was in much deeper than I'd intended and that I was not going to be able to help them. We were going to hell. We were going to see God and be terrified for hours. We'd probably all learn a great deal by the time we came out of it, but we were going to pay a terrible price to learn.

I wanted to sit up and shout to everyone that I was sorry. I'd asked Ramón and Francisco to make a strong ayahuasca but I'd never meant this. I didn't, of course. There was nothing to do but remember to breathe and try not to panic. I was already having a hard time doing both.

I knew what was coming and couldn't get away. I sat and tried to light a cigarette, but the chiric sanango numbness in my lips had spread to my fingers and toes and it took me several tries; even then I couldn't keep the thing in my hands very well. I knew I was just panicking and reminded myself to breathe deeply. I did, and in a few minutes I was calmed enough to try to lie down.

The moment I did the world started crumbling in on me again. The DNA was no longer coming at me, it had me in its spirals. I was dizzy and disoriented.

"Is everybody okay?" I managed to blurt out, though I felt my voice sounded broken and unsure.

"Fine over here," someone answered. "How are you doing?"

"Not great," I said, praying that someone would come over and help me, somehow. No one did. I sat back up and began rocking, thinking I had to get myself together. No more outbursts. I was the one supposed to show the way with my behavior, and if everyone knew I was panicked I could cause some of my guests, if they were on a similarly thin rope, to fall over to the panic side as well. I tried to maintain. I tried to tell myself that no one ever died of ayahuasca, no one ever came out visibly different on the other side of the ceremony, but each time I thought I had reached a point where I could relax enough to let the experience take hold I panicked again. It must have been terribly disturbing to the other guests to have me sitting up, then lying down, then shifting into a fetal position, then sitting up and trying to light a cigarette, then unwrapping a candy. I was palpably freaking out.

"We're here," came the voice I'd been terrified of hearing. It was the doctors, and this time they didn't come with the rush of air, they were simply there. "We're going to work on you tonight and you are going to let us. You need healing."

"I can't breathe. Can't we do it another night?"

"You called us and we've come. It's time to work."

I felt the clutching at my heart and the immensity of the barbs of sorrow race through me as images of all of my failures flashed in my innermost being. "Stop! I can't do it!" I fairly screamed.

"We don't care. This time we don't care if you don't want us to. It's time to work."

## Chapter Five

# A HARD LESSON IN HEALING

I SAT BOLT upright and tried to light another cigarette. It fell from my numbed fingers; I grabbed another, then another, until my whole fresh pack was empty. I ran my fingers on the floor trying to find one but couldn't.

"Hey Pete, you want a smoke?" It was Stephen.

"Yeah."

"You're having a hard time."

"Can you light it?"

He did, saying, "Can I do anything?"

"Just watch the others. I'm in no shape." I clutched at the cigarette and took long pulls, then lay back down, hoping that maybe the doctors would have gone away during my cigarette break. They hadn't. Instantly as I lay down the work began anew and with it my unimaginable terror. It was a terror as chilling as the rapture of being at the place where the four winds start. I was helpless in the face of it. But then I remembered what I had forgotten the last time the doctors visited and asked them: "Are you my teachers?"

"We are doctors."

"But are you my teachers?"

"We are past teachers. We are the doctors."

I didn't know what to do: I thought that the rule was simply to ask if a spirit was a teacher and if it was it would announce itself, and if it wasn't it would go away. This was something I hadn't anticipated.

"So you're not my teachers?" I asked.

"We already told you who we are. If we meant you harm we would have disappeared."

They began to work again. They were merciless and there was little I could do to stop them. A lifetime's pain was dredged up and relived in moments or minutes; I never knew I had felt so much pain in my life. Then, suddenly, they said they had done enough for now but would be back soon because there was so much more to do. And then they were gone. I was alone on the ground and the red world was spinning around me, frightening me, but no longer with the abject horror of being hurled into the unknowable abyss that it had been a moment earlier. I opened my eyes and sat up.

*Kerosene Lamp*

The hut was a scene from a Fellini movie: a couple of my guests were draped over the back of the benches, vomiting violently onto the jungle floor. A couple of others were clutching one another, looking, as best I could make out, as though they felt if they let go they would fly off into space. Nearest me, Mac was fully stretched out on a bench, moaning to Stephen not to go away. Don Ramón and Francisco were tending someone on the dirt floor near the altar. I was still in no position to help anyone, so I just asked if everyone was okay. Those who could speak said they were in hell and hated me for bringing them there. I assured them it would be over soon, and prayed I wasn't lying.

One of my guests, Susan, was having a particularly hard time, and I decided I better try to make my way to her to see if there was anything I could do. I stood on very shaky legs, and took a couple of staggering steps in her direction. I didn't get very far when I thought better of it. But Harry, the man who'd been holding on to her, had seen my attempt, and on his own shaky legs stood and told me to come to him.

"I'm going to try to ground you," he said, reaching for my hand. I reached for him and he told me just to breathe into him, to let myself ground through him into the earth floor. We stood stone still for a few moments, then he let go and turned his attention back to Susan, who was beginning to vomit violently.

I sat down where I was and shimmied back to the place I'd been. I felt awful for everyone that I'd brought them this far and couldn't do anything to help them. But I was still in the full throes of ayahuasca myself and thought it better if I just let it happen. I lay down and closed my eyes again.

Hundreds of spirits appeared before me. I was no longer afraid, and asked each if they were my teachers. One by one they disappeared until there was nothing but an empty red world.

And then suddenly I thought of my snake, and it occurred to me that I'd never asked him—I don't know why I thought of it as a him rather than her—if he was my teacher. I found him in the pit of my stomach. "Are you my teacher?" I asked.

"Of course I am," he answered.

I felt ridiculous. "Why didn't you ever tell me?"

"You never asked."

"What are you here to teach me?"

He indicated a mirror lying near him. "Take that mirror and hold it high. Look into it."

To my surprise I was able to somehow reach into my belly and take hold of the simple oval mirror. I looked into it and saw my reflection.

"You can use that to see the answer to all your questions."

I immediately thought of Chepa and looked into the mirror for a solution to our problems.

"You're on your own there. You can't look for anything selfish or it won't work. Besides, you already know the answer. Stop drinking is the first step."

I chuckled at myself. Bad enough I was in conversation with a snake that lived in my stomach, but he'd just busted me.

"Now climb through the mirror to get to the other side. That's where you will find help for things."

I tried to watch my spirit body climb through the mirror but nothing happened. I tried again. Same result.

"Stop trying to see yourself, let go and just climb through it."

I did as he said and surprisingly, found myself climbing into a pitch black space that felt like a chamber. But my feet didn't touch the ground. Instead, it felt as though I were floating. I reached out with my arms and they made contact with what felt like smooth stone.

"Feel along the ceiling," the snake instructed.

I reached up and did as asked, pulling myself along. I hadn't gone more than a few feet when I realized there was a sort of recessed light in the ceiling. I pulled myself toward it: It wasn't an ordinary light, more like an eight- or ten-inch cylindrical tube about an inch and a half in diameter from which light emanated.

"Take the light stone," the snake said with a touch of impatience when I didn't move to touch it. "Bring it to this side of the mirror, bring the mirror back to me, then wrap yourself in the light."

At the time it made sense to me, so again I did as the snake said. The stone was neutral to the touch, though I thought it would be warm. I took it, made my way back to the mirror, crossed over, put the mirror away, and suddenly found myself on the dirt floor of the hut, wrapping my physical body in a stream of white light that came from the stone. No one else could see the light, I'm sure, though they probably could see me slowly waving my left hand in a circle around my head. As I did I felt the comfort of the light around me.

"Now take the mirror," said the snake, "climb through it and put the light back. Never forget to replace the things you take from the other side."

I did, then thanked the snake for teaching me.

Francisco's voice brought me back to physical reality. "Pedro, if it's alright with you, it's late, so tell your friends to sit up and we will say a closing word for the ceremony." He lit a candle and suddenly the room was filled with the shadows of my guests, none of whom looked ready to have the ceremony end. One or two were still moaning, and another couple were still vomiting.

"What did he say?" Mac asked weakly from her prone position on the bench.

I translated from the Spanish.

"Tell him it's not over by a longshot."

Everyone agreed. I told Francisco what Mac said and he reluctantly blew out the candle, while Ramón began to sing again. Ten or fifteen minutes later I could hear people beginning to move in the darkness, and Francisco once again lit a candle. I was still under the influence, but felt I could function in ordinary reality and turned my attention to the others. Harry was telling Susan that she might be better off in her bunk, sleeping under a mosquito net. Susan agreed and I could hear her gathering her things.

I asked Susan and Harry if they'd be alright, and Stephen surprised me by suggesting that he would walk them back to the sleeping hut, about 100 yards away on a narrow jungle trail. Stephen's mom, Barbara, said she'd accompany them as well. Stephen borrowed my flashlight to lead the way. A few minutes later Stephen returned and then walked a man named Jahn, who said he'd had a wonderful and enlightening experience but was still wobbly-legged. With only Mac, Jean and myself left in the hut, Francisco said that he and Ramón were going as well. Mac looked as though she was still deep in the throes of her experience and I said I wished they would stay. "You know what to do, Peter," Francisco said, and when I objected he simply smiled and said, "Sing." I didn't like being put in that position but Ramón was looking very old and exhausted so I told them to go ahead.

A few minutes later Stephen came back and asked Jean and Mac if they were ready to leave. Jean said she was still under the influence but thought she'd be better off in bed than in the hut. Mac said that she was in no condition to move and I volunteered to stay with her. She asked Stephen to bring her blankets, as she was feeling very cold. He said he would once the others were all settled.

I sat on the floor near Mac and gathered up all of the cigarettes I'd lost during the night. I thought she just needed a few more minutes, but when I asked how she was feeling, she said there were spirits pulling her to the other side and she didn't know if she was strong enough to fight them. I felt her heart and pulse: both were slightly erratic, and her breathing was labored. I thought she'd be better off sitting up but she was unable to move, and being a big woman, I couldn't simply lift her to a sitting position.

"They're pulling me, Peter. I don't know that I can fight them." Her voice had an element of deep fear in it. Of all her group, she was the most experienced with visionary plants and altered states, and short of being deeply terrified she could have handled anything.

"Just remember to breathe, Mac," I said, but when she continued to breathe unevenly I started to sing my simple icaro to give her a rhythm to follow.

Stephen returned with two blankets and we put them over her. "I'm freezing. I'm freezing," she repeated over and over, so Stephen went to get more.

"I've never met spirits like this. I don't know how to get rid of them."

"Just don't forget to breathe."

And again I sang, and didn't stop singing when Stephen brought more blankets, and then water to cool down her forehead, which was burning up.

An hour passed and she was still not well. By then Stephen had picked up a shacapa and was shaking it in time with my singing. If it had been anyone else but Mac, I might have thought they were milking it for the attention, but I knew that I was still under the influence, albeit not with the intensity of the first few hours, and thought she must be as well.

As I sang I tried to look at her. Not at her body, but at her spirit body, to see if I could see anything wrong. At first I couldn't see anything, and I began to feel silly for even trying. But just as I was about to stop it seemed to me that there was a sort of black hole in Mac's upper back and what I can only describe as a kind of energy—it wasn't solid or liquid, or anything I could see with my regular eyes—was leaking out of it. And then I thought I saw another in her lower back, and then another. It was as if they had always been there, but only in my not trying to see them did they become apparent. But seeing them only made me feel helpless, as I had no idea whether they were really there, and if they were, what I could do about it.

Suddenly the voice told me I'd better do something. It was the same voice, with the same intensity it had used when I was fighting for Marco years earlier, and I knew to take it seriously. I thought of the light and closed my eyes. With an ease that surprised me I made my way to my belly, got the mirror, placed it high and climbed through it. I pulled myself along the ceiling of the other side until I got to the stone light. I took it and reversed my steps, and found myself back at Mac's side, singing. In my left hand I held the invisible stone light. Feeling slightly silly, I began to move the light up and down the length of Mac's body, stopping at the black holes that I saw or sensed. Suddenly a different voice, or a group of voices, told me just to touch the stone to the holes; there was something familiar and frightening about the new voices. I realized it was the doctors, but before I had time to panic, they continued.

"Just do what we say. We're here to work on her, not you this time."

Relieved, I did as they said, and the first hole seemed to close a little. I waited for instruction but none was forthcoming, so I moved the stone light to another hole. It too seemed to close a little, though I wasn't sure I wasn't just playing curandero and making the whole thing up.

"I'm not winning this battle," Mac, who'd been silent for nearly an hour, said suddenly. "I think I am going to die."

"You're not going to die, Mac," I said. "Nobody dies from ayahuasca."

"I don't think I can keep going."

I didn't know what to say and didn't think shouting that she was being a baby—which is what I was feeling by then—was going to help. At the same time I knew she was in that terror zone and unable to let go for fear of falling into the abyss, which would be a sort of dying.

"Don't stop singing. It's the only thing I have to hold me here," Mac said, and I realized I had stopped. I began my simple icaro again, and sang it with every variation that came to my mind. And when I could no longer mouth the notes I began to sing regular songs. I sang the old blues songs "Alberta," and "Who Do You Love;"; I sang James Cotton's "I'm Gonna Be Down At Your Burial" and anything else I could remember. All the while I kept moving the light stone from black hole to black hole, and silently begged the doctors to tell me what to do next. Stephen kept an eye on Mac's breath, and kept her covered when the blankets would shift. He fed her water through a straw which she kept vomiting weakly the instant she took it in. Vomiting meant she was breathing, so we took it as a good sign.

Still, by the time three hours or three years had gone by—there was still no sign of false dawn but it seemed like forever—Mac didn't seem to be getting better. Her breathing remained labored, she was running a fever and at the same time was deeply chilled. When she spoke it was either incoherently about the spirits trying to get her to join them on the other side or a request that we tell her son Josh that she was sorry she couldn't make it but he should never forget how much she loved him. Whenever she spoke there was terror in her voice.

I wondered why the stone light treatment wasn't working. It seemed to me that the black holes had all shrunk considerably, and many had disappeared altogether. If they were an indication of the battle she was waging she should have been improving.

"Breathe through the holes to clean them." It was the doctors, returned after an eternity.

I didn't hesitate: I began by switching from singing the notes of my icaro to breath-whistling them over Mac's whole body, trying to clean off whatever ether was clutching at her. After a few minutes I began to breathe deeply and focus a single stream of breath at the first hole I could see, trying to aim through it. Nothing happened, but to my surprise I was able to breathe out for a much longer period that I thought. I took a deep breath and tried again. This time my breath seemed almost solid, and as it passed through the hole the blackness disappeared with it, and when I finally stopped breathing, what had been a black hole of sorts now looked to me like a fast-healing clean sore, as if the hole had somehow really been cleaned out and was sealing itself.

I breathed into the second hole, and then a third. Each time, my breath seemed to be coming from a place deeper within me, as though it wasn't my breath at all but a hint of the four winds that started somewhere in the vast distance and passed through me on the way to passing into and through Mac. The sound was deafening to me, though I don't think Stephen heard a difference. It felt as though I was the conduit for blowing the wind at the beginning and end of the world and each time I blew I felt myself growing larger and larger, until I almost no longer fit beneath the high roof of the hut. I might have been blowing the wind of the universe and each breath seemed to clean and close a dozen holes until I couldn't find anymore. I still didn't stop; I blew the air around her, beneath her, through her hair, until, exhausted, I could breathe no more. Instantly, I shrank to my normal size and was once again sitting on the floor next to Mac and near Stephen.

"Call Francisco and Ramón," I told Stephen, telling him which hut they were staying in. "Tell them we need them here."

I began chanting quietly again, silently thanked the doctors, then visited my snake to get the mirror to put the light stone away. I felt utterly spent.

"Are you there, Peter?" Mac asked softly.

"Still here, girl. How are you?"

"I'm weak and I still feel stoned. I'm still scared but I don't think I'm going to die anymore."

"Good."

"Where's Stephen?"

"He went to get Francisco."

It was better than she'd sounded for several hours.

Francisco and Ramón came in shortly, carrying several *toronjas*, a jungle grapefruit, a knife and a bowl with ice in it. Francisco cut the fruit in halves and began to ice it while Ramón felt Mac's pulse and heartbeat. Then he put his hands on her head.

"She's very hot," he told Francisco.

Francisco handed him the bowl, and Ramon began applying the halved-fruits to Mac's temples. She objected vehemently to the cold but was told to simply bear it because her brain was still very hot. I thought that the silliest thing I'd ever heard and touched her head myself: though she had no fever anymore—her forehead and glands were cool—her temples were on fire. The cold juice gradually cooled them down.

"She was in quite a battle tonight," Francisco announced, as though it was news.

"Why didn't you stay?" I asked. "You knew she was in trouble."

"It was your turn tonight," Don Ramón answered simply.

In a few minutes they left, leaving Stephen, Mac and me alone again. A few minutes later the first light of dawn began to arc across the eastern sky.

"I was really going to die, guys," Mac said. "I've never been that close before."

In another hour Mac had regained enough strength to make it to the sleeping hut, and after a couple of hours of rest managed to make the hike to the road, where a bus I'd arranged for picked us up for the ride back to Iquitos.

When I later related the story to Julio he just shrugged and said, "*Ah, Pedrito*. This is red magic," as if everyone knew what it was and how to use it when necessary.

# PART IV

# AYAHUASCA HEALING AND
# AN INKLING OF DARKNESS

*One family, my family*
*My family, one family,*
*Mama Chepa, Papa Pedro*
*Italo and Marco*
*And my Madeleina.*
*Help me help me*
*Fix my broken family*
*Fix my broken family*
*Heal me doctors,*
*Heal me spirits,*
*Help me Red Magic*
*That lives in my veins.*
*Help me White Magic*
*That fills the sky,*
*Help me Green Magic*
*That gives life to the firmament*
*Help me Black Magic*
*Deep Magic that dwells in the earth.*
*Cleanse my Spirit,*
*Cleanse my heart*
*Cleanse my soul*
*Cleanse my body*
*Help me help me*
*Fix my broken family.*

*—from a gift song from Julio*

Chapter One

# THE DOCTORS AS A NURSE

WE MOVED back to New York shortly after that trip with Mac and her crew, and it was months before I had a chance to return to Peru and be with Julio again.

The next time I drank ayahuasca, my son Marco drank as well and the focus on him—and my four guests—allowed me to have a relatively easy time, with the doctors not even making an appearance. For Marco—who, like Italo, had cultural ties to traditional Amazon healing and had grown up around curanderos and ayahuasca—it was a marvelous, if scary, night, during which I held him for hours.

In the morning one of my guests came to me in Julio's kitchen area and angrily demanded to know how on earth I could have let a 12-year-old drink ayahuasca. "What on earth could Marco have possibly learned at his age?"

"I don't know," I answered. "Let's ask him."

We did.

"Well," he started, "before last night I was always afraid of the dark because I thought that's when ghosts came and I was afraid of ghosts. But last night I realized they're always here, right here with us. Only it takes ayahuasca to be able to see them and hear them and talk with them. So now that I know they're everywhere all the time, and now that I talked with them and see they're not all just trying to kill me, like I thought, I don't think I'll be afraid of the dark anymore."

On the next trip, I brought five guests up to see Julio. They were a terrific group, open to Iquitos, to the overcrowded riverboat, to the filth of the marketplaces, to everything I loved. Among them was a former captain in the US Special Forces who simply exuded strength of a kind most people don't possess. His presence alone pushed me to promise that I would not panic this time when the doctors appeared, not be so cowardly in the face of such a man.

Unfortunately, I caved in almost the instant that Julio blew out the last of the coffee-tin kerosene lanterns that lit the little unwalled area of the hut where we sat. It was a dark night, with a hint of rain in the thick clouds overhead.

In the darkness the twinkle of green lights appeared. I tried to stay calm as they connected into beams, and the beams connected into the great arched cathedral ceiling. And then it all turned red and I knew I was there again, in the world where the doctors worked. I made my way over to a railing by the platform's edge and stood. Julio wasn't five feet away, shaking his shacapa in time with the icaro he sang. I clung to the sounds like a lifeline, breathing deeply to try to get past my fear. I looked out at the jungle past the little clearing around Julio's home and saw that everything was alive and moving and ominous. Julio had called a lot of spirits to join us and they were coming in droves. It was going to be a long night if I could not control myself.

I couldn't, of course, and when a few minutes later I began the wonderful and violent retching, I was relieved to have something tangible to cling to. Up from my stomach came the residue of the ayahuasca I'd drunk; then up from deep within myself came the bile of my life, all of it bursting out of me like great chunks of something filthy I'd been carrying for too long. I roared like a lion, spewing like a waterfall into the jungle night while Julio sang. Over and over I roared, eliminating junk.

There was nothing to see on the physical level, of course, no real vomit to speak of since I'd fasted all day. But with ayahuasca eyes it looked like a pile of bad things at my feet that grew with each violent retch. What a fantastic feeling to eliminate so much so effortlessly, what a gift from the medicine to clean another closet in my personal wasteland.

When I finished, I sat down where I was and made my way over to my original spot on the hut floor. The others were in the throes of their own cleansings, and I hoped they enjoyed them as much as I had.

My joy at momentarily forgetting what I'd come to learn quickly dissolved as I heard the familiar rustling of tall grass. The rustling became louder than Julio's singing; it was filling me up. I crawled across the floor and stood against the railing, facing the jungle again. The rushing grew still louder until I thought my head would burst, then abruptly stopped. The sudden silence was deafening.

"We're here again," one of them said.

"I know," I heard my inner voice answer.

"There is still work to do and not much time."

"I don't know how to let you work. I want you to, but after all this time I still can't do what you want."

"Would it be easier to work on you if we looked like this?" they asked, suddenly transforming themselves from the tiny creatures I'd never really seen into a young woman. I couldn't see her face but felt she was lovely.

"Is this better?" she asked, chiding me.

"You're still the doctors," I said.

"I'm just me," she said plainly.

"It's a trick. If I relax you're going to turn back into the doctors and tear me to pieces."

"Not this time. It's not going to hurt a bit," she laughed.

"Bullshit. I don't trust you."

"Oh, come on. It's not going to hurt at all. It might even tickle."

She didn't wait for an answer. She just reached into me and grabbed my heart and began to massage it. "You really don't have a choice. I've got to get this work done."

I didn't know if I was talking out loud or not, but I knew I was moving around and disturbing the others, so I made my way down the three-step ladder to the clay earth outside the hut.

"*Bien?*" Julio asked as I left the platform.

"*Los doctores,*" I said.

"Yah!" he laughed. We'd never really spoken about them, but Julio seemed aware of them anyway. "Not that far," he said in Spanish as I began to step outside of the immediate area of his voice, drawing me back to the base of the hut.

Outside was as frightening as it was inside, but I had no place else to go so

I lay on the ground and listened to Julio singing as I looked up at the red world around me.

"That's much better," the woman laughed, taking out my heart and beginning to reshape it.

Her voice startled me, but her demeanor was so open and light-hearted that even though I knew she was just the doctors pretending to be a woman, I didn't fight her.

And in not fighting her, the work went easily. She didn't provoke fear. She just seemed to be tickling me. Up came the question I'd been asking for years: How can I make Chepa happy? What does she want? And the old follow up: To make her happy you must be her. I still didn't know how to do that and asked the woman.

"This isn't the time for that. I've still got a lot of anger to take out."

Images of things I'd done in anger, or wished to do, came pouring out. The sourest moments of pain from my marriage came back to life and I was forced to relive them in wretched detail. A hundred things, a thousand moments or hours I wish I'd never lived, were all relived horribly. But something about this nurse, this woman and the joy with which she worked, allowed me to allow her to dredge all those things up, things I'd fought the doctors over reliving for years.

I don't know how long she worked. I remember that it started to rain and my wonderful assistant Corina told me to come into the hut, but I told her I was fine. I was more than fine. I was singing something, an ayahuasca song was coming out of me effortlessly and I was singing it and laughing and anyone seeing me would have surely thought I was crazy. But I knew better. I was letting some of that stuff go, some of that stuff that was keeping me locked in a sour place, and I was getting lighter and more giddy with each bad memory I relived and threw away.

Finally, she said she'd done enough for one night and put my heart back into my chest. I tried to see what she looked like, but as I did she crumbled back into a thousand little doctors, all of them laughing at me.

"That wasn't so bad now, was it?" they asked.

"You should have done that years ago," I said.

"We couldn't. You weren't ready."

And then the rustling of the leaves began and they disappeared, taking the sound with them until only the sound of Julio's singing and the che-che-che of the shacapa remained.

I lay where I was for a long time, until I realized what I must have looked and sounded like to my guests—then stood on ayahuasca-drunken legs and made my way to them one by one to see if they were alright.

They were. Corina, Jairo and MaBel had seen to that.

## Chapter Two

# A CHANGING OF THE GUARD

IT WAS six months before I got another chance to visit Peru, and this time I managed to bring Chepa and our baby Madeleina, who was nearly four. I thought things were getting better with Chepa; she had moved to Fort Worth, Texas—where three of her sisters lived—for a few months, but then moved back to New York. She had been saying that living with me in New York was not her life anymore, but she had stayed and I thought things were pretty okay. We fought sometimes, maybe often, but we drank beer every night and so managed to get a lot of laughter into the mix as well. In any event, I flew one of her sisters in from Fort Worth to watch the boys for a few weeks, and Chepa and Madeleina and I took off for Peru.

To my delight, Chepa wanted to help with the group, and made them a great party at our bar—which we only opened when I was in Iquitos— took them out dancing, and even came along on the river to help me cook and attend to things.

Julio was delighted to see her—we'd left Madeleina back in Iquitos with Momma Lydia—though he did tell me privately that she would be leaving soon and that I shouldn't fight it since she had no control over it. Another impossible challenge I would fail miserably, but at the time I hoped he was wrong and might take a moment to see what it was she needed to make her happy, so that I could provide it for her. I didn't actually ask him to do it; I just thought he would know.

After I'd introduced everyone to Julio—he always stood very erectly for introductions and formally announced his full name to each of my guests— Corina and Chepa went about catching some fish for dinner. While they did,

Jérnan—Julio's eldest son—and a couple of assistants set up hammocks and mosquito nets for my guests at Jérnan's home—a short distance from Julio's—and I did the same for Corina, Chepa and me on Julio's porch.

That night, Chepa and my assistant Juan, Julio's son-in-law who lived nearby on the Aucayacu River, took my guests out night-fishing under the starlit Amazon sky. They didn't catch anything except for a handful of fish that leapt into the dugout canoes, but their catching fish wasn't important. What was important was that by being on the river in those uncomfortable little canoes that tip so easily, they were forced to be perfectly still. And in the silence of that motionlessness, the presence of the jungle makes itself known in a way they could not otherwise grasp. The dark shapes of the trees overhanging the riverbanks and the dead yellow eyes of caymans reflected in a flashlight's glare conjured up childhood fears and excitement. The sounds of fish breaking water, or kingfishers crashing into things, the whistle of bat wings near your face—all call on you to summon up your courage. There could be jaguars on the banks, after all, or boas in the water. Those shapes and sounds of the jungle would never leave them, I knew. They found a way into my guests' blood.

When the canoes returned it was late, well past midnight. Corina gave everyone something warm to drink and a bite to eat, then sent them off to bed.

I got them up much earlier than they would have liked, so that they could go along with Julio to collect the vine and other plants he would need to make the ayahuasca for that night's ceremony. I always brought the chacruna leaves with me from Iquitos, as I never knew whether there would be any nearby. But collecting the ayahuasca vine itself was part of the preparation for drinking.

Julio waited graciously, as he always did, for the gringos to finish brushing their teeth and taking care of their other essentials. When everyone was ready he headed out on a path that took us past his own small fields of yuca and plantains, behind his son Jérnan's house and the soccer field there, past the new blue-painted one-room schoolhouse, and finally up a hill onto a hunter's path. That path took us to where the jungle looks like the jungle of our dreams: towering trees whose crowns joined in a full, closed canopy, through which only dappled sunlight shone; fifty-foot strands of wild orchids growing side by side with lianas, vines as thick as a man's leg. Bromeliads so old they'd dropped root-strands nearly eighty feet. This was a glimpse of ancient things.

The deep forest was interrupted with *chacras*, jungle garden plots, that had been burned out of it to grow bananas, plantains, yuca and a few other things the river people need. We'd come on a chacra and have to climb over and around the half-burned fallen trees, trying not to step on any of the crop seedlings, then we'd be back in the real jungle.

Julio walked in front of us. Despite his age, he still had to slow his pace to make certain we didn't fall behind. When he came on something he thought might give one of us trouble—a plant or tree branch he thought might hurt us—he flicked his machete to cut the path clear. He didn't swing his machete, or hack with it. He flicked it. Walking with Julio in the jungle was like watching a karate master at work: his movements were so economical they seemed more like a suggestion to the plants to clear the way than an actual cutting-and-clearing of them. And the plants seemed to simply separate for him, as if they would put themselves together again once we were gone.

When Julio reached the vine he wanted to use, he smoked it with a mapacho, chanted a little, then cut the sections he wanted. He worked meticulously, slicing several sections of vine for each person. He blew smoke on each then handed them to me. When he was satisfied he'd cut enough, he asked for the large plastic sack I'd brought to carry the vine, and blew smoke in it as well, before allowing me to put the vine in it.

Before we left he blew smoke on the plant again, then left some mapachos at its base both to thank it for its generosity and to encourage it to grow back quickly.

On the way back to Julio's we stopped at a huge and vibrant *lupuna negra* tree. It's one of the giants in that part of the world, with a trunk sometimes a meter-and-a-half in diameter that grows straight and proud for 70-or-80 feet before it begins branching. Its spirit is as powerful as its presence. Julio asked me if we ought to include just a little for the ceremony, but he already knew my answer. For Julio, adding the bark of the tree of light and darkness—which is how he sometimes referred to it—to the ayahuasca was an invitation to the spirit of that tree to come teach us those things we too often keep hidden in the dark parts of ourselves.

It was nearly 8 AM by the time we returned to his home. While we all sat for breakfast—our only meal of the day as we were drinking the medicine that night—Julio told his sons Antenor and Jairo where he wanted the ayahuasca cooking fire and which tree he wanted cut as the primary fire logs. While his sons set off to do as he said, Julio cut two small sections of *catawa* bark from a nearby tree and added it to the bag of vine. Then he sat on a log, laid out the contents of the bag and began crushing the vine sections with a hardwood mallet. When all of the vine was crushed he began to layer his pot with the leaves I'd brought and the vine he'd cut, putting pieces of the barks he'd cut in among the layers.

By nine, the fire was burning, water had been brought from the river to fill the pot, and Julio was standing near the ayahuasca as it heated up, chanting softly and blowing smoke from the mapachos, into the mix.

Not long after breakfast I sent my guests out with Juan for a good hike in the hills, to keep them occupied while Julio worked. They came back at about 4 PM, exhilarated and exhausted.

While the guests couldn't eat because we wanted their stomachs empty when they drank ayahuasca, Julio did what he liked, and he ate a good meal of boiled river fish and plantains with a cup of coffee once the medicine was done.

At about eight, my guests and crew assembled on Julio's porch. Among us were a number of locals as well, who chatted and joked for an hour or more before they disappeared into the night and we were left alone with Julio. Everyone was planning on drinking except for Corina, who would stay in the kitchen area unless she thought one of the guests needed something, and Juan, who would help anyone who needed to maneuver the little three-step ladder from the raised platform to the ground.

My five guests and Chepa and I made a sort of circle on the porch flooring, while Julio sat on a low stool with his back against the porch railing next to the ladder and set up his things.

When he was satisfied the time was right to start the ceremony, he reached for the ayahuasca and the cup, then lit a new mapacho. He asked me for the name of the first person to drink and I gave it to him. He poured the ayahuasca, then began to quietly say a prayer, using the name of the person I'd given him while he called on the spirits to help them in their work. When the prayer was finished he handed me the cup to pass along. It was Chepa, and when she'd finished drinking I passed her the bottle of the protective cumalunga and told her to put it to her nostrils and inhale deeply. When she had, I passed her the bottle of fragrant Agua Florida, and then finally the bottle of Tabu cologne—which Julio always said was ayahuasca's favorite. I also handed her a lemon drop to suck on to help her keep the ayahuasca down long enough to get into her system. The simple ritual was repeated with each of us until Julio himself drank, after which he stood with his book of the saints, made his arcana, then had Juan put out the kerosene lamps, leaving us in utter darkness. Next to me I could hear Chepa breathing.

Julio picked up his shacapa, lit a fresh mapacho, and began to shake the leaf fan. *Che-che-che, che-che-che*, the sound of the leaves was instantly rhythmical and comforting. In a few minutes he began to chant in tune with them. It probably wasn't twenty minutes after Julio had begun to chant when the green sparkling lights began to appear and my familiar panic began to set in. I opened my eyes, hoping I would find myself on Julio's floor in simple jungle darkness, but it didn't help. The lights were still there and they were connecting into the rich green cathedral ceiling as they'd done so often. I felt Chepa's hand on mine and squeezed it, hoping she was alright. In no time the cathedral shifted its shape into a broad endless twisting strand of DNA sparkling in the darkness, inviting me to climb its ladder-like structure. I grabbed hold of one of the rungs and watched it change from green to the familiar dark red hue.

Surprisingly, panic didn't overwhelm me. Perhaps it was Chepa's presence, or how gently the doctors had treated me the last time they'd visited, or that the ayahuasca and Julio were so powerful that there was little time to indulge in trying to hold onto myself. Whatever the reason, I seemed to pass into another space so quickly I didn't realize it had happened. One moment I was squeezing Chepa's hand and hoping she was alright; in the next I found myself leaning out over the platform railing to Julio's right, beginning the familiar cleansing. I watched as my children were vomited out of me, not understanding why I wasn't good enough or strong enough to hold onto them and keep them together. I watched my baby come tumbling out in a heap of questions she wasn't old enough to ask. All of it came rumbling up from deep, deep places and burst from me into the jungle night.

I was still standing by the little doorway to Julio's three-step ladder when the doctors arrived, the rushing of the tall grass preceding them by only an instant this time, not giving me enough time to let my fear of their coming well up within me.

"We'll make this quick this time," they said. "We know you have to take care of people tonight."

Standing where I was, they showed me Chepa and my Madeleina. "We've taught you how to give to them," they said. "Now you have to work at that. You have to learn to do it freely, with no expectation of return."

"How?" I asked.

"Just keep giving. There's no end to it. And nothing will come back, but keep giving. No return. No investment. Just giving like we've taught you."

"Will that bring them back to me?"

"No. But you must still do it. You must give freely or it isn't giving."

I felt a rush of immense sadness begin to wash over me but the doctors didn't give me time to indulge in it.

"You also have to learn how to receive love. To get love. Love and be loved," they said.

They didn't say anything for a minute and I wondered if there was more. I hadn't asked it, just felt the question, but they answered anyway.

"Yes."

"Will it hurt?"

"No."

They transformed into the nurse they'd been the last time, and I suddenly thought they must have been tired of me, tired of still teaching me the lessons they'd started so long ago.

Then, unexpectedly, another voice started talking. A man's voice. I don't remember what he said but he showed me my sons Marco and Italo. I loved them when I saw them.

"You've been a father to them," the voice said. "But now it's time to learn to be even more of a father to them."

Again I realized how second-rate and inadequate I'd been. Even to my boys. I felt wholly useless to everyone now.

"Do you ever ask them what they'd like to do sometimes? Like for whole days? Do you ever ask: 'Yo, guys, what would you like to do today?' So they could have a whole day without hearing you say 'I've got to do this or that'? Just to give them the day with you as a father and not as the father figure?"

I'd never thought of that. It made such perfect sense that fathers ought to do that, that I couldn't believe I never had.

I didn't have much time to mull it over as the doctors interrupted and said it was time for them to go. It was a simple announcement followed by their getting into an open-ended capsule of some kind. Brilliant colors began to glow around them like an aurora borealis and they told me they were leaving. I knew what they meant and my stomach dropped out from under me.

"Leaving for how long?" I asked.

"Leaving," they answered. "We've worked with you and spent time with you and now we have to get on with other people."

I began to panic, realizing at once how much they'd taught me over the past few years and simultaneously knowing, without knowing how, how much more they'd tried to teach me but which was lost because of my fear.

It occurred to me that I'd been taught the lessons of Red Magic, one of the four colors of magic Julio sings about, and that I wouldn't get any more, that they really wouldn't be back.

For a moment I glimpsed the red room, the cavernous room where it seemed to me all the pain and evil of the world accumulates and which the doctors then re-form and reshape into good and positive things. I knew at that instant that if I hadn't been so afraid of them and spent so much time fighting the work they needed to do with me, they would have shown me how to work with that pain to heal. But they were going for real.

Those doctors who were still in the shape of the young woman told me not to be as afraid of The Man Who Tells Me Things, the name they gave the voice, as I had been of them. They told me I missed so much of what they'd come to teach, that I'd only learned a smidgen of what they'd intended, and to do better with my new teacher.

The last thing they said as they closed their capsule was that I'd missed the colors they'd meant to teach me. I shouted back that I didn't know what colors they meant, or what they planned to teach me about them. They answered that they knew that and were sad for me because of it.

And then they sort of blasted off and flew away. Their capsule ship was really more like an upside down bottle cap than any other shape I knew. As it flew it grew smaller, not from the distance it was travelling—it was just that my perception shifted and I saw their ship as tinier and tinier until it disappeared into a droplet of liquid, with a slight splash, and then was absorbed. The liquid was red, almost the thickness of nectar, almost like the nectar of the red flower I'd drunk that had started the red medicine sessions.

The thought of it coming full circle like that hit me like a sharp crack on my consciousness. Was it really like that? Was that all for red magic learning? I wanted to shout "But I don't know anything yet!" But knew it was no use. They were not coming back, at least not then, if ever.

Silence and sadness engulfed me. In the distance I could hear the che-che-che of Julio's shacapa and the sound of his voice. They seemed to pull me like a rope from a far place back to the railing of his hut where I stood.

## Chapter Three

# THE MAN WHO TELLS ME THINGS ARRIVES AND CHEPA DISAPPEARS

I HAD NO idea how long my visit with the doctors had lasted. When my eyes grew accustomed to the dark I saw that my guests all seemed to be either in the midst of their ayahuasca dreams or sleeping. I made my way past Julio to my spot on the flooring next to Chepa. She was huddled up in a fetal position and shaking. I leaned close to her and asked if she was alright. She didn't answer so I asked again. Corina heard me from the kitchen area and came over and shook her, also asking if she were alright.

Chepa seemed lifeless, until she suddenly turned her head and told us to leave her the heck alone and to stop interrupting her dream.

I sat back, embarrassed, and lit a cigarette. Just then the voice of The Man Who Tells Me Things spoke: "I can teach you some things. But I'm not as patient as the doctors. If you lie to me or hide things I will take you to hells you never imagined. You will wish the doctors were just tearing your heart out."

"I won't hide from you," I said, lying.

Instantly, faster than that, I found myself in a place so wretched, so awful, so full of the stink of things, so evil that even the doctors couldn't reshape them into something worthwhile. It was as if it was a place not of pain, but of fears. A place where fear and the malice that creates it are born. It was overwhelmingly horrible.

"I am not fooling. I am stuck here teaching you and I don't have time for games," the voice said, bringing me back to Julio's hut.

"I'll try," I said, shaken at the power he'd unveiled.

154

"Good. I'll be back soon."

And with that the voice vanished and didn't reappear that night.

I spent the remainder of the ceremony keeping an eye on my guests. I helped Juan and Corina and Jairo in getting them to the bathroom area and supplying tissue when they finished vomiting.

When they came out of their dreams, Juan walked them over to Jérnan's and their mosquito nets and hammocks. After they were all gone, Julio lit a kerosene lamp, gathered up his things and said goodnight.

I stayed awake and listened to the jungle for a long time. The image of the doctors disappearing like a drop into a bowl of soup was fresh in my mind, as was the sadness I felt at their leaving.

A week later, after my guests had all returned to their homes, I returned to New York. Chepa had said she'd stay for a couple of weeks with Madeleina as she needed to take her mother to the cancer clinic in Lima for a checkup.

The two weeks passed, during which time we spoke often. But when she was due to return, she didn't. I called the airline to see if she had made the flight. I was told she'd changed the tickets and flew to Fort Worth, not New York. It was six months before I saw either her or my Madeleina again.

# Chapter Four

# PREPARATIONS FOR A JUNGLE JAUNT

ON THE home front things were harder than ever. We'd moved just two months before Chepa and I went to Peru, so Italo and Marco were already adjusting to a new space in a new neighborhood when I returned without their mom. When she finally called to say she'd moved to Fort Worth to start a new life near her three sisters there, things got really difficult for them. They never dwelt on it, but I'm sure they wondered what I'd done this time to make mom move so far away. And while at first Marco would remind Italo and especially me that mom had moved away before but would soon return because she couldn't live without us, after a couple of months he was wondering if this time was the exception.

I did the best I could, but lived with the damned failure every minute of the day. I was working hard at both my family and my writing and I'd given up hard liquor two years before. I was producing some of the best political journalism I'd ever done, had a good connection deep within the US government who supplied me with information no one else had. I was loving my kids to death and calling Madeleina nearly every day. But since I didn't really know what it was I'd done wrong this time, I couldn't give my boys an answer or even change anything to make things better for them. That Julio had told me this would happen and that there was nothing I could do was no consolation. That the doctors had told me to give and keep giving and not to expect any return was something I worked at, but which didn't give me any consolation either. In my mind, and in our lives, I'd just fucked things up to that awful point, and nothing made it easier to bear or understand.

In April, four months after she left, I sent the boys out to visit her over their Spring break. In June, out of desperation, I filed a custody suit for Madeleina, which forced Chepa to return to New York for a few days for the hearing. There, it was as if she'd never left and we'd never argued, as if the past three years had never occurred. For three days we laughed and played. There was no animosity at the hearing and we came to terms easily. Madeleina was in heaven with her brothers, as they were to be with her and their mom. But when the weekend was over, Chepa didn't stay. I just wasn't her life anymore.

At the end of July I had a trip lined up. I invited Chepa to come stay with the kids, but she was working and couldn't, so I brought her sister Amelia into town to take care of them.

I hated leaving my boys but I had to work and determined to do it well.

I arrived three days before my guests, reassembled my crew and worked furiously to get things ready. Hammocks were washed and hung out to dry in the Amazon sun. Several new ones were bought in place of those that had gotten a bit shabby. Foam matting, blankets, mosquito nets, jungle boots, kitchen equipment and everything else we'd need was scrutinized and either scrubbed or replaced. Corina, my right-hand man Jhonny, and my mother-in-law Lydia did the scrutinizing and were also the beneficiaries of what was tossed, so nearly everything had to be purchased new. Half-a-dozen day laborers I knew scrubbed down my bar, since it had been closed for several months. Corina saw to stocking the bar's fridge with food, and I took care of beer and exotic jungle liquors my guests might want to try.

Though one or two guests always arrived a day early and found me at the bar, I generally had them come in on a Saturday, got them settled into their hotels, then brought them to my place for an orientation dinner followed by a huge party.

The group that assembled for this trip included Larry, an accountant who was ready to take on the world; Alan, a young seaman looking for an adventure; Brian, a young fellow searching for himself; Angelica, an artist and visionary who was caught between living in France and the Southwest U.S.; Bonnie, a counselor and a healer in her own right; and Lynn, a hotshot telecom consultant and former NASA scientist whose software still graces our space shuttles. He'd come in a last-ditch effort to save his marriage; ten minutes with me and I suspect he knew he'd come to the wrong place for that kind of healing.

Over cold beers at the bar I went over our itinerary and answered some questions, but before long the gringos in Iquitos began to make their appearances. Alan Shoemaker brought his lovely wife and kids. Jim King, a lumberman with a huge laugh and his wife Pat, who nursed more sick and hurt jungle animals back to health than all the do-gooders in the Amazon combined, came in. Ryan R., a snake-farmer and former government operative put out to pasture in Iquitos—or at least that's what a lot of us thought—showed up to keep an eye on the DEA agents who made their way through the gauntlet of rowdy dockhands gathered around the bar door. Some oil men I knew came with their local wives or *chicas*, and a couple of DynCorp crop-dusters—the pilots spraying herbicide on the coca plants in Colombia as part of Plan Colombia—showed.

A lot of the insight I'd gotten into good political stories came from guests like those at my bar that night. Special Forces soldiers and DEA agents and pilots working in Colombia knew what operations were planned by the U.S. government because they were part of them. And they were a long way from home. They'd get drunk and want to do the confessional thing with the bartender, me. I'd remind them that I was a journalist and that I might end up printing what they told me. If they told me anyway, they'd been forewarned. I wouldn't attach their names, but if I could verify what they told me—which is where the source in the U.S. government came into play—I'd print it. I was often out on a limb, because what I was being told was very different than the way the stories appeared in the U.S. press, but I knew I had the real goods.

Also making appearances that night were Duke—the fellow who'd been on the first trip I'd taken with guests, a former SEAL himself—and Jake, a former Navy captain who was a fan of mine from my days as a writer and editor for High Times magazine. Both Duke and Jake had been living off and on in Iquitos for several years, Duke to study medicinal plants, and Jake, a chiropractor, who was trying to get healed from kidney cancer. He had already beaten the timetable the docs gave him. There were also a few tourists who'd heard there was free beer and food—when I opened my bar for guests the first night was always free—most of my crew, and a contingent from my extended family.

I'm sure we were quite a sight, but as my groups rarely included your average tourist, no one seemed to mind. Stories flew, music blared, dancing happened, food got eaten and beer got drunk. I stayed in the only safe place I knew, behind the bar, taking it all in joyfully.

The party lasted a long time, until it was just Lynn, Alan and myself, along with a couple of my crew who were watching out for me, locking the place up before heading to sleep.

The following morning, despite the lateness of the night before, I got everyone up early for a trip to the teeming marketplace of Belen, where we picked up mapachos for Julio, the chacruna leaves I'd ordered from an herb-seller friend a couple of days earlier, flashlights, fishing line and hooks, shotgun shells and a number of other things we'd bring as presents to the river.

By late morning I'd had everyone in my group taste salt-dried wild boar, drink a glass or two of *aguardiente*—hard cane liquor—and generally get the smell of jungle-goods in their souls. We walked in muck at the docks where local boats brought in those goods, and where the stench is overwhelming. We'd begun, starting with the party, the process of stopping their worlds so that they could be open to the experience they'd come to have.

By noon I'd taken them to the far end of Iquitos, where the Nanay River meets the Amazon, for something to eat and a cold beer in the bar built for the movie Fitzcarraldo. Along the way we'd stopped at Iquitos' largest port, Masusa, to clamber aboard a flat-bottomed riverboat like the one we'd take to Julio's the following evening. As it was Sunday and the port was closed, the boats were nearly empty and permission to board easily obtained. Seeing them empty, lined up like that at the port on a Sunday, it was hard to imagine that all of the goods coming into or leaving from western Amazonia were shipped on the 80 or so boats operating out of Iquitos. But except for a couple of oil tankers anchored a few miles away and the little that moves by air, everything moved on those riverboats.

At the Fitzcarraldo bar we ate broiled river fish and seasoned rice at a table overlooking the glorious Amazon. I didn't usually run into anyone I knew there, but that day was surprised to find Jake sitting in a corner with his new girl and her mother. He joined us briefly, and as I was sitting he noticed a small brown growth in the center of my scalp.

"Better have that looked at," he said.

"I know. It's ugly, right?"

"How long have you had it?"

"I don't know. Couple of months, I think, since my kids noticed it."

"Have it biopsied. I'm not fooling."

Jake was sort of the resident doc among the gringos in Iquitos. He was bright and funny, but he could irk me with his pushiness, so while we were friends we'd never gotten close. And sure enough, just after his impromptu medical examination—I later had the growth removed—he insisted I come over to his table to tell his girl's mom that he really was a chiropractor. I did, but she didn't believe me, and Jake wanted me to stay and insist that he was until she did. I begged off, wanting to get back to my group, and he complained that I always treated him in a second-rate fashion. I told him that I simply had guests to attend to, and he asked why my guests should be more important than my friends.

After lunch, I set the group free with a plan to meet up at the main square in a couple of hours for a sunset canoe ride in the Amazon wash around the floating houses in lower Belen. All but Angelica agreed. She said she had made plans with Duke the night before to go see a healer he wanted her to meet. I said okay, but inside I seethed a little. Our personalities clashed almost from the time I'd met him, and after I let him go as an assistant following the first trip with guests I'd had, things got worse between us. He always seemed to be trying to one-up me, and his inviting one of my guests away from a planned event seemed like just another incidence of that. Angelica was capable of making her own choices, so I let it go. Still, I thought it was rude of Duke to do that.

The evening trip went calmly, and I sent the group out dancing later that night—an outdoor spot with an 18-piece band and thousands of locals— with several of my crew, to give them another snapshot of life in Amazonia. I set a time for meeting in the morning.

My plan was to have Corina and a couple of others on my team take my guests to the local zoo. I knew that in the jungle we'd make too much noise to see many animals, so this was their chance—even though none of them were fans of zoos—to see jaguars, capybari, anacondas, tapir and other Amazon wildlife. While she did that, I would be in the market with a couple of assistants buying our food for the next several days.

But at the morning meeting time, Duke was there with Jake and announced that both Angelica and Bonnie would miss the zoo because they were taking them to the university to see something important. Again I seethed a bit because this was not the way to get a group interacting, but the women wanted to go, so there was nothing I could do.

Corina took out the four remaining members of our group, and I went shopping. At about two, my group showed up at the bar, packs ready for the trip. The riverboat was scheduled to leave at five, giving us plenty of time to go over things. At about three, in the middle of counting everything one last time before it was packed into duffel bags and boxes, Angelica and Bonnie showed up with Duke and Jake and a man I'd never met.

I'd never seen Duke take a drink but he asked for a bottle of beer and a couple of glasses. I told him to help himself as I was busy, but he insisted that out of respect for his friend I bring them myself, along with a glass for me. My guest Lynn offered to do it, but I said I would and stopped what I was doing and did as Duke asked. When I arrived at the table Duke presented his Peruvian friend as a curandero. He was dark complexioned, thick and strong with a good handshake that lasted an unusually long time. I told him I was glad to meet him then excused myself to go back to my preparations.

Packing was critical because Julio lived several hours by boat from the nearest town with a store, and whatever we forgot we wouldn't easily be able to get once we got there. Half of what I brought, of course, we'd never need, but had to have in case things went wrong and we got stranded by the weather or a faulty boat and had to stay longer than expected.

While my team and I packed, half a dozen friends showed up, and by about 3:30, an hour before we began transporting our things to the boat, an impromptu party commenced.

At some point Jake came over to re-inspect my head, then showed it to the healer he and Duke had brought in, who made a comment I didn't hear over the din. I thanked Jake for his concern and assured him I'd have it looked at first thing in New York.

Angelica commented that she'd had a great time with Duke and his curandero and hoped that Julio would be as powerful a man. I laughed and said I hoped her experience with him was good too. Duke leaned in and told me not to worry, that he was confident that Angelica would bring the angels to the ceremony, and that he'd be there with us in spirit. "I'll be there with you too, brother," he said.

By four, my chief boat organizer, Mauricio, had taken the duffel bag of hammocks across the street and down the long steep stairway to the boat we'd be taking, secured a space, and began setting them up. Not long after I hired several dock hands to carry the rest of our stuff over, and just before five, I locked the bar and we all headed over.

Chapter Five

# THE RIVER, THE BOATS,
# THE WORK BEFORE CEREMONY

IT WAS MAYHEM, as usual. The 60-foot-long, 12-foot-wide, wooden stairway down to the water was crammed with people headed to the two large riverboats leaving from that port that evening. Each boat held about 300 passengers and a couple of hundred tons of cargo, and everything was being loaded by way of the stairway. Dockhands carrying refrigerators, mopeds, hundred pound sacks of sugar and salt, toilet bowls, school desks, cases of soda and a thousand other things strapped to their backs and heads fought through the crowd, shouting for people to make room on the rickety stairs. There were family members saying goodbye to their loved ones and dozens of vendors selling food, soda, gum, crackers and anything else they could carry crammed onto the stairway and the boats anchored at its foot.

Just after five, our boat sounded its whistle, and everyone not leaving on the boats raced across the gangplank between the bow and the stairway and we backed out into the river. Fifteen minutes later we were on the Amazon. The boat was a spider web of hammocks and lines, and to reach the little area Mauricio had secured we had to crawl on hands and knees beneath dozens of low-slung hammocks and around people who slept on cardboard on the boat's deck. I recommended we all head for the roof, which would be windy and cold at night but glorious for the next several hours.

It was. There is something magical about sitting on the roof of a riverboat travelling on the Amazon, gliding past the jungle at river's edge. I never grow tired of seeing the villages or the fields of plantains and yuca interspersed with the trees, the canoes anchored in the river at the base of steps carved by machete into the vertical mud banks, fishermen and slash-and-burn farmers bathing with their children on balsa rafts tethered to stakes buried in red clay that underlies much of the area. It is the real Amazon jungle, not like in our imagination, but the way it has probably been for as long as humans have lived there. Each farmer builds his own home, makes his own canoes, fashions his own fishing gear, clears his own field. The homes are built on stilts from logs tied together with *soga*, jungle vine, covered with leaf roofing sections. It's plain and not very pretty, but it is the real Amazon jungle.

The hours passed easily. At some point a few pairs of magic mushrooms from a local cow field appeared, and most of my guests took up the offer to enjoy the night under their influence. Overhead, the sky was ablaze with stars. We all just laughed and laughed until it was time to head down and brave the uncomfortable crawl to the hammocks.

We arrived at Genaro Herrera at sunup and commandeered a friend's kitchen, where Corina made us a jungle breakfast feast of broiled fish, scrambled eggs and fried plantains. By noon we clambered aboard my friend Fernando's peque-peque, and headed for Julio's.

The trip up the Supay and through Supay Lake was glorious, as always. At the far side of the lake we made our way through the reeds and into the Aucayacu, and I was home again. Colorful kingfishers flew about; pairs of macaws flew overhead; monkeys we'd disturbed with the *peke-peke* sound of our motor yelled at us and an occasional sleeping turtle slid off a sun-drenched log and into the river at our approach. We arrived at Julio's by three to find that he wasn't yet home from his chacra. But Jairo, was, as was his wife Asteria, and they welcomed us warmly. I sent Mauricio off to set up the hammocks for our guests at Jérnan's, while Corina set to getting hot water ready for coffee and tea, then began to go through the food supplies, selecting things for dinner.

Julio arrived home carrying a machete and an armful of plantains. He handed the green bananas to Asteria, then climbed the three-step ladder to the unwalled platform that was the primary living space, and disappeared into his bedroom. He emerged with a clean shirt and a laugh in his eyes.

*"Ah, ya. Pedro,"* he smiled, hugging me. *"Bien, bien, Pedro."*

I introduced my guests, gave him a bag of mapacho cigarettes and a couple of lighters, then told him I hoped we hadn't disturbed him but that we'd come hoping he might have time to make us ayahuasca.

*"Yah. Yah, Pedro."*

I don't know what my guests thought of the visual of Julio. To me he was an immense human being, with eyes that seem to know everything you were going to ask as well as most of the answers. He was a man who was so clear that he had become almost see-through over the years, and I imagined that when he finally died he would just vanish, as if he'd just be too clear to see on this plane anymore.

On the other hand, he was an old, oddly handsome guy with a shock of white hair and a white mustache, huge ears, and a head much too big for his 4-foot-eight-inch, slightly hunchbacked frame. His clothes were always clean but ragged and hand-patched, and while his feet were size 9, he always wore a pair of size 11 or 12 jungle boots. When I brought him clothes, he always gave them all away to his sons except of a pair of pants and a shirt he'd keep to wear to Iquitos once a month to collect his army pension.

He was simply magnificent, and it never took long for most of my guests to get that. Bonnie came away from simply shaking his hand on meeting him saying that she'd already gotten some of the answers she'd come for.

Over the course of the next few hours, while we had dinner and talked, we were visited by a couple of his sons and several people who lived on the river near him. Each time someone new arrived I'd reach into one of our packages and take out a present I'd brought for them: hard bread for some, crackers for others, matches, batteries, a flashlight, fish hooks. Simple things that Moises Vienna had taught me to bring years ago. "It's not the money," he always said. "It's that it takes a whole day to go to Genaro Herrera by canoe to buy batteries, and for you it's nothing to bring extras."

That night I sent the guests out in the canoes, and in the morning we went with Julio to collect the ayahuasca and the other barks he wanted to add. The walk was as glorious as usual and I took the opportunity at some point to tell them about a study a botanist named Brian Boom had done some years earlier. For his dissertation he and a partner had registered all of the higher plants found in a hectare of jungle. The number was enormous. But what was most interesting to me was that for many of the plants there was only one example in that hectare. That, to me, explained the frailty of the Amazon more than anything else could. If, for instance, we had to walk nearly an hour to reach a Banisteriopsis caapi—ayahuasca—vine, then it was probably the only example of that vine for a couple of miles in any direction. Imagine if instead of an ayahuasca vine, that was a particular type of fruit-bearing tree whose fruit was the food of a particular species of monkey. If someone cut that tree down, that monkey would have no reason to enter those several square miles any longer, and would change its feeding route. In turn, the insects that fed on the waste produced by that monkey would no longer be found there, nor would the animals that depended on those insects for food.

And if that particular tree only occurred every three miles for some reason, and if each were cut down over a 20-mile area, there would probably be no seeds dropped by those monkeys to ever propagate that tree in that area again. So the ants that fed off its bark, the monkey that ate its fruit, the insects that ate the droppings, the animal that ate the insects, and so forth, would all be seriously affected.

## Chapter Six

# GETTING SPLOOCHED, GETTING ANSWERS

WHEN WE returned from the hike, Julio began to prepare the ayahuasca while my guests ate and then went out for a hike with Juan. By the time they returned and bathed in the river, it was nearly time to gather on the platform. Julio had made the ayahuasca with the vine he'd cut and the leaves I'd brought, then added the usual catawa and lupuna negra and capirona barks. When it was time, the group took spots around the platform, and Julio took his seat on his stool by the platform gate. As usual, Juan and Jairo would watch the door and Corina would stay in the kitchen to watch for anyone who needed help. But just as we were about to start, Juan surprised me by saying he needed to drink as well. I'd never seen him drink ayahuasca before. When I questioned the wisdom of that, given that he generally helped people navigate the little ladder, he said he really needed an answer to something, but that I shouldn't worry about it.

I switched my place to one near the door so that I'd be available to help and just told everybody to be very careful maneuvering the steps.

Because of my position I was first to drink that night and I had him pour me a smallish three-gulp portion, maybe four. Nonetheless, before he'd finished the circle and served himself I could feel the first waves of the medicine washing over me. Neon-green lights appeared like iridescent fireflies and I felt the usual panic begin. I had a moment when I could have vomited the ayahuasca out before it had taken full effect but decided not to do that. Instead I concentrated on Julio and looked around the space at my guests to see if they were beginning to feel it as well.

Julio finished his prayer, moved the bottles to the corner, then flicked out the kerosene lamp with his shacapa. The darkness was sudden and utter, but in moments it all seemed lit up to me as the green lights intensified. It couldn't have been more than a few minutes before I found myself in a landscape that seemed to be constructing itself from what looked like a kind of gigantic, cartoonish Lego blocks that moved in slow motion. The sidewalk where I seemed to be was maybe two bricks higher than the street being built to my right. To my left a wall was going up about five bricks higher than the sidewalk, as was another across the street. Everything was coming together in a slow, syrupy fashion, as though the bricks were not quite solid yet, still undulating and distorted as they found their spots. There was something odd about the consistency of the moving landscape that didn't feel right. It occurred to me that the world had not become red this time, and that was peculiar by itself. But more than that, the colors of the bricks—red, blue and white—were more solid than the bricks themselves. Accompanying the motion was a buzzing in my ears, a deep metallic sound that might have been the grinding of huge gears.

Time passed in the real world, in which I felt myself unable to move.

Julio sang beautifully. The speed of the moving landscape changed as his songs changed. Chepa appeared and I watched her change horribly and saw how rottenly she'd treated me. I threw that out as fast as I could. I didn't want to go there at all.

Suddenly The Man Who Tells Me Things asked "Do you remember you were told you couldn't really love Chepa and Madeleina because you're giving them things you think they need and not what they really need?"

"Yes," I answered.

"Do you remember you were told you can't love them until you are them?"

"Yes."

"Do you want to know how to love Chepa?"

"Yes."

"Then come with us," The Man said, and instantly the sidewalk I was on began to move, sliding up the street toward a dark bend while the street and wall on either side of it and me simply undulated where they were, so that the sidewalk seemed to be like a conveyor belt. The colored blocks passed like pouring molasses and The Man said, "First you have to learn to accept unconditional love," but the way he said it didn't sound like a joyful experience was about to occur. It had more of the ring of the doctors telling me they just had to take my heart out and cut away the bad parts. I was instantly

167

AYAHUASCA IN MY BLOOD

petrified.

The Man ordered me to relax. "It's just love you have to get," he said.

"Are you going to play tricks?" I asked.

"I am asking if you want the answer to the question you asked years ago. Do you want to know how to love Chepa and your baby?"

I felt silly, because she didn't love me, but the voice continued. "It might be the next Chepa. We can't promise to bring her back, but she might come back or there might be another and at least you will know how to love her."

It was a very sad thing to hear but it was also so honest that I began to really relax, even though I was still afraid. We'd been moving up the street and around the dark corner during the whole conversation and continued to move further into the dark space. Still, I was ecstatic because I believed that I was finally going to learn how to love Chepa and Madeleina in a way they needed to be loved.

Then suddenly, out of the blue, I felt something land on my right shoulder, toward the back. It startled me completely. It was like a baby's puke that simply pops out of its mouth without warning, except that there was no baby there and that it seemed as if it had come from regular reality to land on my shoulder in the other reality. It was just suddenly and abruptly there and spreading and when I looked I could see a mouth sort of spitting it from the real world and entering the ayahuasca world. It was an evil and invasive goop, brown and full of hatred. A *splooch* of something intended and wretched.

The ayahuasca world was instantly gone. The Man, the sliding sidewalk— just gone, and I was at Julio's again, near the little railing. Nothing like that had ever happened to me before. I'd never even heard of anything like that happening.

All of that took less than an instant to see and feel and experience several times over in a series of replays, and it terrified me. I sat bolt upright on the platform and knew I'd been attacked. Someone purposefully *splooched* a glob of evil goop on me from the real world and I turned to see who it was and Jake appeared, looking cold and jokerish. He was so clearly there I felt I could have touched him—though he wasn't there physically—and I realized he had done it. I asked him why. He just grinned in a horrible way, then said, "Because I can."

I wondered what I'd done to make him do that but he'd already answered all he was going to. But his line—"Because I can"—told me instantly that yes, he could do that, and he could have done it anytime he wanted.

And then the image of Duke leaned in over my left shoulder and said, "I'm here too, brother," and smiled coldly, and the realization that they wanted to harm me was awful. I wanted to get away but there was no place to get away to, so I skittled next to Julio and opened the platform's gate and sat with my back to my group, facing the jungle, my feet on the first step of the little ladder. I wanted to grab onto Julio's legs to have something to hold on to, but didn't dare. I wished he would sing loudly and get that awful icky stuff off me. There was nothing there physically, but it was very real to me. I was reeling, really reeling from what Jake and Duke had done and how cold it was. I thought maybe it was a game people who used ayahuasca and learned to do tricks did to each other, but I didn't play that game. I barely understood it.

But I wanted it off me. I looked at it closely and in the goop I could see things with points and sharp edges like strangely shaped thorns starting to go into me and I realized they put virotés—magic, invisible darts that ayahuasqueros talk about sometimes—in with the splooch.

I lit a cigarette and realized that Julio had stopped singing and was snapping his shacapa leaves like a whip while he shouted *"Vete! Vete! No moleste este hombre! El es un hombre bueno! Vete!"* "Get out, get out. Don't bother this man. He's a good man. Get out!"

He was shouting to the space between and around us and I knew he'd seen what happened and I was grateful. But at the same time I knew I had to do something to get rid of the spreading *ick* and the virotés. And even as I knew that I saw more and more virotés in my arms and hands and legs and stomach and heart, thick thorns and nails sticking into me, or into the spirit-me where I sat. I started to try to pull them out, but each one that came out went in again as soon as I let it go.

I started singing softly, the first simple song I ever got from ayahuasca. I was singing to give myself courage, and I lit another cigarette off the first and began to sopla myself with the smoke. I felt lost since I knew nothing about this or what it meant or if it was real or I was crazy or it was a game or I was going to die. I heard Julio telling me over and over to keep smoking, not to let the cigarettes go out. And while it was comforting to hear him—I'm sure he was talking silently—it also meant that he was taking it seriously, which meant I wasn't terrified for nothing.

I started to sing out loud. With my back to the group I was singing out toward the jungle, and hoped they wouldn't hear me, or if they did, that they wouldn't be too disturbed. I had never interfered with Julio's ceremony before, but didn't feel I had a choice. I gave up any guilt about it pretty quickly and just decided to do whatever I needed to do.

I lit a third cigarette off the second and saw the faces of Jake and Duke in front of me while I pulled out the virotés. I began to see other people as well, some of whom I'd never cared for and some I thought were friends in Iquitos. I realized that they were all contributors to this, though it was Jake who could do it and did actually do it. I sang louder and began to bounce a knee in rhythm with the notes coming out of me. The virotés were easier to pull out the more courage I had, and the louder I sang the more courage I got.

I lit another cigarette and sopla'd myself. I blew the smoke on my hands and held them to my body to get the smoke everywhere. I smoked the *splooch*, my shoulders, my face, my head, my arms and legs, my feet and heart. I was scared, but getting stronger. I knew I didn't know what I was doing but had to keep doing it. Some of the virotés were shaped like talons and hooked into me. I was pulling them out and coughing them up and wondering what to do to get rid of them and I heard Julio saying over and over *"No mas moleste! No mas! Vete!"* and telling me not to let the cigarettes go out no matter what.

Suddenly my feet started jumping up and down like a nervous kid's, only they were moving in unison and with purpose and suddenly my song was getting faster and stronger, faster and stronger, than it had ever been, and out of the top of my head I felt something coming. None of it was my doing that I knew of. I couldn't move my legs that way or sing that song so powerfully and with so many variations, and I certainly had no control over the thing that came out of my head. It was like a monster, all limbs, and it somehow took all the virotés I'd taken out of me and went straight to Jake and began putting them in him. And when it did I felt the doing of it and the satisfaction of inflicting the pain they caused him, so I knew the monster was connected with me, or was me—I just didn't know how. The me of me was just sitting on Julio's porch, uncontrollably bouncing my feet in time to an impossibly fast rhythm of a song that had taken on a life of its own. Still, I enjoyed the feeling of putting those sharp things into Jake, and as I did I heard myself saying: "Here. Do you want these?"

The monster that had climbed out of me was getting stronger and I put some of the virotés in Duke as well, in his arms and legs, and I felt like I was strong enough to kill them, strong enough to push the virotés in one side of them and out the back. I wanted to do that, and my song was strong enough to give my monster the power to do that, and my legs were moving fast enough to let me do that and it seemed like something I was going to do. But then I heard Jake saying, "Go ahead. Then you'll be one of us."

I knew what he meant and stopped everything instantly. He wanted me to do it. He wanted me to be as mean as he was, to inflict pain as joyfully as he'd *splooched* me. But I didn't want to do that or be that. Which left me in the awkward position of wondering what to do instead. Then I felt the doctors near me and remembered that in the red room the doctors turn the evil to good. As I thought that, I saw the red room to my left and reached in and grabbed a handful of the red gloopy clay there, and put it on Jake. I started piling him with it to stop him from coming back without having to kill him and becoming like him. I began to push more virotés into him but only half-way, and then covered them with more clay so he couldn't take them out. I did the same with Duke and then put clay on me as well, all the while lighting cigarette after cigarette and smoking myself and tapping furiously and singing loudly and with power. In the distance I heard Julio yelling at me, ordering me to close myself. *"Cierra, Pedro, cierra!"* I turned and saw him motioning for me to call back the monster, to put it back inside and seal the opening. He was commanding, and I did as told. I smoked my head and back and head again, and hoped what I was doing would work. I felt the monster returning through the opening, and closed the gaping space in my head.

Just as I finished, Jake suddenly smiled and said he wasn't done yet. Out of the dark night birds of prey started swooping down, talons out, tearing at me. I grabbed for their talons and turned them in on themselves until the birds screamed then told Jake not to send any more or I would send them on to him and Duke. I don't think I'd ever felt as strong and wanted to revel in it, but realized that Jake could do this anytime he wanted, so that I could never win a war like this, a war that an hour or a lifetime earlier I never knew could even occur. I kept singing faster and faster and more and more clearly to push the image of Jake away, at least for the night, to make him flee.

I don't know how long it took but finally Jake was gone and it was over and I knew he wouldn't be back. I waited a little while longer, still singing, to make sure I wasn't premature, and then turned to tell Julio it was over. As I did I saw that he was already turning away from me and back to my guests to sing for them again.

I lit another cigarette then stopped singing and was quiet. I felt beat up and dirty but wonderful, and glad I didn't kill anyone and become like them and still proud and scared and exhausted. I stared out into the pitch of the jungle.

Then, from the far right, from the position of one o'clock, at maybe 30 yards, my oldest sister, Pat appeared and said, "Hey, Peter. I want you to know I was keeping an eye on you." A flush of warmth came over me. From behind Pat, her husband Steve, who'd been with me in the jungle 15 years earlier, appeared and said, "So was I." And the warmth grew. Then from my direct left my baby sister Regina appeared and said, "I don't even know what I'm doing here, but I guess I am." And then she hugged me. And then my brother Mike was there saying, "Hey, Baldy," and my sister Barbara and her husband Paul came. "Hey Peter, it's Barbara," she said and Paul added, "How are you?" From straight in front of me came my other sister, Peggy, with her husband George, and Peg said, "We're here too." And then their kids and their kids' kids came and I was being hugged by everybody, and then came my Madeleina who snuck up in the crowd to grab onto my chest and she said, "I love you, daddy." Chepa was behind her and I felt her warmth but couldn't see her face, so I knew she loved me but couldn't be with me, and behind them were Marco and Italo. Even Jhonny, my right-hand man who had been in the background among the faces backing Jake and Duke, appeared. He was pretending to hug me but he had a sharp viroté with him and I turned it back on him and he cried out and I told him he shouldn't treat me like that anymore. And then my mother-in-law, Momma Lydia, who loved me but hated me came, and I asked her why she did brujeria on me. She shrugged. I told her not to do it anymore or I'd turn it against her. She said okay, so I hugged her too and suddenly I was laughing and feeling this intense love coming at me—a feeling of unconditional love coming to me from so many people, even some people I don't even make time for. I was so complete and rich, and I realized that Duke and Jake could never get me, could never have gotten me with that many people loving me and surrounding me.

It occurred to me that if the red room was around and available, maybe the red flower syrup would be too, so I put out my hands and got some drops and smoked them and put them on all my family, including my mother and father, who were in the space above everyone else. I blew the smoked red nectar drops into a red healing mist that rained out over them all. Then I lit another cigarette and wondered if in that second of love I had any access to healing power. Hoping I did, I reached over to Corina and blew smoke into her head for an easier life and then opened my sister Pat's head and put some drops in there and told them to heal her physical ailment then closed her up. But her head was too full to close so I reopened it and looked inside and saw that a kind of red viscous gelatin had come to the surface. I reached in and took out the phlegmy stuff. I held it in my hands and wondered what the hell to do with it. And Bertha had always said you couldn't just take a sickness out and throw it away because it would land on someone else. It had to be neutralized. So I smoked it and put it in the red room so the doctors could turn it into something good, then shut Pat's head again and closed it tight. I did the same with Momma Lydia, trying to take her cancer away.

I put some drops in my heart and lungs and on Madeleina and on Italo and Marco. I realized Chepa had been hurt too and put some on her as well.

Then I blew some more on everyone and they all said goodbye and disappeared until only Chepa and my kids were left. I tried to turn Chepa to me and blew smoke on her. A little of the darkness left her and she turned toward me a little. I did it again and she turned a little more, then again, but she still wouldn't turn to me fully so I took her head in my hands and turned her until she was looking me in the eyes. "Chepa," I said. "I love you, and will take care of you, and protect you from Duke and Jake and everything even if you are not with me."

And in that instant I realized that that was what she needed all along, even if she didn't recognize it. She needed to feel that protected all the time, and when I was drunk she didn't. The answer to the question was that she never felt protected since her own family fell apart when she was a youngster. Her father had lost everything by an accident of fate and it tore everything apart. And if it could happen to her father, her immensely powerful father, it could also happen to me. And my drinking was a constant reminder to her of how weak I was, how little protection I had to offer, how little chance I had to satisfy that need in her. The awareness of that simple truth was almost unbearable. I simply had to protect her unconditionally and love her unconditionally. That was the answer to the question all along of how to love her. And the same for Madeleina, who had watched me destroy our family. She needed to know I would be there, always.

I started to laugh out loud in the real world, like something was tickling my soul and I couldn't help myself. I told Chepa she could go and she suddenly smiled a little and called me a nickname I hadn't heard her use in years. And Madeleina hugged me and said, "I love you, daddy, but I have to go now," and then she and Chepa were gone and Marco followed them but before he disappeared he turned and said, "Don't worry dad. She can't live without us forever." And Italo added, "Now you know what to do you just have to do it, dad." And then they were all gone and I was spent, spent, spent.

And then, right in the middle of all that love and exhaustion, Jake popped up again. "Or," he grinned, "we could go after Madeleina."

Suddenly I let go and found myself coming out of my head again and heard myself roaring, roaring like a lion and letting him know not to dare, not to dare touch my family. That I wouldn't stop my monster next time, that I'd let my monster kill him on the physical plane. I started to smoke the whole universe furiously, white smoke bursts of power that I hoped carried my message to Jake and Duke and anyone else. "Don't you dare touch my family!" I roared, sure no one would defy me. But Jake reappeared, smiling and nonchalant, like he could do what he liked. He was just so arrogant, so secure in his power, that it utterly disarmed me.

Then, unexpectedly, my feet quit moving, but my left hand began beating my thigh in a fast straight rhythm: *bang, bang, bang, bang, bang, bang, bang, bang.* I didn't know why my hand was moving like that, I didn't seem to be in control of it at all, but the *bang, bang, bang* kept up until I recognized it as the sound of the beating of birds' wings, birds I hadn't realized I'd sent to Jake and Duke. Thousands of birds beating their wings around them, slapping the air around them to my hand's rhythm like thunderclaps, until both of them were cowering from the power of the birds and Julio was again entreating me to close my head. *"Cierra! Cierra!"* he ordered.

I kept up the beating but softened it and took some red drops and smoked them and sent them to Jake and Duke to heal their hatred, or at least neutralize it, and when it touched them they vanished. I knew the fight was over, at least for the time being, so I smoked the air and laughed.

I realized that the birds my monster sent were the same bird, multiplied a thousand times, that I'd flown with the very first time I'd ever had ayahuasca. I knew too that what The Man Who Tells Me Things said I'd get I'd gotten. I found out how to love Chepa and Madeleina after I had gotten unconditional love and accepted it.

I could still feel the horror of that glob of pain and hatred being spit on me, that awful *splooch*. But I felt like I would make it for the night, that Jake and Duke would not come back. So I closed myself again as best I could and smoked some more and listened as Julio turned his attention back to the others.

Funny, but I was sure I'd ruined everything for everyone with all the noise I'd made but when I turned around to look at my guests they were all still lying down, not yet out of their ayahuasca dream. I took a moment to sopla Julio, and then it was over.

Chapter Seven

# A GUEST LEARNS THE
# POWER OF THE MEDICINE

LATER, AFTER all of my guests but Lynn had gone back to Jérnan's house to sleep, we stayed awake and talked awhile. I was glad he was there as I wanted to relate some of what had occurred to someone. I was just so amazed at having been attacked like that. I told Lynn about it and told him too that I'd sometimes heard curanderos talk about other curanderos shooting them with virotés. One had supposedly killed another that way after several battles at the nearby city of Requena not long ago. I didn't put much stock in the stories, though. None of the curanderos I respected would waste their time harboring enough hatred to kill someone. Besides, it was the Amazon. If someone wanted someone dead, they just generally whacked them with a machete or shot them with a shotgun. It wasn't as if the police were going to get involved, not unless they did it in the middle of town anyway.

But why Jake and Duke? And why had both of them made a point of being around me much more than usual in Iquitos? And why had Duke said he'd be with us and then showed up in that fashion? It was all odd to me.

"What are their military backgrounds?" Lynn asked, while we sat on a log outside of Julio's in the darkness.

"Well, Duke's a former Navy SEAL who did a couple of tours in Vietnam," I said. "And Jake was a captain in the Navy. I think he said he had something to do with Naval Intelligence, but he also claims to be the youngest guy ever to have command of a certain type of ship."

Lynn looked at me with disbelief. "Are you missing something here, Peter?"

"Yeah. Why would they do it? I mean, they're both okay. It's not like we're best friends but I don't think they hate me. Or didn't, anyway."

"Peter, did it ever occur to you that your political writing about the secret operations the U.S. government does down here might really piss some people off? Just go with me for a minute here. What if somebody in the government wanted you dead?"

"I think they'd have somebody shoot me. But if they did, they would have and they didn't. Who cares what a journalist writes?"

"That's not how they work. Did you ever hear of something called psy-ops, Psychological Operations?" I told him I hadn't, and he launched into the story of a program the U.S. had run during the 1970s, in which an attempt was made to develop the paranormal to where it could be used as an instrument in war. One aspect of the program was to develop the abilities of people who had a propensity for mind control in the hopes that they, given a specific target, could make that target—presumably a military higher-up at a critical moment—make a wrong decision.

Lynn said that Congress had shut the program down at some point but that the scuttlebutt was that it had simply gone into the government's black hole where it continued to flourish.

"So you've got a former SEAL and a Naval Intelligence Officer who work with ayahuasca. They both decide to hang around you. They get close with one of your guests, bring a curandero to your bar that you've never met who physically inspects your head, then tell you that your client is going to 'bring the angels to the ceremony.' And then this happens. Don't you get it? They did try to kill you. They just tried it from an angle you never expected."

I didn't tell Lynn, but I thought that was about the craziest thing I'd ever heard.

What I thought was that it was just what Jake had said, "Because I can." Like a prank or a challenge. But it hadn't seemed like a prank. It might have been somebody else who really did hate me who used Jake and Duke's faces so that I wouldn't see who it really was. It could have been a million things. Whatever or whomever had done it, I knew it was real because it wasn't on any list of 10,000 possibilities I could have imagined. I was just glad that with Julio's help I'd been strong enough to fight it off. And I was really happy to finally have an answer to the question of how to love Chepa and my baby.

For all of my experience that night, Lynn said that he'd gotten nothing.

"It was fantastic to be in the ceremony with Julio, but I didn't get anything.

"Nothing?"

"Well, hardly anything," he said. "There was one point where I was sitting there thinking 'Come on, Julio. Show me something, anything,' and he turned to me and shook his leaves at me and the whole darned hut filled with colored lights and he grew to about 14 feet tall and he was glowing. Then his chakras lit up and began spinning and throwing off sparks that went flying all over the room. I just stared at him in amazement and after a few moments he asked, 'Now can I get back to the work I was doing with the women?' And then he returned to normal size and turned to work with the others. But that was it."

"That's not bad. Anything else?"

He thought for a moment. "Well, there was just one other little thing," he said. "I was thinking about Gail"—she was his wife, the marriage with whom he wanted to save—"and a voice said, 'Lynn, it was never about you. It's about Gail!' But that's about it." He paused, then remembered something. "Oh, there was this one vision I had for just a minute, where I saw Julio take my heart out and put it in Corina's breast, and take her heart and put it in me. Then I saw myself getting married to Corina, and she was dressed in a beautiful white gown. I know it's silly, but that's all I got. I guess ayahuasca just didn't want to teach me anything tonight."

Eight months later Lynn married Corina. As always, ayahuasca didn't give him what he wanted, but it did give him what he needed.

## Chapter Eight

# APPLYING THE LESSONS TO LIVING

W E STAYED with Julio for two more days and had a second ceremony,at which I didn't drink, then returned to Iquitos. There, I made a point of running into both Jake and Duke, and asked them about the incident. Both denied any part in it, though I didn't know whether to believe them or not. I do know that Jake went through something difficult just after we spoke, and for months was too frightened to leave his hotel room, while Duke, who'd planned on staying in Iquitos a while, changed his ticket and left the day I returned. Shortly after going home, his house burned to the ground. I have no idea whether there was any connection with that night to those events, or whether it was just coincidence.

What I do know is that there was no telegram or email from Chepa when I returned saying that she'd had a dream and wanted to put our marriage back together, and though I didn't expect one, I was heartbroken that none awaited me.

A couple of weeks later I returned home to New York, and shortly thereafter Italo and Marco made it clear that if I wanted to be around Madeleina I would have to move us to Fort Worth, where Chepa had settled in her new life. Six months later we did, buying a small house on a lovely piece of land in the town of Joshua, just southwest of Fort Worth. A few months after that, thinking I could do better, I quit alcohol—though who knew how long that would last?

Not long after I did, I was lying in bed one night, feeling lousy that I hadn't been able to fix things. In fact, I was considering a legal action to try to get full custody of Madeleina. It wasn't something I wanted to do, because for it to succeed I would have to make Chepa out to be an unfit mother. And though we had our differences about child rearing, she was not an unfit mother. But I was having a hard time having Madeleina live away from her brothers even if we weren't too far apart now. It was an issue I'd wrestled with for weeks. Anyway, for some reason the image of Julio popped up in my mind. It was nice to see him. He smiled at me, and the phrase "More Joy, Less Pain" came into my head. I repeated it over and over, trying to get his meaning.

It took some days, but when I did, it was simple and clear: Do whatever I had to do, but whatever I did should cause more joy and less pain for all of us. Which meant, of course, not taking the legal action—but that would probably mean never having Madeleina live with her brothers or me again, and that was horrible. Still, that seemed like the first step.

I was secretly hoping that that was the final test, and that since I'd obviously passed I could now have my family back together. It didn't happen. And so a couple of nights later, again lying in my bed, I called to Julio and asked him what was up. And then, unexpectedly, a new ayahuasca song came out of me. A song with words. I'd never had a song with words before. It was plain and beautiful and I sang it as though I'd known it my whole life. The words were in Spanish, but translated to English they read:

*One family, my family*
*My family, one family,*
*Mama Chepa, Papa Pedro,*
*Italo and Marco*
*And my Madeleina.*
*Help me, help me*
*Fix my broken family*
*Fix my broken family*
*Heal me, doctors,*
*Heal me, spirits,*
*Help me, Red Magic*
*That lives in my veins.*
*Help me, White Magic*
*That fills the sky,*
*Help me, Green Magic*

*That gives life to the firmament*
*Help me, Black Magic*
*Deep Magic that dwells in the earth.*
*Cleanse my Spirit,*
*Cleanse my heart*
*Cleanse my soul*
*Cleanse my body*
*Help me, help me*
*Fix my broken family.*

It took me a little while to come to terms with the idea that though I was asking in the song to fix my family, it wasn't going to be fixed like in my fantasy. But that didn't mean it couldn't be fixed some. And though it's not perfect, though we don't all live together, it is still a family. We are healing the best we can.

PART V

# AYAHUASCA AND THE GLORY

*Be tranquil, little body*
*Be tranquil, little body that is here;*
*Your soul is flying far away,*
*Your soul is flying far away,*
*Flying with the medicine,*
*Flying with the best doctors,*
*Be tranquil, little body,*
*Your soul will soon return.*

*—from one of Julio's songs*

⊛

Chapter One

# A LIE, A THEFT, A LUCKY SAVE

NEARLY TWO years passed after I'd been *splooched* before I could return to Iquitos again. The move to Texas had been harder than I expected. On the positive side, the boys and Madeleina were all living with me. Chepa had gotten her own place and was living near her sisters not far from us, so she visited regularly and we got along but weren't together. Momma Lydia also lived with us. Unfortunately, she was very ill. She'd come up on vacation but hurt so badly after a few days that I took her to an emergency room and they ran a battery of tests that showed her cancer had returned and metastasized to her lungs. By some luck of the draw the hospital agreed to treat her for free when I explained our circumstances, then got her radiation treatment for free at the best clinic in Fort Worth. Italo and I shared the duties of getting her there daily for weeks, and we all shared the duties of keeping her busy and happy when she was home with us. Nights she had me put my hands on her back to take as much of the heat away as I could. It always surprised me how a "cold" disease like cancer, which is how Julio described it, could produce so much heat. Daily my hands blistered from it, but the treatment—which included mapacho smoke and singing—allowed her to get to sleep. It was only a question of time until she'd be gone.

An additional problem I was facing was reinventing myself as a 52-year-old freelance journalist. Having left New York essentially severed all ties with *High Times* magazine, and none of the editors I knew when I had been a freelancer 15 years earlier were still at their old magazines, so there was no work from that quarter either. Within months of buying our little house in Joshua I was two months behind in the mortgage and at risk of losing it. I managed to get lucky when a friend had an editor at the *National Enquirer* call out of the blue—I'd never written for them before—and give me a few weeks' work. But that didn't last long and I was soon behind again. I sold a couple of stories to the alternative paper in Fort Worth, but that only kept me going for food money. Friends bailed me out with loans and I pawned my guitar and my grandfather's pocket watch. I took a loan out on my nine-year-old 1994 Ford Ranger, applied for jobs at every factory and warehouse in town, applied at restaurants, and even went to work at day labor for a month just to keep the house. I was not going to lose it, regardless of what I had to do.

So when a couple contacted me to ask if I had a trip coming up, I lied and told them I did, then hastily arranged one. And when they sent the money I put it to the house, hoping against hope that I'd somehow be able to repay the theft by the time the trip date arrived.

It turned out I couldn't. Worse, no more trip guests materialized. As the day of the trip came closer I thought of just not going at all. My friend Lynn was already in Iquitos, taking care of some family business with his new wife, Corina. I was tempted to call him to ask him to explain to the couple that I had gotten deathly ill and so the trip was cancelled and they would get their money back at some point in the future.

But it wasn't in me to do that. Instead I decided to tell my guests the truth face-to-face, that I'd used their money to save my house and borrowed money for airfare to get there to tell them that. If they needed to kill me or hate me, well, they'd at least have me there in person. So I left Texas for Lima with $100 in my pocket and arrived in Iquitos with about $15 after buying a ticket from Lima to Iquitos.

Lynn was generous enough to give me $100, which I used to get drunk my first night in town—after more than a year of being sober—and then got robbed of the remainder. But in the morning, amazingly, Chepa got in touch to say a $1,000 check from a magazine for an article I'd written had arrived in the mail. I wasn't expecting any check but thanked the heavens for it. Fantastically, when she forged my name my bank cashed it for her and she was able to wire it the same day. So I had been saved from having to admit to my guests, who flew in that afternoon, that I'd embezzled their money.

The couple, young Russians who'd recently immigrated to New York, were lovely. Alyona was a walking light stick, full of energy and joy. Pasha was smart and intense. He'd read a lot about ayahuasca and was full of questions about it, many I considered irrelevant. But he insisted on asking them so I did my best to answer. Lynn backed me up by noting that what was in the books was not necessarily connected to what actually happened in ceremony. I offered coffee, for instance, and Pasha asked about the caffeine-ayahuasca interaction. I told him to forget everything he'd read and just be with Lynn and myself and most of all, Julio.

Two days after Pasha and Alyona arrived, they, with Lynn and Corina and myself, boarded the riverboat to Herrera. Nearly twenty-four hours later we arrived at Julio's.

He was delighted to see us. And yes, he'd be delighted to make ayahuasca next day.

## Chapter Two

# THE MAN WITH THE HAT

THE AYAHUASCA Julio made looked magnificent. But by 8:30, when I took my seat near the little front gate of Julio's platform, I was nervous. I didn't want anything, anything negative to attack us during the night as I'd been attacked two years earlier.

To that end, about 30 minutes earlier I'd walked slowly around Julio's house, *sopla'ing*—blowing Agua Florida—to create a wall beyond which nothing with negativity was invited. All good spirits and angels, however, were welcome to come. It was meant to be an *arcana* around Julio's arcana.

I'd made the ceremony up on the spot. It seemed almost silly, coming from me—with Lynn walking behind me blowing mapacho smoke—but it also seemed like the right thing to do. So despite feeling silly, I just made the wall and hoped it had power to work.

There were one or two moments when it seemed that while I was telling negative spirits to stay out that one of them was saying it was already there and would get me later. I brushed that aside as best I could.

Julio began right-to-left with me first. Not long after I drank, my panic set in, and not long after Julio made his arcana I was outside, knees knocking, feet tapping, hands shaking. "I can't do this. I'm not ready for this!" I was shouting to myself. No good. Worse, the buzzing in my ears began, disorienting me.

I did make an attempt to be brave: I told myself that if my college roommate Phil were here he'd calm me down like he used to if LSD got a little strange and say: "Hey Peteball! You can do this standing on your head," or something like that, and instantly I would be confident I could get through anything. But Phil was not there.

I stared open-eyed into space to keep a level of stability for fear of disappearing if I let go. Suddenly, colorful lights appeared in front of me. Colorful lights that were sort of like Christmas lights but compelling. They filled my vision and read a simple A.

A bright "A"—and I heard myself saying something like "Oh, sure, and what does that stand for, anaconda?"

And as I said that, I moved from the ground to sit on one of the three cut log pieces that made up Julio's steps and of course I realized the "A" stood for ayahuasca.

As I realized that, the "A" pulled back and revealed that it was just a crest on a hat. A pointed black crushed-velvet hat which sat atop the head of a giant of a being dressed in a similarly made crushed-velvet cape that swept to the ground and reached to the heavens and was dotted with what looked like jewels. When I looked closer I realized they were jewels in the shapes of the planets, stars, the moon. They glistened fantastically. And then I realized they were not jewels or lights on the cape at all but that the cape was the entire universe and the glistening jewels were actually cut-outs in the material that allowed the light of the universe to come through the cape in the shape of the stars, planets, and moon. It was the cloak of the universe itself, and if it were removed the universe would be revealed to be all light.

The being was male and overwhelming, though he didn't threaten me. Just his enormity, his unknowableness itself was terrifying. This being was strong and stately and elegant and definitely a "he."

He came down in size to the point where I could see his hat again, though he still appeared to be hundreds of feet tall, and asked if I was ready to follow him. I said I wasn't, that I was too frightened.

He told me not to be frightened, just to follow, that it was time to work. The work, he said, involved learning the next part of becoming a curandero. I'd never thought of myself that way, but as soon as he said it I realized that it was something that had been happening without me asking for it since that night when I battled for Marco.

I said I couldn't. I was not ready for ayahuasca work that night.

He was disappointed but not angry. He wanted to know why I couldn't work, why I was afraid. I told him I wasn't ready to give myself up to being torn apart by ayahuasca and blown to bits by the universe.

I knew that If I could summon up the courage to follow him something immense and fantastic would occur. But I couldn't manage to let go—of my fear, my ego, myself—and allow myself to follow him.

I told him I had things to do before I could follow. I had to fix things with Chepa and with my work so that my kids could be taken care of. I had too much to do to follow yet and go through the world and change.

He turned and started to stride away, then turned back and said, "Go fix your problems. Come back when you're ready to work."

He said it plainly, then turned and walked away. No rancor, no anger, no sadness. Just plainly.

I apologized silently to Julio but believed that what the man said was true: I should come back when ready to work, which meant follow him to wherever and through whatever hells I had to go through to get somewhere new.

Just after the man disappeared, I vomited. Good, strong and clean. Up came the ayahuasca and the cup of lemon water I'd had a couple of hours earlier, out onto the dirt in front of me.

I looked at the damp spot on the ground.

Suddenly a man dressed identically to the first but of a more normal size, was standing to my right.

"Go ahead and leap into it," he said.

"How?"

"Put your intent into it and leap."

The vomit had become a Merlin mirror. It was the first time I'd seen it. I'd heard about it and often told people about how their vomit might become a sort of magic mirror through which they could leap to travel anywhere in the universe. And now, suddenly for the first time it made honest, physical sense.

The vomit was only a few inches wide but the portal—clearly that was what it was—was as large as I needed and all I had to do was intend through it to be in it. I thought about it for a minute and then looked at it again and saw the caped man's face looking up at me from it, grinning a devilish, dark grin, and of course I got scared and stepped away. And with that the portal closed. But I knew the portal had been real, and was ashamed to be so afraid. All those years waiting for that door to materialize and when it did I was a small, small man unable to jump into and through it. Ah, nuts. Julio had just been wasting his time with me.

There is a gap after the Merlin mirror missed opportunity. I remember my shame and then coming out of that space and listening to the other guests, seeing that they were alright—although Pasha seemed to be vomiting quite a bit—then finding a spot outside Julio's hut but near the stairs where I could lie down. The doctors came and worked on me a little. Sort of a guest appearance, and then things got sexy for a while with cartoon-sized women prancing and preening, and then the beautiful world of ayahuasca tickling me, making me laugh. Bittersweet because I knew I'd lost an opportunity but it was way, way over my head.

But then, out of the calm I found myself being walked up large stone steps by the same being who'd been with me at the portal. He brought me to a set of doors. Tall doors, very tall. They had rounded tops and a very high window. You would have to be a giant to look through that window, maybe 20 feet high. The doors were made of simple but strong oak and were reinforced with crossbeams set perhaps every six feet. I think there were three of them. They were like castle or cathedral doors.

"This is where the wishes are," he said, indicating I should enter. "There is still time to do the work."

This is where the wishes are, I repeated to myself. Of course, just as I thought that it occurred to me that I hadn't asked for wishes. I had wished for Chepa's heart to be cleaned, of course, so that there would be a chance she would realize she loved me and didn't need to be afraid of being in love, but I wanted to do the conquering so it would be real.

What other wishes? To have enough work to keep the house?

But behind those doors lay something bigger than that, I knew. The wishes. Maybe all the wishes in the universe lay there. How? Like Christmas presents? That made no sense.

And in the moment of thinking that, a row of demons came through the doors—without opening them—and roared past us. They were human-like but tall, and all of them were eating furiously. But they had no fronts on their bodies so as soon as they ate the food fell to the ground. And in seeing them I realized that the wishes that were probably in that place were only base desires. Desires for wealth, power, fortune, fame. Desires for Cadillacs, for oil, to run the world. Or desires before they took shape. I shivered: I felt that behind those doors probably lay the very heart of man's desires. All the lurid evil imaginable. The willingness to trade in lies and lives, the deals with the devil himself.

The demons that had passed were creatures of unimaginable and insatiable hunger. Desires in creature shapes that could never be satisfied, creatures who could eat a universe and never be full.

I might have those base desires but I didn't want to be one of those ever-hungry creatures. No, I did not want to go through those doors at all.

The man did not urge me. He had brought me there but did not insist I enter. When he understood I would not pass through those doors he grew sad.

"There is still enough time to do the work tonight," he said again. Then he walked me down the stairs and into a kind of living computer.

We moved through living wiring and tubes at the speed of light. "Would you like to see the cell that powers your soul?" he asked.

And into the heart of the living machine we flew. I was sad and disappointed that there was a machine that ran my soul. I'd always thought souls were living things, spirits that were given life. And now, in an instant, the man had let me know I was just part of a machine, nothing of my own.

We traveled for what seemed like a long time, finally stopping at the entrance to a small room. Inside there was a pedestal, topped with a wire-framed glass box. Inside that was a tiny, tiny box. "That is the cell that runs your soul," he said.

He made it start to turn one side toward me. A tiny speck in the box began to glow. The tiniest speck. It began to throw off light until in a moment it began to blind me, engulf me with searing brightness.

He turned the box back away from me, cutting out the light.

"Now, would you like to see the part of your soul that runs that cell?" he asked.

I was dumbstruck. What was this?

I didn't need an answer; I knew. Our souls were powered by the machine of the universe which was in turn powered by our souls, which in turn were powered by another machine...endlessly. I almost laughed.

The man opened his hand. In his palm was a grain of sand. Like the cell it began to emit light. But as bright as the cell's light had been, this was brighter, much more powerful. A glimpse and I was knocked to the ground. The power was way too much to witness, so I opened my eyes and lay on the ground near Julio's home.

A little while later the man told me he could have given me so much that night. He was sad when he said it. I asked: "Why don't you come in forms that don't terrify me? Like the doctors, why not come as a nurse and tickle me? Why do you spirits always play to my fear?"

"Because your fear is what you need to deal with."

And then he took me to a place where something was gleaming. It was something golden and red and green and it was like a crown as wide as my sight and taller than my sight.

"I could have shown you the *corona*," he said.

I looked at the crown presented to me. It was so golden it radiated light and life. It shimmered. When I looked at it for a few moments, I realized it was moving. It looked like a crown in the shape of an impossibly huge pipe organ so large you couldn't see the sides or top or bottom of it.

Closer, the pipes were each alive and pulsing. Some were like serpents, others were made of strings of stars and planets, still others were winding DNA stairways 100 feet wide and infinitely tall. Millions of dots of light made up others; growing flowers on long orchid-like strands made up others.

It was the most glorious *is-ness* I'd ever seen. I was in absolute awe. This was life at a level normally impossible to perceive, what our eyes are not programmed to receive. I was speechless, in speechless awe of this life force, this universe center, this pulsing core of *is-ness*.

And I knew that though I was seeing it, what the man meant when he said he could have shown it to me was that had I had the courage I would have been in it. Would have felt it pulsing through me, would have known all things knowable and unknowable, felt all things feelable and unfeelable, been all things be-able and un-be-able.

The man left me with a glance and disappeared. With him, the crown pulled back and disappeared as well, until it was a single star that rolled its edges into itself, became a cluster of interlocking gleaming rings, then disappeared and left all darkness.

I stayed on the ground and laughed and cried. I had gotten more than I could have imagined, yet knew I'd missed something unimaginable.

꧁꧂

The sound of vomiting suddenly took my attention and I stood and walked up the log steps to the hut platform. Alyona was sitting peacefully, as were

Lynn and Corina, but Pasha lay on the floor, writhing, still vomiting. I checked on him. He was fine, just having a difficult time with the cleansing. But it didn't stop. For perhaps two more hours, as Julio chanted, Pasha suffered through what was the most physically difficult time with vomiting I'd ever seen someone have under ayahuasca's influence. And he wouldn't get up and let me take him outside. He just rolled around in his own vomit—I put towels under his head so that he'd at least be reasonably clean, and Corina, who had not taken the medicine, tended him wonderfully, wiping him down with moist towels and wetting his lips but not otherwise interfering with him.

Julio chuckled at one point and said: "I don't understand a man who vomits in a living room." He laughed again, "Well, maybe it's just impossible to do anything else." And then he began to chant again.

Chapter Three

# JULIO SAYS "GRAB YOUR BALLS"

THE NEXT morning Pasha and Alyona wanted to ask questions about what they'd seen. I explained that they would most likely get no response. They insisted and I said alright, so after the morning bath in the river to put everyone back together, and after Julio had sweet, light coffee with several dried bread rounds, we gathered around him on the floor of his living space.

Alyona said she'd seen herself, no, had been herself riding on a horse...

I translated her first phrase and was surprised when Julio interrupted.

"What color was the horse?"

I was amazed. He'd never done that before in 20 years and 100 visits.

I asked Alyona what color the horse was and she told me it was blue and white. I translated for Julio. He looked at me, impossibly deep eyes gleaming, and said that was good. Blue and white was a good color for a horse to be.

Alyona continued. She had ridden into a Greek temple, through vast columns, but she had arrived nowhere as the columns continued endlessly.

I translated the vision and Julio thought for a moment. I imagined he was going to do what he always did when I spoke: listen attentively and then ask what I'd said. He didn't. He said the riding of a blue and white horse into a columned building signified success, but as there were no walls to the building and no place arrived at, it signified that she hadn't chosen what to do yet. He assured her that ayahuasca had said she would succeed at whatever she chose but told her to choose soon as Pasha had two enemies at his work who might cost him his job.

Pasha interrupted to say that was true but that he had not told anyone.

Julio just laughed when I told him what Pasha said; he told me to tell Pasha to watch his back; one of the enemies had already put something negative into him.

He urged Alyona to pick something, anything, to do, as things were very auspicious for her. He echoed the fact that she might have to carry Pasha for a while if his enemies succeeded in unseating him.

As for Pasha, he said he had not seen much of anything because he'd been vomiting for so many hours and demanded to know how it was that he'd had such an awful time while his wife was having wonderful visions.

Julio explained that he'd wanted to paint Pasha with the colors of ayahuasca but that when he got inside he saw that Pasha was like a room filled with broken old furniture and peeling paint and garbage in the corners. "Who could paint in a room like that?" he chuckled. So instead of painting Pasha, he'd spent the night preparing him. "There was a lot of junk to clean out. But tell your friend that now he's ready. Tell him I'll paint him next time."

Pasha didn't believe a word of it, but I knew what Julio meant.

Though I rarely even tried to tell Julio what the medicine had shown me, that morning I needed to, so I showed Julio the pictures I'd drawn: the hat with the letter "A," the man in the cape, the doors, the hungry creatures.

Julio said the man with the cape was one of his guardians and that he'd sent him to me. He asked me what I'd done when I met him. I said I'd sent him away out of fear. Julio shook his head in dismay for a few moments, then asked if the man had said anything before he left.

I told him the man said to come back when I was ready to work. Julio said that was both good and lucky. He said I should stop being so frozen with fear, that I should be fearless.

I told him about Merlin's mirror and how I was too afraid to go into it and he repeated that I should stop being afraid. I must be fearless.

I told him about the gears and the slow-motion blocks that form when the sound begins to hum in my ears and that it makes me feel afraid and overwhelmed. He said the sound was the sound of the gears of the universe, the mechanics of the whole shebang—he used a phrase that I didn't get—and that again I shouldn't be afraid. These were all good things ayahuasca was sharing with me.

I then told him about the doors and the wishes and how I knew there were perpetually hungry creatures inside that would come out and overwhelm me, consuming me over and over with base desire if I opened the doors.

Julio was ready to explode, partly with laughter, partly with frustration. He said that it was rare to go to the doors, but that if I'd had the courage to enter I would have met three men at a table. I could have asked them for anything I wanted and they would have given it to me.

"Anything?"

"Whatever you want. They can give it to you. Just ask them and you get your wishes."

"But what about the creatures I saw there?"

"Yes, they were there. Forget them. Forget your fear. All of these spirits are *bravo*, aggressive. They're like Indians. They challenge you. If they are *bravo*"—aggressive—"you be more bravo. If they are 100 feet tall, make yourself 200 feet tall. Then they will respect you."

He laughed, then told a story of himself as a younger man working with ayahuasca. "There was a man, a fierce spirit, blocking my path. He wouldn't let me pass and said he was going to kill me. I was afraid too, but I was determined to pass him. So I told him to kill me. And the man stabbed me three times. But each time he turned the knife around at the last second and stabbed me with the butt of the knife. And then he let me pass."

Julio laughed. "You must do the same."

I thought of the Matses Indians and how Moises had stood toe-to-toe with Papa Viejo, and told Julio I would try to be more brave. He said I was doing all this work and not getting what I could, even when he was help-ing by sending a guardian to assist me. *"Tienes cojones, Pedrito? Agarra tus cojones,"* he laughed, seriously. "You have balls? Grab them." Two days later I got the chance.

## Chapter Four

# CONVERSATION WITH
# THE GUARDIANS

URING THOSE two days I came up with the phrase: "I am Peter Gorman, son of Thomas and Madeleine Gorman, father of Italo, Marco and Madeleina Gorman, spouse of Chepa, and I have business here. I have been invited here by Julio Jerena."

I must have repeated that phrase a thousand times between Thursday morning and Friday night, determined to implant it to the point that even if I was disoriented I could say it. I hoped it got my gumption strong because I was determined not to be so afraid of everything on the other side of ayahuasca.

Which didn't mean I was confident I could pull it off, of course. But still I practiced that phrase and concentrated on the feeling of loss and how awful it was each time I refused something ayahuasca offered out of fear and then later realized it was a gift I'd lost.

The night we were to drink, only Lynn and I were going to participate. Alyona had gone to bed. Pasha and Corina sat with us, though, although neither wanted to drink.

Julio began the ceremony with his prayers and we had him pour a huge portion for Lynn: he'd never really gone to the other side and needed to. I took a regular portion. Julio took just enough to keep us company.

I wasn't long before my world began to shift: the sound of the gears began to grate in their slow, metallic fashion.

Instantly I was afraid, but found the courage to say my mantra: I am Peter, son of Thomas and Madeleine, father of Italo, Marco and Madeleina, husband of Chepa, and I have business here.

I was spinning upside down when I tried to say that to maintain order, and instantly on saying it I found myself in a dark void. Pitch black, empty. Nothing.

I got my bearings—that is to say I felt myself stand in that vacuum, and began to walk across it, thinking there must be someplace to get to if I kept walking. I wasn't walking toward anything but more nothing, but still, I'd never been in a space that didn't go somewhere sooner or later, so walking seemed like a reasonable thing to do.

Going was slow and frustrating since nothing appeared on the horizon, so I decided to make myself 40 feet tall to make my strides longer. I did, and began walking with giant steps across that void and in no time found myself in a forest.

I had no idea what forest or where it was but kept on walking through the trees on a kind of path.

In a few moments I found myself nearly stepping on a *sachavaca*, a small white tapir with bright yellow stripes on its fore-quarters and back.

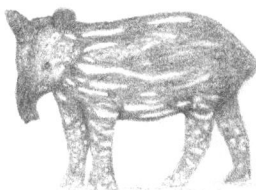

*Sachavaca*

"Are you ready to work tonight?" she asked in a lovely, friendly voice.

I said yes and added the mantra that I am Peter, son of Thomas and Madeleine, father of Italo, Marco and Madeleina, and I have business here.

She laughed and told me that in that case I should follow her.

I knew it was a trick, of course. I knew the moment I stepped behind her on the jungle trail she would turn into a giant tapir or monster and kick me into hell, so I left a little space between us and silently repeated my mantra.

She didn't do what I thought she would. Didn't do anything mean.

In a little while she came to a black hole in the ground and hopped over it. Then she turned—the sachavaca was definitely a she—and said: "Why don't you jump into that?"

Surprisingly, I did.

In the hole was a thick clear sort of gelatinous goop—I should say the hole was made up of the viscous goop. It wasn't wretched or slimy or constricting or something that prevented me from breathing. It was just goopish, but so clear that it was black.

Down I went into the thick stuff, afraid but excited. Down I went in and through until I reached a sort of bottom where the sachavaca was waiting for me.

"Come," she said, and I followed her down a hallway of some sort into a room where I saw planets and the stars. Like a 3-D projection of a mini-universe. The sachavaca asked if I would like that. I didn't understand. She asked if I would like the power of the planets and I said okay, but still didn't know what she meant.

"Okay," she said, and started to leave the room.

"What do you mean?" I asked.

"From now on all you have to do is want to be on a planet and you will be," she explained.

I thought I would try and thought of Saturn: Instantly I was a giant, standing on the rings of the planet, looking out at the universe. Some of the rings were narrow and some were thick. Some were made of gray dust while others were smooth like glass. I stepped from one to another and nearly fell because they moved at different speeds.

I jumped onto a reddish ring and was nearly knocked down because it was made in part of huge stones that moved beneath my feet.

It was glorious.

I tried the moon, and got to a cold, dark place and looked down at earth, so close, so huge.

Then the sun, and felt the heat of its fires roar around me, though I don't remember hearing them.

"Just want to be there and you will be," she said, bringing me out of my reverie.

She walked out of the room and into another chamber filled with plants.

"Would you like this?" she asked.

"I would like to know how to heal with plants," I said.

"Okay," she said.

"You mean I can do it now? You just say okay and I can do it?"

"Yes. I just gave it to you."

"But how do I do it?"

"You just have to talk to them and they will tell you how to use them."

I don't remember if I said anything, but do remember her saying: "The problem is most people don't know how to talk to plants. They ask the plants: 'What good are you?' And of course the plants, being perfectly themselves, are already good, so that is not a question they can answer. They don't have to justify themselves to anyone or anything, so they won't even answer that. But if you say, 'Excuse me, I need help. What use might you be to humans?' then they will tell you. Some are good for food or beauty or firewood, others are medicines, and all sorts of things. You just have to remember the right question."

"And I can do that now?"

"Yes. I gave you that present. Of course you won't do it so well yet. You will have to practice to get good. You should touch them and feel them and then ask them. You can sleep with them or near them too. They will tell you how to use them. You should start with the trees in your back yard. Ask them what use they might be to humans."

We left that room and I wondered if any of it was real. I mean, I know it was beyond my imagination to invent all of this, but still, I wondered if I were really being given things, if I might ask for X-Ray vision or mind reading and such.

Sachavaca answered my silent thoughts. "You are being given gifts but you can't use them selfishly. That doesn't mean you cannot benefit, but that's not the reason you have them. You can't see through girls' clothes. I won't give you that. It's not important. You can have mind-reading but only in limited fashion. If it is important that you get something from someone's mind, not something selfish but something important, then you will have the ability. But circumstances will dictate.

"What's important to remember is that we are lending you these powers. They are not yours. You must use them or we will give them to someone else. You must not abuse them or we will take them away. At the most inopportune time. Use them, don't abuse them, or lose them."

She took me to a room with animals and serpents and said I could talk with them if I wanted. I said okay, and we were leaving the room when a fish appeared underwater and told me not to forget him and talking with fish, too.

I asked her why I was getting these presents. She said they'd been watching me for a long time.

"Everyone gets watched. We've been taking care of you for a long time."

"What do you mean?" I asked.

"Like guardian angels. Why do you think you have always managed to escape harm when you invite it with drugs and drinking?"

"I don't know."

"Because we're watching. Do you remember the other night in your room? At the hotel?"

I cringed. It was the night I'd arrived and gotten drunk on Lynn's $100. Afterwards I had taken a prostitute to my room. I asked her for a blow job then passed out. When I awoke my money—about $60—was gone, but nothing else was touched. Not my passport, camera, tape recorder, nothing. It was just a stupid drunk thing to do.

"I remember," I said.

"Well," said Sachavaca, "you have no idea how close you came to having your penis cut off by her."

"What?" I asked, shivering at the image.

"You were just one too many fat, middle-aged, white guys who made her suck your smelly, unwashed dick. You were the last straw. So she took out her nail file and was about to cut you when we intervened and told her spirit that it would be better just to put the file away, take your money and go. She almost didn't. And then she was going to take your camera and medicines and we reminded her that if she just left with the money you would live with it and your own stupidity. But that taking your things would make you go after her. She rethought and took the money and left."

"Buy why are you protecting me?" I asked, secretly hoping that there was something special about me or my reason for living that would be explained.

"When you were a little kid with rheumatoid arthritis and you were so fat and sick, well, we felt sorry for you and decided you needed looking after. So we did and do."

I was a little crushed with the idea of a sympathy guardian angel. Not what

I was hoping for at all.

"You're not a bad guy. You just don't do some things so well. Like money. How many times have you gotten to the end of it with no way out and something saves you? That was us."

"What about when I get home?" I asked, knowing I was two weeks away from losing the house again. "Can I have more work?"

"The work will be there when you get back. Have confidence. You are a good worker. It will be waiting."

For some reason, I believed her.

"What about songs? Can you teach me icaros?"

"No. You're not a curandero so you don't need your own songs. When you do need one you will have one. Just open your mouth and it will come out. If you use them enough you will learn a lot. Have faith. We're taking care of you."

"Can you fix my family?"

"Do you want Chepa to be back and in love with you?"

"Yes! No! I mean, I do, but I want to do that. I don't want you to do that."

"Are you sure you don't want me to do it?"

"Yes. That's my work. I may fail but if I succeed I will know she really loves me again."

"Good choice."

"Do I have a chance?"

"Keep not drinking. That's very important. Don't clutter yourself."

"Can I have more children with her?"

"We might help to have two more but what good would it be to give you two more angels if you are going to keep smoking and die before they get the good from you?"

"But it's hard to quit."

"We'll help. Your cigarettes are going to start tasting bad. Over time you will hate them. But you will still have to finally quit if you want to live. And of course you have to decide if you really want Chepa. She may take some time to be free for you and you could already have Gina."

Gina was a woman I'd met and begun an affair with in Iquitos during the several days I was there before we left for the jungle.

"She'd be great for you."

"I know," I said. "But I would rather Chepa and my family get better."

"Then don't confuse things with Gina. Don't try to have both or you won't have any."

I wanted to get up and go out to pee and have a cigarette.

"You could do that," she said, reading my thoughts. "But I might not be here when you get back. If I were you and you were giving me all these presents, I think I would wait on the cigarette rather than risk losing you."

She was right, and I didn't go anywhere.

"Good choice," she said again, smiling.

We began walking again and suddenly we were out of that world in Merlin's mirror and in a more familiar ayahuasca space.

"I'm going now," she said. "But I will be there when you need me."

She started moving away and the man from two nights earlier, the man with the moon and stars and planets in his hat and cape, appeared.

"I am Peter, son of Thomas and Madeleine, father of Italo and Marco and Madeleina, spouse of Chepa, and I have business here. I want to go to the room where the wishes are."

I don't know that the man laughed at me for my carrying on, but I don't remember him being impressed, especially as he was one of Julio's guardians and he'd come to help me at Julio's request.

I moved with the man until we were on a long narrow sort of walkway. Devils and horrid creatures lined the sides of the walk but I kept repeating my mantra and they never really formed. Except for one of them who leapt onto the walk blocking the path. He was big and scary and had two heads and then bodies formed from his left and right sides, completely blocking the path. He would not let me go.

"I am Peter, son of Thomas and Madeleine, father of Italo and Marco and Madeleina, husband of Chepa, and I have business beyond you."

And then I was beyond him, like Julio said I would be, and at the huge doors.

I knew the hungry creatures would be in there but for some reason had courage in the mantra and willed myself through the doors.

The creatures were indeed there, but they were only a foot tall that night and they rushed by me easily. They did not frighten me.

I looked around the hall for the table Julio said I would find. It was just around a bend in another room. At it sat three men, thick and strong, all with broad hats like sombreros and scarves pulled up across their faces so only their eyes shone.

They greeted me and shook hands. The middle one, though imposing, shook softly and I wondered why. Just then he put out his hand again and took mine and squeezed hard.

"Is that better?" he asked.

I laughed at myself.

"What do you want?" he asked.

"Julio said to ask you for anything I want," I said.

"We already gave you everything. You want more already?"

"I want to be a curandero. I want to talk to plants," I said.

"You already can. Sachavaca gave you that and a lot of other things."

"But Julio said to ask you," I protested.

"You did. She is one of us. When you asked us to come in a shape that wouldn't terrify you we sent her. The only problem is that she will be your guardian forever and she's not very macho."

The men all burst into laughter.

"But she is one of us, don't fool yourself. And do as she said: Use the gifts. Don't abuse them or you will lose them. And if you need more gifts, now that you know where we are, you may come back when you need to. We will be watching you."

"And my kids?" I added.

"They are being cared for, too. So is Chepa. Sachavaca is very good. Don't let her fool you. She is very powerful for such a little thing."

The men laughed again.

And then I was outside the doors and Sachavaca was waiting and said she would be watching and that was the end of that and I was just back at Julio's, lying on the floor of his living room, listening to him sing.

The next morning I tried to talk to Julio about what happened, but ran into the same problem I did most of the time: I spoke, he nodded and asked what I had said. I repeated, he nodded and asked "What was that?" I finally gave up and began breaking camp for the return to Iquitos.

When we were set to go I went to Julio to give him a hug. He took me by both arms and looked into my eyes. "*Yah, Pedro*. You did alright." Then he chuckled. "Your guardian, Sachavaca is *muy bonita*, very pretty."

PART VI

# INTO THE FRAY

*Chiric Chiric, Sanangaton;*
*Chiric Chiric, Sanangaton;*
*La jïtima medicina,*
*Le jïtimo doctorsitaning.*

*Chiric Sanango,*
*Chiric Sanango,*
*The best medicine;*
*The best doctor.*

*—from one of Julio's songs*

# Chapter One

# MARVELOUS HEALINGS, A WRETCHED ATTACK

SACHAVACA DIDN'T lie. As soon as I returned home, work started coming in. A new magazine from Canada called and asked if I would write a drug war column for them on a regular basis; my local alternative paper began assigning me stories more frequently, and a third magazine called to ask for a cover story.

I worked hard and began to get caught up—not on what I'd borrowed, but on the bills as they came in. Marco was amazed when one night a few weeks after I'd returned from Peru, I put a pot roast on. "We're not having chicken for the 400th time in a row? You must be doing good, dad."

What was awful was that Momma Lydia was dying and didn't last till spring. I continued to work on her every night and in the mornings as well, and when she went she went peacefully. It was a deep blow to Marco and Italo, who she'd helped raise, but it was good that she died with us rather than down in Iquitos. She had all of her daughters and most of her grandkids around, and that helped ease everyone's pain.

Within days of her death, a woman named Susan got in touch with me for a trip. She told me she was dying of cancer. She had only a couple of weeks to live and wanted to die in the jungle. I told her not to come, that that wasn't my line of work.

She insisted and insisted and when another couple asked me for a trip that would begin the day Susan's ended, I relented. It was a selfish decision based on finances. I had enough miles for a free ticket.If I only used a skeleton crew, mainly depending on Julio's daughter MaBel, and her husband Gerald, who were living with Julio at that time, the two couples back-to-back might generate enough for me to pay a month's bills at home.

When I met Susan and her partner Steve, I couldn't believe she was dying. She was about 50, tall, blond, slim and lovely. She looked vibrant and very much alive, which I was glad for, but Steve said that what she'd told me was no exaggeration: Her doctors had said her body couldn't take any more treatment and to expect to die in weeks.

*Julio*

Before we headed out to the jungle I made her promise to try to stay alive until we got back at least, and that I would push for her to have one more Christmas with her daughter—six months away. She agreed to try.

When I spoke with Julio about her cancer, he reminded me that ayahuasca didn't cure cancer because cancer was cold and ayahuasca was hot. Still, he said he would do what he could.

The evening's ceremony was one of the gentlest I'd ever been part of. Neither Susan nor Steve got ill at all, and I only vomited once.

When it was over, my guests said they'd felt nothing, but loved Julio's presence and his songs.

I knew that though they'd felt nothing the ceremony had been much more than that. Julio had sung wonderfully, and all night he shook his shacapa at Susan. I watched as fine white lights came off the tips of the leaves and shot into her body. He mostly worked her mid-section but sometimes worked on her head and neck as well.

At one point early on in the ceremony a voice asked me if I would like to know how to cure cancer, and I said yes, thinking of Momma Lydia and how I hadn't been able to help her.

In moments my vision changed and I began to see inside Susan's body, where Julio's lights were moving things that looked like pins in her stomach, sending what looked like electrical impulses throughout her insides.

Julio worked for two or three hours. I was mesmerized. And then, at the end of the night, the voice asked me again: "Would you like to know how to cure cancer?"

Before I could answer, the voice answered its own question: "Watch Julio."

In the morning, Julio sent his son Jairo—who had his own house nearby—out to collect bark from the *medio renaco* tree and made a two-quart extraction from it in aguardiente. He told Susan to drink a little of it every day for two weeks, until it was finished.

I didn't hold much hope despite the work I'd seen the night before, but was glad, when they finally said goodbye and set off for Brazil, that she was drinking the medicine, and was happier still that she had not died in the jungle.

Nearly two years later I got a phone call in Texas. It was Susan. She was motorcycling around the Italian Alps, having a great time. She was still dying, she said, but had had not one but two extra Christmases with her daughter.

⁂

Something odd happened during the first ceremony with the second couple. I had made my protective wall with mapacho smoke and Agua Florida, as I had every time since I began doing it with Lynn. It was a very tranquil ceremony for me; some light visions, but nothing extraordinary occurred. I was lying on my back, listening to Julio's icaros and *che-che-che* of his shacapa, feeling warm and content. The calm of the night was broken, however, when I heard a crash: I sat up and looked in his direction: He was lying on the floor in a fetal position, his mapacho burning an inch from his mustache.

I thought he'd fallen and got up and started to help him up.

"Don't touch him!" yelled MaBel. "He's been attacked! Sing, Peter. Sing. Here's a mapacho. Protect my father!"

Her voice had an urgency I'd never heard from her, but I did as she asked. I sang and smoked and ordered whoever had done this to leave the space. MaBel handed me a second mapacho before the first was up, then gave me the bottle of camalonga to clean Julio. I don't remember my guests even moving; they might have been deep in their dreams and didn't notice the

211

change in the space. I did. It was like there were spider webs on everything, and especially on Julio. I sang and shook his shacapa and smoked and sang some more. Songs I'd never heard came out of me and I thought of Sachavaca's promise that I'd have icaros when I needed them. I had no idea what I was singing, I just let them out.

I don't know how long it went on, only that MaBel kept handing me mapachos and urging me to sing more forcefully, to get rid of whatever had attacked Julio.

Finally, Julio stirred. MaBel asked if he was alright and he said yes, but that he was too weak to sit just yet. So I sang some more and smoked some more until he, with MaBel's help, was able to sit and move onto his little stool.

"*Oye, Pedrito*. That was some battle. But I won. Thank you for your help."

"I didn't help at all, Julio."

He chuckled and lit a mapacho. "You helped a lot. When they first got me and knocked me down, I didn't see it coming. But then I let my other self come out and do battle."

"Who were you battling with?"

"Two spirits. Very strong. *Fueron*. They're gone now."

And then he resumed the ceremony.

In the morning he would only say that sometimes people got jealous and struck out at him. I couldn't get any more from him, so I asked his son-in-law Juan what might have happened. He told me that there were several curanderos who were jealous of Julio.

"What for?" I asked.

"Ah, who knows why people are jealous? Because he has a large family? Because you and other people bring him clients? Because of anything." He paused. "You know Julio's guardians, don't you?"

I said I knew one of them, The Man with the Hat.

"Julio has a lot of guardians. And other curanderos are jealous of that. So they attack Julio, hoping to make him look weak so they can take those guardians for themselves."

"Why don't they just get their own?"

"That's just how some people are. Maybe they don't have the power to get their own or maybe they think they'll be better than Julio if they can take his guardians. You know the jungle. That's the way people are. Even if they have a boat they still want your boat."

Juan turned and walked away and I thought that was the end of the conversation. But he came back. "You don't know everything about ayahuasca."

"I don't know anything."

"You know a lot. But there is one secret that you don't know—well there are many, but there is one you don't know about guardians."

"And...?"

"Yah. *Escuche*. Listen. When a curandero dies, whoever is with him can take his guardians for themselves. And Julio is old. He's getting too old to fight. When he was young no one dared to attack him. Most still don't interfere, but there are a couple who are trying to kill Julio. And when he is dying they will come like friends and try to get his guardians."

"The guardians will go with them even if they killed him?"

"If they can dominate them, yes."

"That sucks."

"When you make your arcana around the house for ceremony you have to make it stronger. They got through it to get to Julio. You didn't know their power. Now you do, that's your responsibility.

"Oh, and they will try to get you too, because they are afraid that if you are with Julio when he dies, you would get the guardians."

He was serious.

✦✦✦

That was the last time I ever drank at Julio's house on the Aucayacu. When I returned to Iquitos a few months later for the start of two more groups, I discovered that MaBel and Gerald had built a small stilted-house for themselves and Julio in a patch of Iquitos that was just being settled. It was tiny but workable. MaBel explained that she and Gerald and another of Julio's sons—also named Julio—who lived there, could take care of Julio better in Iquitos than they could out in the jungle. "Last month he fell while everyone was in Herrera," she said. "We came back the next day and he was still on the ground. That's no way for my papa to live."

She also said the attacks were continuing. "Sometimes they try to get him while he sleeps and he wakes up screaming. Sometimes he just goes white and can't breathe."

Julio, better than 85, still looked strong to me. He'd developed a sort of hunchback over the last few years, but his eyes were clear, his chuckle infectious. And he was more than willing to accompany my guests and me to the Aucayacu—where we used Juan's house, just a 10 minute walk from where his had been—as he missed the river and friends there.

***

With the regularity of the trips—I liked the back-to-back idea and began doing two in January and two in June and July—my team came together fantastically. Except for three—Jhonny, Gasdalia and Mauricio, all of whom had worked at my bar—all of them were related to Julio. Sons, daughters, grandkids, in-laws. They knew their jobs, had grown up on the river with Julio, every one of them knew plant medicine, and three of them, Juan, Jairo and Antenor could all run ceremonies.

But Julio was the center of it all. He didn't run ceremonies, he worked with the medicine to effect healing. He was the maestro. And he was dad and grandpa, and he loved being with nearly all of his family for a week or so at a time several times a year.

For me, using the whole team made things more difficult financially than they should have been—paying 12 or 15 people to care for six or eight guests is not a good business model—but it was worth it to see Julio so happy.

And his work was as potent as ever. The healing some of my clients got was extraordinary. One woman told me weeks after she returned home that she'd suffered from irritable bowel syndrome for her entire adult life but that it disappeared the day after her first ceremony with Julio. Another fellow, a wealthy man, wrote me six months after the trip. "Before the trip every day I woke up and wondered if today was the day I should put the pistol in my mouth and end it all. Since the trip every day I wake up and thank god I'm alive."

# Chapter Two

# SPLITTING INTO PIECES

I DIDN'T REALIZE it at the time, but after the night when Julio was attacked, our relationship began to change. For the first time he began pushing me to learn things. He had me help make the medicine and sing into it. He'd have me stir it and dole out the portions to my guests. He'd ask me things about what Sachavaca was teaching me and tell me when he thought I wasn't being strong enough.

One night, perhaps a year after Susan and Steve's trip, I had a group of seven men. I wasn't planning on drinking with them, but during the days leading up to the trip Sachavaca and The Man with the Hat kept telling me I needed to drink because they had something to teach me. I asked them what it was but they wouldn't say. "We'll tell you when it's time" was all I could get out of them no matter how much I pestered them for a hint.

During the day of the first ceremony, I helped Jairo and Julio make the medicine. That evening I thought about skipping drinking again, but the guardians would have none of it. "We're going to teach you things. It's going to get a little crazy but trust us and you'll be alright."

That meant it was going to be hell, but I knew I had better listen to them. Julio must have heard them too because he served me first and urged me to drink every drop.

Julio had gotten very *mareado*, drunk, on the vapor of the ayahuasca during the day, and as he prayed and smoked each cup before handing it to me to hand to the guests, he inhaled deeply several times, making him more and more ayahuasca-drunk. It seemed as though it was taking 10 minutes to serve each person and I was afraid I would begin to fall under the medicine's influence before we were done serving. I told Julio to hurry up a little.

"*Ah, Pedrito…buena medicina…yah…*" he chuckled, nearly toppling off of his chair.

By the time he was serving the fifth person the medicine was coming on strong and I wanted to run off, but couldn't. Still, I could hardly pass the medicine any longer: everything was splintering and multiplying itself. I couldn't tell which of my 20 hands was the one that actually held the cup and which of the 20 cups was the real one. I told Julio I couldn't help any longer but he suddenly perked up and said: "Keep working. You have work to do."

The sixth guest couldn't keep the medicine down. He just spit it up after he drank. He drank a second time and just puked and ran off the hut platform. I told him, as best I could with lifeless lips, that it wasn't his turn, that I was losing it fast and he might be needed to help my team with the other guests.

I'm sure I simply scuttled from Julio to the last guest on the seat of my pants in order to get him served. I was vibrating out of this world like a comic book of the Flash when he sped up to go through a wall. My body was losing solidity. Julio's face was doing the Lego block dance and I was trying to tell a guest to sniff the camalonga and the perfume without being able to speak.

By the time a very shaky Julio made his arcana and flicked out the kerosene lamps with his shacapa I just wanted to lie down. Ayahuasca had simply knocked me cold and I could do nothing but fall down and dream. The machine that runs the universe was grinding its gears in my head; giant red, white and blue Lego blocks were vibrating, building things, forming snakes whose tails were snapping back and forth. Faces appeared, grins without faces grinned at me.

"Sit up. Stand up. Go outside and take a guard position. You have guests to guard tonight." It was Sachavaca.

"I can't. I can't do anything."

"That's the work you need to do tonight. You must be here, but be with your guests as well."

"I can't even move."

"Yes you can. Just split yourself in two and do both things."

"I don't know how to do that."

"You will after you do it. That's why we told you to drink. You need to learn this."

I did the best I could, getting first onto my hands and knees and then crawling to the platform edge and down to the dirt just below it. From there I felt in the darkness for a post and gradually inched my way up until I was leaning against it. Faces were everywhere and there was a sudden and overwhelming scent of sex and decadence in the air. The world had stopped splintering and was undulating with a sort of pre-orgasmic recklessness and I realized I was sweating and sweating. I wanted a cigarette but couldn't manage that. I couldn't manage anything but trying not to run away or scream. Sachavaca told me not to do either but to watch what was unfolding.

Gasdalia, a beautiful woman who'd worked at my bar years earlier and now helped out with some of my trips, appeared, Kali-like and sensual, sexual, vibrant. Her features were devilishly distorted and her body was serpentine. She kissed me with a kind of black serpent tongue that had a tiny spade at its tip. It was not a human kiss. It was hot and sensual beyond all sensuality, as if her tongue reached down inside of me and licked me from my insides out. I felt myself instantly hard. At the same time I realized that this entity, whether it was another side of the real Gasdalia or was just taking her familiar form, thrived on sexuality. It felt as though it might have been her *is-ness* to get me to plumb the depths of my physical desires, to allow me to revel in my fantasies, my wildest dreams and hungers. She leaned in and I kissed her deeply, richly.

"Your desires make you strong," she said. "Strong enough to do what needs to be done."

"What is that?"

"Join us."

I pulled away.

"Know man," she said.

Instantly, images of human horror filled my vision, images that showed me being part of the awful mayhem. I told her that that was not me, not what I had come to do.

A voice asked me to trust them, and I said I would but only if the work was good, not evil.

I was hanging on for dear life. Now and then I'd have a momentary respite when I found myself back at Julio's, leaning on the platform's post. I looked at the guests and Julio; I would hear someone vomiting powerfully, or being helped off the platform by one of my team, and then I'd be back with Gasdalia in that other world. At one point Gasdalia kissed me with her serpent tongue and my own mouth opened to let my snake out and I felt a little calmer. I was told to take several steps forward.I was intimidated because I didn't think I could take a single step, much less several, and if I could and did that would put me in the middle of the mandarin orange tree behind the platform and the tree would wrap its branches around me and pull me in to some other place, far removed from Julio's voice.

Sachavaca told me to grab my balls and announce that I was Peter Gorman and had business there. I remembered that earlier in the day Julio told the story of a time when a giant frog once tried to eat him in a dream. He said he told it he was not a grasshopper to be eaten by a frog and the frog had simply gone away. So I grabbed my balls and stepped forward awkwardly and made my way to the tree and into it. I knew something terrible was about to happen and waited for it to wrap me up. Instead, it caressed me and her scent was lovely and I thought "that's not so bad" and a voice, not Sachavaca, told me that things were not going to be what I expected and that I should step forward again. I grabbed my balls again and did, and realized I was climbing up the steps behind a packed stadium from the top of which I could see light and hear people cheering but didn't know what I'd find inside when I reached it.

The voices told me to keep trusting them; if I did I might earn the right to be an apprentice. I argued that I was not going to live on the Aucayacu for my whole life, that I was just a dad getting through as best I could. They told me I should quit what I had and start a new life.

Sachavaca told me not to let go of my balls. I wondered why she'd said that but before I could finish my thought the human misery was presented to me again. Awful, vile things men do to one another. There was war and there was the crushing of babies under boots; there was rape and limbs being torn from bodies; there was unimaginable screaming, the sound of human pain through an amplifier as big as the machine of the universe. I wanted to throw up from the sight and sound and smell of it all, but Sachavaca told me not to dare get rid of a single drop of the ayahuasca.

And in the middle of the mayhem there was sudden silence. "You must know pain to heal," Sachavaca said. "You need to learn the awful things too."

"They're too awful to need to know."

"They are what men do."

The horror was relentless. It might have gone on for an hour or years before it stopped abruptly and Sachavaca told me it was over. "That's enough for now. Now, let me take you to where you get the medicines."

In a moment we stood in front of a low-ceilinged building and walked inside. The smells of thousands of different plants hit me and was overwhelming. "This is the market, where you should come to get your plants."

The dark market was vaster than I could see. Boxes of leaves and roots and barks and unboxed piles of flowers and vines extended forever. "I don't even know what these are," I said. "I'll never find the right plants for things here."

Sachavaca laughed. "Just tell them what you need. Just shout out what you need to heal. Try it."

I shouted out "the flu" and almost before it was out of my mouth dozens of citrus fruits and other plants holding signs with their names on them jumped up from different parts of the market.

"That's all it takes. Just ask them and they'll tell you what you need. Don't forget this place. It's important."

Sadness came over me unexpectedly. I didn't know what was wanted of me. I would have loved to be a curandero, but was not going to move to a river and minister locals for the remainder of my life. Heck, I'd starve to death because of how little I knew of the river and jungle, despite how much time I'd spent there.

Julio stopped singing and I was back near the platform, still wrapped in the mandarin orange tree. I could feel disappointment coming from him. I'd been learning for nearly 25 years, albeit slowly, and come all this way to quit?

Gasdalia urged me to keep climbing the stadium steps and told me she'd been encouraging me for 10 years and it was time to just dare it or I'd be sorry for the rest of my life. If I did it and didn't like it I could quit, but I would at least have done it. So I reached down and grabbed myself again and said, "I'm Peter Gorman and I'm holding my balls. Let's go."

I stepped forward to the top of the stadium and there was the machine of the universe and I stepped into it and as I did Julio began singing again. I marched forward through a dark tunnel in the machine until I came to the far side, and there was the stadium, full of lights and people cheering me on. I realized I was supposed to jump and started to get afraid. But I remembered that my body wasn't with me and from somewhere courage surged through me and I leapt into the air.

The machine caught me almost instantly. Sachavaca said that was good.

And then I was back in the tree and made my way, wobbly legged, back to the platform's edge. Suddenly Daniel, one of the guests, was coming toward me. I put out my hands to grab him. He said he was alright, that he was just going to throw up and didn't need help. It occurred to me that he probably imagined I'd been in guard position all along, when I'd been so, so elsewhere. But Sachavaca said that that's what Julio did and what other curanderos did: They were in both worlds or dozens of worlds at once, and in each of them fully capable at all times.

Julio went silent again, and when he didn't begin to sing in a few minutes, I thought he might have fallen asleep. I shook his arm. No response. I wondered if I should sing, if Julio was just not able to anymore that night.

His eyes opened and he stared at me. "Never doubt me or what I'm doing," he said, though I don't know if he actually said it out loud or just in the ether. "The guardians can give you songs and medicines and information but none of it will ever be yours until you dominate it. You must have the courage to do that."

I realized then why Julio's songs so often talked of dominating the spirits, dominating the angels and demons. It wasn't enough to have had a glimpse of them, or to have met them and run away in awe or fear; you had to dominate them, or dominate your fear of them, before they would work for you.

When Julio's physical body still didn't move after what seemed like a long time, I began to sing, just a whisper. Sachavaca told me "If you want to sing, sing fearlessly. Sing like a coward or fearful boy, and your songs will have no power."

I began to sing more forcefully.

Not long after I did, Julio began to sing again, so I stopped. "Sing, *Pedrito*," he said out loud, and so I did. I sang with him and sometimes he stopped to let me sing alone; I never felt my voice like I felt it that night. Not loud, not lovely, but focused, with the sounds coming out with intention and moving into people, through their skin and into them.

"Now breathe in and see," he told me, and I breathed in during a song while my voice was inside one of the guests and suddenly I realized I had followed my voice inside with my in-breath, and was seeing the person from the inside. Or maybe it was that I was following my voice with the in-breath and was sucking their life force into me, inhaling it. I could see things that were right and things that needed fixing. Those that looked bad I pulled out and gave to the doctors in the red room. The parts that were good I exhaled out of me and back into their rightful owners. It was a fantastic feeling to suck that life into me, to be able to see what was good and what was wrong with it. It almost made me giddy.

I looked at Julio and began to breathe him in, but as soon as I did I realized that was way out of line. He was Julio and it would take someone with a lot more experience than me to be able to take in that life force. I blew him back into himself.

As I did I felt a change in the air. A deep eerie chill took hold of me. I looked around. At the top of the protective wall I'd made with mapacho smoke and Agua Florida around the ceremony hut there were hundreds of spirits looking in on us. *Lookey-loos* peering in at what we were doing and seeing everything. I looked at them and thanked them for not coming into the space.

But they weren't the cause of the hair rising on my neck. They were just curious spirits. I looked more closely. Out of the corner of my right eye I saw part of the wall I'd built behind the mandarin orange tree. There was no one staring over it, but there was a large chink in it, near the top, and in that chink I could see the eye of a giant looking in at us. His eye took up the whole opening. It looked like a real eye, not a spirit eye, as though it were human. And it didn't have the same feel as the lookey-loos. It was mean-spirited and seemed full of bad intent. I told it to go and began mentally bricking up the opening with mapacho smoke. But I still felt awful and clammy and it occurred to me that that eye really did have evil intent; worse, the opening that allowed it to peer in at us was caused by me, in the moment when I so stupidly began to suck in Julio's life force. Whoever it was couldn't get to Julio—he was too strong—but by me doing my stupid and arrogant breathing I'd directed the person right to him, through me.

Just before I got the hole bricked up, the eye winked. There was something sinister about it and a chill ran up my spine.

## Chapter Three

# BRUJERIA

I DIDN'T MENTION the eye to Julio, but I did think about it. It hadn't felt like a spirit eye at all—whatever that would feel like. It was like a real person's spirit had come and intended something bad. Fortunately, nothing happened for the remainder of the trip, though that wasn't the end of it.

I had run into Gina on that trip before my team and I left for the jungle with our guests, and as she was free and I was alone at that time, we had wound up romantically involved after a few years of not relating that way.

Three or four days after my guests had gone she was in my room one night. Before dawn she woke me to tell me she had to leave to get her kids ready for school. I said okay and lay back down as she went to the doorless bathroom to wash and put her makeup on.

Moments after I put my head back down a man's voice shouted in real time: "You think you can play in that world? You don't know anything about that world!"

As he said it I saw a huge hand, a hand probably as tall as a man, begin to swing down from outside of the hotel. I knew, knew that that hand belonged to the man who had looked in at the ceremony with such evil intent and I sat bolt upright, wide awake. I watched as the hand moved through the hotel wall, swinging to the bathroom. I called "Gina! Watch..." I didn't have a chance to finish and she didn't have a chance to react. The hand walloped her, knocking her off her feet and against the far wall of the bathroom. She flew several feet sideways off the ground and hit the wall with a loud crack as her head hit the tiles, then slid to the floor.

I was there in an instant. She was conscious and not bleeding. "What was that?" she asked, shaken, holding her head.

"That was *brujeria*, black magic" I said. "Let's go get you X-rayed."

Fortunately, after the X-rays and a visit to a doctor we were satisfied that there was no serious damage to her head. In a couple of hours she was even joking about it, asking who I'd pissed off so much they'd wallop her like that. For me it was no laughing matter: I was shaken deeply. I had experienced some bad luck brujeria when we had our bar, but I had no idea that anyone could have the power to do what I saw happen to Gina.

❦

That wasn't the end of the brujeria. On a trip not long after that, Julio showed me his left ankle and calf. They were horribly swollen.

"Virotés," he said. He said that some days earlier someone had shot him with the invisible darts and while he'd gotten nearly all of them out he had not been able to find the one in his leg, hence the swelling. "Can you find it, *Pedrito?*"

Sure I couldn't, I still looked at his leg. It was like looking without staring, just sort of glancing for something different, something that didn't belong there. In a few moments I saw a bump, reached down, pulled at it: a sort of thorn—of course you couldn't actually "see" it because it wasn't solid—came out and Julio's leg began to drain from the very real hole it left.

"*Ah, bueno, Pedrito. Ahhhh….*"

MaBel, whose job it was to take care of Julio when we were on the river, took over. In an hour the swelling was gone.

Foolishly, I didn't remember to get rid of the thing in the red room—don't ask me how I forgot—and I wound up feeling awful. It was as though some invisible spider web had attached itself to me. It was dirty. Both Julio and his son Jairo cleaned me but couldn't get rid of it all. Worse, when I returned to Iquitos and my room there at the Hotel Isabel, Jhonny, my right-hand man in Iquitos who used the room when I went to the jungle, said he'd had several sleepless nights.

"The other night there was a man standing by the bed," he said. "I'm not kidding. I got up to turn on the lights and they wouldn't turn on. I lit a mapacho and told him to get out, then blew Agua Florida on him and he finally left. After he did the lights came on."

He urged me to be careful after he returned to his home and I was alone.

223

"Someone has some *mal espiritus*—bad spirits—looking to hurt you, brother."

I didn't pay it much mind. I was pretty used to spirits. Heck, they were everywhere all the time, and I didn't really think anyone had anything in for me. Why would they? Because they were jealous of me? Jealous of what? It wasn't like I had any money or power to be jealous of.

Nonetheless, Jhon's warning was a nice heads-up when later that evening and all through the next day or two I caught glimpses of spirits ducking around the corner between the living and bedroom areas of my hotel room. Some were quite clear. On the second night I woke when Jhon called to me to tell me he'd decided to sleep on the old couch. I got up to say hello and of course he wasn't there.

Things got more odd when one of the trip guests met me on the boulevard where I was having some drinks and said they'd been given a doll by a stranger for me to give to Madeleina. It was just a small red plastic doll wrapped in plastic in a cardboard box and I didn't think twice about it until a couple of days later when Jhon and some of my team—Sidalia, George, Ruber—woke me when they came into my room in the morning. I stood and reached for my shorts, felt a horrible pain in my chest, then just felt my heart giving out and fell down, stone-cold out. They got me up in seconds and over to a doctor who said I'd had a little heart attack. "Nothing horrible. Just a little one."

I felt fine in a few hours, but wondered what the heck had happened. What was I doing with a "little heart attack"?

My team felt sure someone had sent virotés to hurt me. I told them that was silly. They asked if I'd brought anything into the room that was new or from someone I didn't know. I showed them the doll. No one wanted to touch it.

"Someone wants to hurt you with that," said Jhon.

"That's brujeria, hermano," said Ruber.

"Well then, let's open it," I said.

I opened the box and took the plastic wrap off the little red doll. It was kind of a boxy, 1950s spaceman-looking doll, not really something you would give a 10-year-old girl. When I got the plastic off I realized it came apart and thought there would be a smaller version of the same doll inside. Instead, there was a doll with a knife in its left hand and the knife was pointed at the larger doll's chest from the inside. I took out the little doll:

it had a chain around its neck and a little medallion on the chain read: "To my enemy, I will kill you. I will plunge this knife into your heart until you are dead."

I guessed somebody didn't like me after all.

It was just a plastic doll, of course, but the idea that someone had bought it with the intention that I get it and get hurt from it sent a chill up my spine.

# Chapter Four

# BRINGING BAD ENERGY HOME

I LEFT FOR the states a couple of days later, after the gang had done their best to clean the spider webs off me, and had a great flight home.

Once on the ground, however, things got shaky fast. Italo met me at the airport in the newer of my two pickup trucks, an eight-year-old Ford Ranger. Most reliable truck in the world. But when he went to start it, it wouldn't start. It wouldn't even begin to turn over. We sat there about 15 minutes before it would start and when it did it ran fine. It was just taking a rest. Or so I thought.

Once home, I brought my bags in, then opened the fridge. As I did, both Italo and I heard the freon pipe crack and the gas escape.

"What did you bring home with you, old man?" Italo asked.

"Just bad luck, I guess."

Except that when I went to turn on the electric stove, it shorted out, and a few minutes later the microwave had flames shooting out of it. And when Madeleina got there an hour later, the ceiling fan in the living room fell, nearly hitting her.

Whatever I'd picked up from either the bad intentions in the viroté in Julio's leg or from the person who gave me the doll was definitely not aligned with regular electrical objects. In two hours I was out nearly $2,000 in appliances.

"Italo, you got to clean me. Get this junk off before I set the damned house on fire."

"I don't want to go near you. You're a catastrophe."

"Just get to work."

"What do I do?"

"You've seen me do it. Get the shacapa, light a mapacho, smoke me, look sort of sideways at my back and use the shacapa to scrape off anything you see that looks weird. I know it sounds crazy, but just do it."

He did as he'd seen Julio and others do a thousand times, taking it seriously.

"You're a mess. You got black junk all over your back."

"Well, let's get rid of it."

In 20 minutes I felt like a new person.

But stupid me, just like with the viroté, I again forgot to put the junk in the red room. I didn't even think about it until the next day. Chepa had come over and was taking the gang, which by then included her two new babies and Italo's live in girlfriend Sarah, out to a movie.

She was driving one car; Italo was driving his. Just as they were getting ready to pull away Italo came back to the house, saying he'd forgotten something. A minute later he came from his room, nearly doubled over.

"What's the matter, buddy. You look sick…"

"I'm going to throw up, dad."

He stepped to the front porch and began to vomit. But it wasn't just vomit. It was the roar of an ayahuasca purge. Over and over, from deep in his belly it came rushing up and bursting out of him.

"What's going on, dad? Why am I feeling like I drank ayahuasca?"

"I don't know."

In a few minutes he couldn't stand, and was talking almost incoherently, asking what all the spirits were doing around him. I told Madeleina to get my things, and while she got the mapachos and shacapa and other things, Chepa and I helped Italo to a far corner of the yard, a quiet space near a fire pit we occasionally sat around.

He was deep in the throes of a full-blown ayahuasca dream, and he wasn't liking it. I smoked him and tried to calm him down with singing and the shacapa; Chepa held him and sang her own songs to him.

In about an hour both Chepa and I realized that something really nasty had hold of him. Italo was frightened, and it was more than ayahuasca-frightened. "What's going on, dad? Why can't you fix me?"

I began to look at him to see what might be there. In a few minutes I saw something at the top of his head and stuck my hand out and into him—or at least that's what I tried to do—and grabbed hold of whatever it was. Whatever it was, it was not happy I was trying to pull it free, and it fought me. When I finally did manage to pull a little of it out of him, I realized I had my hand on the back of someone's neck. That doesn't mean it was a person, just that my brain had to compartmentalize whatever the energy was and my brain turned it into what looked like a little man. I pulled harder and got his whole head out from Italo's head.

"Fuck you! Fuck you! Fuck your mother!" he screamed, though only I could hear him. I pulled harder and got him out and held him tight in both hands. He struggled furiously as I mentally opened a door to the red room and asked the doctors if I could get rid of him in there. I didn't wait for an answer but just began shoving him inside.

"I'll kill you! You can't do this! Fuck you and die! Fuck you! Fuck you! Fuck you!"

And then he was gone. I closed the door quickly and washed my hands with mapacho smoke and Agua Florida, then cleaned both Italo and Chepa and Madeleina, who'd watched us work, then took whatever *ick* I could find, gathered it up and put that in the red room as well.

Italo sat up.

"You okay?"

"Yeah. What the freak was that?"

"I messed up after you cleaned me. I forgot to get rid of what you took off me, so it got on you."

"That was really weird and scary. Someone must really hate you, dad, if they put that on you. We're lucky the darned car didn't blow up."

A few minutes later, everything seemed back to normal. No more appliances shorting out, no more unexpected ayahuasca dreams.

✿

Chapter Five

# WORKING ON JULIO

BUT EVERYTHING wasn't back to normal. I returned to Iquitos in early January, 2007 for the start of two trips. I'd only been in town for a couple of hours—I had my usual large room at the Hotel Isabel—and was visiting with a former client named Aaron, when Juan came to the door.

"Hola, Pedro; hola Aaron," he said. *"Tengo mal noticia."* He had something bad to say. I told him to go ahead and say it. He explained that Julio had been ill and taken a sudden turn for the worse. He feared Julio was dying and wanted me to go clean him, to see if there was anything I could do to help.

In a minute I'd put together a little bag of mapachos, a bottle of camalonga, another of Agua Florida, a third of his favorite cologne, Tabu, and an old shacapa.

As I collected the things I realized that I was flattered that Juan had asked me—and the moment I realized that I was ashamed to have felt it. Who the heck did I think I was? I wasn't going to be able to do anything, didn't know anything, and now I was flattered that my dying friend's son-in-law had called on me?

If there was a hole nearby I would have crawled into it.

That pathetic ego demonstration recognized, I asked Aaron—who knew Julio and had been working toward learning shamanism—if he wanted to come and help.

"Do you mind if I bring some *palo santo*?" he asked, referring to a fragrant wood often used in ceremonies to clear the space of negative energy.

"That's fine."

Juan had one of his three-wheeled *motokars*—a sort of motorized rick-shaw—waiting outside the room. The three of us squeezed into the single broad seat and the driver, Juan's son, Kay, started the motor.

On the 20-minute drive, Juan explained over the motor's din that the attacks on Julio had been stepped up in recent weeks, and were now almost continuous. He said Julio had nearly stopped eating, was weak and in constant pain. I asked if he and Julio's sons had worked on him and he said they were too close to help much. "The same people who are attacking Julio are making it impossible for us to see the virotés. But you've been away for months, so they probably can't get you the same way."

We arrived on the unpaved Independencia Street in lower Puchana, a suburb of Iquitos, and clambered up the ladder to the stilted home. To my surprise, Julio's wife—whom I hadn't seen in years—was there, and after hellos she invited me into his tiny room.

Julio looked worse than Juan had explained. He lay on his bed, frighteningly gaunt. His face looked pasty and his breathing was very, very shallow. I touched his forearm and he felt stiff, as if rigor mortis had already set in.

I lit a mapacho and sopla'd him with Agua Florida. He still didn't move. I put some of the bitter camalonga on my hands and held it to his nose. Slowly, his eyes opened. They were distant and watery and it took him a few minutes to recognize me. When he finally did he smiled a little.

*"Ahh, Pedrido...viene un doctor..."* he chuckled.

"Here comes a doctor indeed, Don Julio. And this doctor says the first thing that has to happen is for you to sit up. So sit up."

He stared out into space for a few minutes. Either he had stopped recognizing me, didn't realize I was there, or was just in his own world of confusion.

*"Vete...Vete..."* he said weakly.

His word meant "get out" or "go away" but I didn't think it was aimed at me. I began to sing, ordering who or whatever it was to leave. In a few minutes the air seemed less oppressive and in another few minutes I felt Julio's hand grab my right wrist.

*"Quien?"* Who?

"It's Pedro, Don Julio. Your friend Pedro."

*"Ahhh...Pedrito...has venido?"* You've come?

"Yes, Julio, I've come."

"*Bueno…bueno…*"

His eyes stayed somewhat alert and he made weak motions to sit. He was unable, so I put my arms around him and lifted him to a sitting position. It was like moving a baby, where you have to keep your upper hand on both their back and neck. He looked so frail that I thought the weight of his head could break his neck if I didn't move it in tandem with his torso.

His wife came in and saw what I was doing. "Be careful, Pedro. He's too weak to sit. He'll just fall back…"

Julio made a weak effort to cough and his wife wiped his mouth.

I told her and Juan that he needed to be in the sun a little, and that we should move him to the front room. Someone got a chair and we carried him there and put a blanket around him.

He was in his underwear, with just a sleeveless undershirt. His shock of white hair was as handsome as always, but his mustache had not been trimmed and his face had several days' worth of stubble. That was not how Julio carried himself. He was always elegant by jungle standards, and well shaved. And no matter how many patches he had on his pants, he always looked ready to step into fine company.

I didn't like seeing him so powerless, so weak.

Aaron had lit some palo santo and its sweet scent filled the air. I began to sing and both Aaron and I shook shacapas. Julio sat in the chair, eyes closed, not moving.

The first few minutes of song were a little intimidating. His son Julio, whom I didn't know well, had arrived and sat on the room's little balcony. His wife, whom I hardly knew either, also stood by. Then there was Juan, and MaBel and then Julio's wife…I wondered what they must have thought to hear this gringo singing for their father's health.

It didn't take long to get over that. Sachavaca had told me that weak singing had no power and I was there to try to help Julio, and that meant with all my might.

I began to sing more strongly. I smoked him with mapacho. I sopla'd him with Agua Florida and put the Tabu and camalonga to his lips and chest.

In about 20 minutes or so I put down the shacapa and began to look at him with that sort of sideways glancing. The virotés were in plain sight. I took one out of his left calf, then another from his left shoulder, and one from near his sternum. With each I removed I asked the doctors to take them and put them in the red room, then washed my hands in Agua Florida and mapacho smoke before continuing. Aaron held up the singing and the shacapa while I worked. I forgot that anyone was in the room but Julio, and the more I worked the more virotés I found. Some were difficult to remove; they were buried deeply in his body and had no intention of being pulled out easily. Those I had to suck out. As I did I tried to make a little wall at the back of my throat to keep them from coming into me. The first one I nearly choked on and began to cough. Aaron slapped my back hard and it popped up from the back of my throat and into my hand.

I don't know how long we worked but it was probably an hour-and-a-half to two hours and when we were done, Julio looked no better than he had when we started. But Aaron and I were spent.

The family thanked me and I told them we would come back at the same time the next day to work again.

Back at my room, Aaron insisted on cleansing me with smoke and the palo santo. In turn, I cleaned him with mapacho and Agua Florida and he told me he'd come back at the same time tomorrow.

The next day, when we reached Julio, I was pleased to see that he woke much more easily and his eyes took much less time to focus and realize that I was there. He even made an effort to sit up, and his wife said that he'd had a little soup just after we had gone.

Too, someone had shaved him and when we started to move him to the front room he insisted on putting on pants. He was still terribly weak but was much more cognizant than he had been.

Aaron and I worked again, this time with confidence from the beginning. What anyone thought of my songs didn't matter. I just opened my mouth and let them come out, just as Sachavaca had said they would. All that mattered was that despite having taken several virotes out of Julio a day earlier, I knew there were more that I'd missed.

That second day I found them more quickly. I took one from one of his ankles and one from his feet; others I found in the palms of his hands, and in his torso. I had someone stand him up and turn him around and found several in his back. The ones I had to suck out were difficult and I choked several times, but Aaron took care of me with hard swats to my back to keep me from swallowing them.

At some point during the work Julio opened his eyes and smiled a little.

It was nice to see.

We knew we were done again for the day when we simply had nothing left to give. Again we promised to come back the following day. Three days was generally what Julio used for bad illness, and it seemed to make sense to do things the way he would have done them.

The following day Aaron and I returned. To my amazement Julio was waiting for us and when I went to help him sit up in his bed he brushed me off and managed it himself. Standing was a different matter altogether, and walking was out of the question, but still, he was more alert, and looking forward to the session.

His wife said that he'd not only eaten some rice and fish after Aaron and I had gone the day before, but that he asked for an egg for breakfast. I was glad.

Aaron and I sang and smoked him and perfumed him and held the camalonga to his nose. He responded with growling sounds from deep in his throat, like he was clearing something but it wasn't phlegm.

There were not many "visible" virotés remaining in his body, and all of them that I could find had to be sucked free. I choked on them and managed to get all of them out of my mouth and into my hands and I put them into the red room.

All but one. It was in his neck. I leaned my mouth against the spot and began to suck. I had a moment when I imagined that when I was done he'd have a hickey and I laughed at the idea. I heard others laughing too. It must have been a sight to see Pedro sucking their dad's neck.

The viroté didn't want to leave. Of all that I'd removed this one was the deepest and had the most intention. This was the one that was doing the most damage—or at least that's what it seemed like to me.

So I sucked harder and tried to catch it in my teeth when I felt it pull free. I missed and it flew past my throat and into my belly. I began to choke, then stepped away and vomited violently. It didn't come out. I made a mental note to have Aaron help me get rid of it later, then continued to work on Julio.

Surprisingly, he called for a mapacho and began to smoke, then clenched his fists and stretched his arms out in front of himself. He growled again, shaking his head as though shaking cobwebs off. He called for Agua Florida and put it to his lips, then sopla'd his chest, doused his hands and wiped his face in the sweet water, and patted the top of his head to seal his corona.

"*Yah, Pedrito...bueno...*" he said with surprising strength.

I continued to sing but he waved me off. "*Ay, no mas...*" he said, telling me the work was done.

I stopped singing, cleansed myself and asked how he was feeling.

"*Bien...bien...casi normal...*" He was good, almost normal.

He turned to his wife and told her he was hungry.

We stayed in the little front room for a while, enjoying each other's company. MaBel came up the ladder and saw her dad looking more like himself than he had in some time and she threw her arms around him. He laughed and pointed to his neck and asked if there was a mark. He said Pedro had kissed him hungrily there.

When we went to leave, he made an effort and managed to stand. "*Yah, Pedrito...gracias por todo...*"

His wife and MaBel began to steer him toward the bedroom in the back; he said no, that he needed the air and wanted to stay in the front room, overlooking the street.

Aaron and I shook his hand, then I gave him a hug and we left.

Aaron came back to my room. He, like I, was amazed at what the work—and eating a little, and the attention we gave him—had done.

I told Aaron about the viroté I'd swallowed and told him my stomach was hurting. I excused myself and went to the bathroom to try to vomit it up. It felt like I got a good deal of it, but not quite all of it. When I came out Aaron swatted me, then cleansed me and after another bout of vomiting it seemed to be gone.

I made sure to clean up as much of the invisible goop as I could find and put it in the red room.

## Chapter Six

# A SAD GOODBYE

MY GUESTS came in the next day and I had to turn my attention to getting things ready for our trip. I spoke with Juan about the possibility of bringing Julio out to the river but both Juan and his wife Lady were against it. "My papa's too weak," she said. "If we bring him he'll just die out there."

"And if we leave him here?" I asked.

"At least there is a hospital here," she said.

She was right. But that left the question of who would run the ceremonies. Juan wanted to bring in a man named Alberto, a former student of Julio's who was a very well known and respected curandero in his own right. I didn't. I knew the man's reputation but had never done ceremony with him. Also, as he'd never been part of the team, he wouldn't know how we did our business.

I asked about Julio's son Antenor, but Juan said that Antenor had recently become involved with some missionaries and so thought the ceremony was blasphemous and wouldn't do it.

Which left Juan or Jairo.

"No Pedro. You do the ceremony," he said.

"Yeah, sure…just what my guests want. Hello, everybody, I'm not just your tour leader but I'm also your curandero…"

"You are. Not a strong one yet, not Julio, but you are."

"Jairo can do it. He's been studying with his father since he was born. And he's already part of the team. Do you think he's ready?"

"He's not as good as Alberto, but he's good."

"Okay. My guests will hate me but I suspect Julio's spirit will be around to make sure things go well."

❋

The guests took the news in wonderful stride and two days later we set off up the river. The trip was good and Jairo was strong, stronger than I thought he'd be. I was pleased for him. And Julio's spirit was definitely around.

When we got back to Herrera to await the big riverboat back to Iquitos we got the news. Julio had died the night before. The cause of death was said to be tuberculosis. It made the trip back to Iquitos a sad one for me and all of his family. The same as when my parents died, I wished I could have had another day with him. Another year with him. But I couldn't.

❋

The wake was lovely. As many as 100 people came from the river and different parts of Iquitos to say goodbyes at the little stilted house. There were flowers everywhere. His body was in a small white casket with a glass plate over his head so that people could look at his face one last time. He looked strong and peaceful and I almost thought he might wake up at any moment.

Women and men cried, laughed, told Julio stories. Some talked of the healing he'd done for them; others talked about his still making babies when he was 70 years old. His oldest son, Jérnan, asked me to tell one funny story about him and I told everyone about one night when my friend Lynn and I were at his home on the Aucayacu. I had guests who were deep in their ayahuasca dream while Lynn and I were finished and had stepped outside to look at the glorious moon.

"Julio came out while Lynn and I were outside," I said. "He excused himself and turned to urinate. We turned away to give him privacy. It sounded like he was *mareado* because it took forever and felt like he was walking around while he was peeing.

"When he finished he said 'Gracias,' and stepped back up into his house. A moment later Lynn and I were amazed to discover that he hadn't just peed: In the light of the moon we saw that he had written the name JULIO in urine in two-foot-tall letters."

Jérnan nearly choked on his laughter. "That was my papa!" he said when he caught his breath. Then he said it again, this time tears welling up with his

236

laughter. "That was my papa!"

The burial was just as crowded as the wake if not more. All of Julio's children were there, including two middle-aged sisters I had only met once who had come in from Pucallpa. And there were dozens of friends and extended family.

Julio's casket sat on rollers in the back of a hearse. I asked Jérnan and Jairo who would be carrying it to the burial site. They said they'd hired four school kids. I turned around and saw them: They had no relation to Julio and couldn't have been more than 12.

"Why don't you two carry it, with Antenor and Julio Junior?" I asked.

"No Pedro. We can't."

"Well then, could I help carry it?"

"Yes, you're not one of his sons."

Ruber, Julio's grandson, was nearby and he said he'd like to help carry it as well.

When it was time, I pulled the smallish casket from the car and two of the school kids and Ruber and I hoisted it to our shoulders. It was nearly weightless. Julio couldn't have weighed more than 80 pounds when he died, and the casket was a lovely but simple one made of cedar.

But as we began to follow the procession into the Puchana cemetery the casket began to get heavier. And heavier. The walk couldn't have been more than 50 yards to the gravesite, but each step became more difficult. I nearly stumbled two or three times and prayed that I wouldn't drop it.

The casket wood was digging into my shoulder and my hands were slipping. I nearly called out for someone, anyone, to help me when my knees began to buckle. The last 10 steps were complete agony. I had no idea what was going on but was thrilled when two men waiting in the grave reached up for the coffin and took it from me.

After the simple ceremony, I pulled Ruber aside. "I don't know what happened, but I just couldn't carry that. Thank you for helping."

"Me? I thought you were carrying all the weight," he said. "That was *bruto*! That was impossible. I almost fell with every step."

He pulled back his shirt to show a deep red line where the casket had dug into his shoulder. I did the same.

We asked the two school kids and they said it was nothing. It was like carrying air, they said.

I found Jérnan and Juan and told them how heavy it was. They both laughed. "That's why his sons can't carry it."

"But when I took it out of the car it weighed nothing."

"Yes," said Jérnan. "But when you walk, all of the spirits connected with a person gather.I didn't think it would affect you because you're not his son. You weren't carrying Julio, you were carrying his spirit, the illnesses he took out of people, his guardians, his good deeds and bad deeds. You were carrying his soul."

"And now," said Juan, "you need to drink again, soon. You need to let your guardian clean you of all of this."

Drinking without Julio was not something I was looking forward to doing.

# PART VII

# BLACK MAGIC

*Black magic, profound magic,*
*Magic deep within the earth and sun;*
*Black magic, profound magic,*
*At the center of everything.*
*Black magic, profound magic,*
*Teach us of the heart of things,*
*Black magic, profound magic,*
*Don't allow us to be led astray.*

*—from one of Julio's songs*

## Chapter One

# JAIRO AT THE HELM

M Y SECOND trip of that January was cancelled, and so I returned home without drinking again. But I returned a few months later with a new group for the start of three back-to-back trips.

I didn't feel comfortable drinking while Jairo was still so new at being a curandero. He was good, and really had studied hard at his father's side for a lifetime, but I didn't know if he had the power to control things if anything went wrong. That, plus being terrified of going back to that space where the serpentine Gasdalia would be, kept me from drinking during the first two groups. I'd take a little, just to be able to see where the guests were going, but asked the medicine to be gentle, and she was.

The first group was lovely. The second group was difficult, however. One of the guests had had Juan bring several cases of beer into the little camp— which was verboten—and another of the guests thought it was mine and raised hell with me for it. Still another of the guests was caught using our drinking water to wash her hair daily, leaving us short of good water. There were several others who were gems to have along, but the few that truly hated me for one reason or another made everything difficult. They complained about the food—which was an amazing array of fresh fruits and vegetables, beans made daily, juices, rice, plantains, a bit of chicken and fish—and the rain and the mosquitos and not having showers. It seemed like every day at least one, sometimes two people called me aside to tell me what was wrong with me and the trip. I was partly responsible, because I'd gotten drunk a couple of nights in Iquitos. It was my own time, after the end of the workday, but it was a dumb thing to do, and not the first time

I'd done it. But for some reason, a few of the people on that particular trip imagined I was giving them less than my best—or that I'd snuck beer into camp—and that just made things hard.

On the first night that group drank, several people had wonderful experiences and a few had a difficult time. Another few didn't feel they'd gotten much, but I assured them that ayahuasca had been working on them, whether they got to see the fireworks or talk to spirits or not. It was why my trips generally had three ayahuasca ceremonies: most people wanted to see the colors and lights and spirits. And on one of the three ceremony nights, they almost always did.

By the second night the group was divided. Seven people thought the trip was wonderful; six couldn't wait till I got swallowed by an anaconda. Those six decided not to drink the second time.

I told them that was fine, but that if they chose to stay in the ceremony hut they would have to stay until the end of the ceremony. I didn't want anyone rending a tear in the protective wall I would be building around the hut to keep the lookey-loos out. If I remember right, four of the six said they wanted to stay; two returned to the sleeping quarters.

Unfortunately, during the evening, one of the people not drinking made their way out of the ceremony hut. I thought she was just headed to the toilet—within the walls I'd made with Ruber and George's help—but instead she walked back to the sleeping quarters. She was too far away for me to catch her, and I couldn't call out to her to stop without disturbing everyone's ayahuasca dream, so I watched helplessly as she walked through the protective wall. Instantly the wind from a thousand spirits rushing through the opening roared onto the platform, and the people sitting on the platform were knocked flat on their backs. The energy was instantly wild and frenetic. It was as if you were having the most exclusive dinner party in town and suddenly the gates were opened and 1,000 people who wished they'd gotten invites poured in. It was mayhem.

Jairo saw it and began ordering them to leave. I shored up the opening and then helped remove the remaining lookey-loos and in about 10 minutes, order was restored.

The same thing could have happened if Julio had been running the ceremony, but I don't think the spirits would have had the same boldness they had without him there.

Still, Jairo was coming into his own, and while he did not seem to heal my guests as deeply and often as Julio did, that began to soon change. On a trip less than a year later—with good trips in between—one fellow said after ceremony that he hadn't felt or seen much at all.

"It was a beautiful night, Peter, don't get me wrong. It just wasn't a life-changing one."

"Well, Tom, the medicine will keep working, and sometimes people find they've been healed of things long after they get home."

He went down the hill toward the river to the sleeping quarters, while I hunkered down in the kitchen area—where I generally slept so that guests who needed to talk during the night could find me easily.

I woke sometime later to the sound of someone vomiting. Hard, beautiful elimination. "Good," I thought, then went back to sleep. Or tried to. But the vomiting continued, deeply buried awful things welling up and bursting out. I looked over and saw it was Tom.

When he continued to vomit I thought that maybe I should go see how he was, but then thought better of it. He was already involved with spirits a great deal stronger than I was, so I chose not to interfere.

He didn't stop till dawn, and then slept through breakfast.

When he finally got up he nearly danced over to the kitchen.

"That was some puking!" I laughed.

"I thought I was going to die," he said. "I got so dehydrated I couldn't even stand but I couldn't stop it. It was awful. Terrible. Fantastic."

"Good combination."

"At first I didn't realize why I couldn't stop. I really thought I might die. But then, after a while I realized what was coming out. Remember I told you I worked for a couple of years as a councilor for death row inmates?"

"Uh-huh…"

"Well, I realized that what I was eliminating was all the pain I'd taken in from them. I didn't know I was carrying that around with me, but once I saw it for what it was, I almost didn't care if I died. What horrible stuff that was. And now I feel lighter than I have in years! If I hadn't gotten that stuff out it probably would have eventually killed me."

Good for Jairo, I thought.

## Chapter Two

# THE NEXT MAGIC

ON THE VERY next trip, Jairo told me he was going to drink a full dose on the night of the first ceremony. Without hesitation, I told him I'd drink on the second night.

"When I'm *mareado*, Pedro, you sing..." he said. I understood.

The night he drank, he got very mareado, and went into a deep dream for maybe an hour or so, during which time I sang and smoked the guests, hoping the change in songs and the rhythm of the shacapa didn't interfere too much with their dreams.

When he was a little more grounded he took over again and finished the ceremony beautifully. In the morning none of the guests even mentioned that they'd noticed the change from Jairo to me.

Two days later it was my turn. The night was dark. There were clouds overhead, obscuring any moon or starlight. We served the guests first, and then the cup was passed to me. I drank the thick, foul tasting liquid in half-a-dozen gulps, then smoked myself with mapacho, inhaled the vapors from the camalonga, wiped my face and head with Agua Florida, then put a few drops of Tabu on my neck and hands.

In a few minutes, the world began to split apart. I felt a shiver up my spine, then reminded myself of who I was and that whatever happened, I could not only handle it but dominate it.

It was one thing to think that, and another when the splitting continued and I began to feel the me of me disappearing. Then the sound of the gears of the machine of the universe began. I started to flush.

Outside the unwalled hut, the trees began to sway. Lights that only I could see flickered in them. I stepped off the platform and moved on unsteady legs toward the trees, thinking I would vomit soon. When I didn't, I sat where I was. I could hear Jairo's singing and the sound of his shacapa and it was good.

The splitting stopped and the building with the thick, syrupy blocks began. This time they built a wall, a golden red wall as wide as my sight and taller than I could see. Two stations that looked like thrones were built in front of it and then two entities began to take shape. On the right was the Gasdalia-like entity, the essence of sensuality and desire; on the left a male. Both were dressed in black or colored black and had bodies that were serpentine, with long tails that undulated behind them.

"Tonight's the night," the male said.

"For what?" I asked.

"To join us," said Gasdalia.

"Join you how?"

"To accept that you've always been one of us. Just accept it. See your wings, allow yourself to feel your tail…"

The two of them were standing on their tails, tall and imposing. I made myself their height.

"Who are you? What does accept that I am one of you mean?"

Gasdalia leaned close to me and opened her mouth for a kiss. "Kiss me. Be me."

I leaned in and kissed her deeply. Like before, her kiss was beyond sexuality. She licked me from the inside, triggering an excitement I'd never felt. And as she did, I began to feel the *is-ness* of her, a kind of selfishness of desires fulfilled. When we separated she purred. "There are things you know nothing about, Peter. Good things…All you need to do is accept that you are one of us."

I was frightened of the depth of desire I felt. There was a baseness to the feelings flying through me. I didn't know what to do, so I reached for a cigarette.

"Don't be afraid," said the male. "Why are you always afraid?"

"Because you guys always come to me in ways I find frightening."

"We are who we are. Just representatives of a group that already includes you. You just need to realize it."

"What group?"

"Us."

"Who is us?"

"We are. Join us."

"What does that mean?"

"You'll find out after you are with us."

"No. Show me who you are."

"That was last time. This time is this time. This time is the time."

"You're not making sense. I have to go take care of my guests."

"No you don't. We've taken care of them for you. They won't even move tonight."

I turned and looked at the ceremony hut behind me. All of the guests were still; Jairo was singing and my team was sitting on the platform edge.

"They don't need you tonight, Peter. You need you tonight. And we need your full attention."

"If I'm already one of you, then why don't I know it? Why don't I even know who you are?"

"You know who we are. Just accept it."

I tried to let myself see if I was hiding anything from myself, to see if I were one of them, whoever they were. I couldn't feel a thing. But I did begin to feel swallowed up by them, as if I was being sucked into something thick and dark.

"Just let go, Peter," she said. "You will get so many things. Money, power, you'll get anything you want. Do you want to read minds? Do you want to know what people are thinking? Do you want Chepa back still? Do you want to fuck her?"

I felt she was telling the truth. All I had to do was be with them, be one of them and I would get those things. But I never wanted those things, not that way. I never asked for those.

I thought of Sachavaca and The Man with the Hat and asked them to tell me what to do.

"You're on your own tonight. We're just watching," Sachavaca said.

"But who are they?" I asked.

"They are who they say they are."

"But are they good? Why are they offering me money and power and my ex-wife back?"

"That's up to you to decide."

The machine of the universe had never stopped the grinding of its gears. My head was ringing. I was hot and sweating.

"Stop talking," said the male. "Just feel us."

The world began to pulse. The sexuality, the sensuality beyond human experience rushed over me. Around me, like a cloak, was the feel of power, of command. It was rich and thick and intoxicating. I saw myself with money and women; I felt electricity surge through me.

These entities were not human. How could I be one of them if I were human? And what would that power or money or even getting Chepa back mean if I had to give up my humanness to acquire it? Why was I even being asked to join them?

I suddenly saw Julio's face high up on the golden red wall. He smiled at me and chuckled. *"Ahh... Pedrito..."* he said. I wanted to talk with him, to ask him what to do, but he disappeared before I could.

But at that moment I knew why he appeared. I wasn't supposed to join these two, I was supposed to dominate them, to get beyond those base desires and beyond that wall. This was the black magic Julio used. This was the molten core of the earth, the core of the universe, the thing that held everything together. But what was being offered didn't feel like the profound magic he spoke of; this felt like base desire and selfishness. This was the trap that so many fell into.

I thought myself through that wall; behind it would be the real black magic, the deep, deep healing.

Nothing happened.

I thought through it again.

Again nothing happened.

"You think you can dominate us?" asked Gasdalia, snarling. "You can't dominate anything and you can't get past us. I dominated you with a simple kiss!" She hissed the words and her malevolence became more apparent.

"Don't even try to dominate us," said the male, slashing his tail at me. I felt like I'd been hit by a baseball bat.

"We're offering you everything," said Gasdalia, softening. "Why not take it?"

"I don't want it."

"Oh yes you do. Come, join us. You will love it."

"You're already one of us!" shouted the male. "Stop denying it!"

I wanted to run but couldn't even stand. "I can't do this anymore. I want you to go away. I want Sachavaca. I want The Man with the Hat. I want the real magic, not the selfish magic."

"You don't know anything!" shouted the male. "You don't know what we are offering, and you don't know what hells we can make your life if you refuse us."

I felt a surge of my own power run through me. It was clear and clean. "You don't know me either! You can't do anything to me. I am Peter, son of Thomas and Madeleine, father of Italo and Marco and Madeleina and I have business here."

My mouth opened wide and my snake came rushing out. In a moment he had consumed them both. I opened my mouth to take him back in. As I did, another voice began to speak. "Do you know what you just did? Do you know what you just missed?"

"No. But it was selfish and I don't want it."

"After all I've given you? After all I've given you? How dare you?"

I tried to move again but still couldn't.

"It's your turn to work for me," she said.

It felt like the voice of ayahuasca, but I'd never heard her talk like that.

"What do you want?" I asked.

"Bring me fresh meat," she said in a voice that echoed through the universe.

"What?"

"Bring me fresh meat!" She said it hungrily and I thought for an instant of my guests and thought at the same time that I was already bringing her fresh meat. As that thought formed, I thought "no," that I had never thought of my guests as fresh meat. I wouldn't bring them if I did. I brought them to make positive changes in their lives, to get healing, not to become fodder for some entity, no matter how powerful she was.

"I will never bring you fresh meat. These are my guests, and they are here for healing. They are not your meat."

"You don't know anything," she said in a surprisingly sad voice.

And then she was gone, and I was sitting on the damp clay outside the ceremony hut. I looked at the trees and the beautiful dance they were doing. I looked at the lights of the spirits flickering through them.

I turned to look at my guests. None were moving. No one was vomiting. My team was in the same place they'd been when I'd last seen them.

I slowly got to my feet and made my way closer to Jairo's voice.

❦

I wondered for a long time what she meant. On the surface, it was a simple and selfish request. But if everything was sentient, as I believed, and everything had will and intent, then why wouldn't everything have desires as well? I'd never thought of it that way, but it made sense. But why would ayahuasca, if that's who it was, want to think of the people she was healing as fresh meat? Or was all the healing, all the teaching, just a lure for humans to draw us into her world, to get us to spread the word, giving her fresh meat?

And why had her tone been gentle and sad when she told me I didn't know anything? Had I missed the whole point? Did the fresh meat mean me? That I was not clean enough? That I was still drinking too much, not working hard enough, not fresh enough to have the power to dominate those spirits that had visited that night?

❦

I got a glimpse of an answer some months later. I had a very small group and decided to drink with them. In no time the grinding of the gears of the universe began to pull me to pieces. The same golden red wall with the two stations began to construct itself. The same two entities, Gasdalia and the male, appeared. But surprisingly, they were tiny. They made the same entreaties to join them and promised the same power and money and other things, but their voices were barely audible. They were powerless. I realized that in the world of black magic, if you had no desires, you could not fall under the spell of desires. That was the trap of the magnetic field of black magic.

Suddenly I was beyond those little creatures and beyond that little wall. I began tumbling into a thick, black mass. Not a solid mass, but something so dense it might as well have been solid. It began to crush me. At the same time it had a fantastic force, a wonderfully dense life-force. There was nothing selfish about it. But it was going to crush me and I fled before

249

I disappeared into it.

But I knew then that at its core, black magic, profound black magic, is the dense and molten magma that that holds the earth together. It wasn't just something that Julio said or sang. It is what holds the sun and the universe together and keeps it all moving in the right rhythm. It's the magic that keeps our bodies and the bodies of plants and fish and animals and everything else from falling apart.

Just a taste of that power might give someone the power to lure things like money and power and fame to them, even without working at it. That was the trap of black magic. It's simply too dense for most people to work with it at its deepest levels—though I have no idea how deeply they go as I only felt it for a few moments—so they work with tiny selfish strands of it.

I couldn't believe what I was feeling, what I was being taught. This is the center of things, I thought. This is middle of the middle of it all.

# EPILOGUE

M Y WORK is certainly not finished. I know that the next time I drink I will be pulled back into that dense material. To learn from it I will have to let it crush me, let it make me part of it. That's a frightening idea.

And I might encounter what I thought was the voice of ayahuasca again as well. I hope I do. I want clarity on what "bring me fresh meat" means.

But no matter what I learn from the experience, my regular life will take most of my time. My marriage is over, but my children still need me to do those things that keep their world turning: paying the mortgage, getting Madeleina to school on time and going to her band recitals. Italo and Sarah just had a baby girl and they'll need me for advice and babysitting duties. Marco is joining the Navy and he'll need me to pray he stays out of harm's way and to send the occasional package of treats from home.

And though Chepa and I are not together, she still needs me to help care for her two little ones, a job I do with joy.

The first 25 years of dreaming have been a challenge. Knowing Julio was a genuine pleasure. And working with my team, taking people to the deep jungle and watching the medicine work with them has been one of the great experiences of my life. And yes, the gifts I've been given are real and available in those moments when they are needed. I'm grateful for that.

But I know there is a lot more work to do.

The always elegant Julio Jerena-
-Peter Gorman

Julio Jerena cooking ayahuasca
-Steve Flores

From left: Roger, Chino, Moises Torres Vienna and Chepa Aguilar (later Gorman)
in front of the Rey David, Peter Gorman's first boat -Peter Gorman

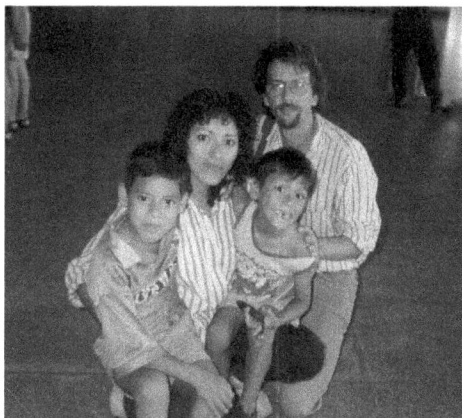

A young Peter Gorman with his wife, Chepa and sons Italo (in soccer shirt) and Marco at the Iquitos airport -Lydia Cahuaza

A young Madeleina with her grandmother, Momma Lydia

A young Peter Gorman getting nu-nu, a Matses snuff, from Pablo -Chepa Gorman

A current day Peter Gorman with Alan Shoemaker in Iquitos -Milan Bogdonovich

# AUTHOR'S BIO

Peter Gorman has been medicine dreaming with ayahuasca for 25 years. He is also an award-winning investigative journalist who has covered stories from the streets of Manhattan and the slums of New Delhi to Peru's Amazon.

If you'd like to keep up with what the author is doing, Peter Gorman's blog can be found at thegormanblog.blogspot.com. To see what he's written about in the past, please visit petergormanarchive.com.

And if you want to find out where the heck he came from, please visit his website at pgorman.com

Lightning Source UK Ltd.
Milton Keynes UK
UKHW011826210519
343075UK00002B/20/P

9 780557 484423